T0317603

Option Spread Trading

Founded in 1807, John Wiley & Sons is the oldest independent publishing company in the United States. With offices in North America, Europe, Australia and Asia, Wiley is globally committed to developing and marketing print and electronic products and services for our customers' professional and personal knowledge and understanding.

The Wiley Trading series features books by traders who have survived the market's ever changing temperament and have prospered—some by reinventing systems, others by getting back to basics. Whether a novice trader, professional or somewhere in-between, these books will provide the advice and strategies needed to prosper today and well into the future.

For a list of available titles, please visit our Web site at www.Wiley Finance.com.

Option Spread Trading

A Comprehensive Guide to
Strategies and Tactics

RUSSELL RHOADS, CFA

WILEY

John Wiley & Sons, Inc.

Published by John Wiley & Sons, Inc., Hoboken, New Jersey.
Published simultaneously in Canada.

For general information on our other products and services or for technical support, please
contact our Customer Care Department within the United States at (800) 762-2974, outside
the United States at (317) 572-3993 or fax (317) 572-4002.

Wiley also publishes its books in a variety of electronic formats. Some content that appears in
print may not be available in electronic books. For more information about Wiley products,
visit our web site at www.wiley.com.

Library of Congress Cataloging-in-Publication Data:

Rhoads, Russell, 1967–
    Option spread trading : a comprehensive guide to strategies and tactics / Russell Rhoads.
        p. cm. – (Wiley trading series)
    Includes index.
    ISBN 978-0-470-61898-1 (hardback); ISBN 978-0-470-94432-5 (ebk);
    ISBN 978-0-470-94431-8 (ebk); ISBN 978-1-118-018934 (ebk)
    1. Options (Finance)   I. Title.
    HG6024.A3R52 2011
    332.63'2283–dc22

2010032261

Printed in the United States of America

10 9 8 7 6 5 4 3 2 1

This work is dedicated to the three most important people in my life—my wife Merribeth Ann Rhoads and daughters Margaret Susan and Emerson Arlene. You are my partner, first friend, and little pal.

Contents

Preface   xi

Acknowledgments   xiii

CHAPTER 1   Essential Option Knowledge   **1**

The Option Basics	1
In-At-Out of the Money	5
Intrinsic and Time Value	6
Spread Basics	8
The Greeks	9
Payoff Tables and Diagrams	10
Option Pricing Calculators	12

CHAPTER 2   Spreads Using an Underlying Security   **15**

Covered Call	15
Covered Call Using LEAPS®	22
Systematic Covered Call Strategies	25
Cash-Secured Put	26
Systematic Cash-Secured Put	31
Protective Put	32
The Collar	33

CHAPTER 3   Synthetic Positions   **37**

Put-Call Parity	39
Synthetic Long Positions	40
Synthetic Short Positions	44

Arbitrage in Put-Call Parity 50
Individuals Using Put-Call Parity 52

CHAPTER 4 The Greeks 55

Price-Related Greeks 55
Time-Related Greek 61
Volatility-Related Greek 65
Interest Rate-Related Greek 67
Conclusion 69

CHAPTER 5 Straddles 71

Long Straddle Mechanics 72
Short Straddle 81

CHAPTER 6 Strangles 89

Long Strangle Mechanics 89
Short Strangle Mechanics 98

CHAPTER 7 Bull Spreads 107

Bull Put Spread 107
Bull Call Spread 114

CHAPTER 8 Bear Spreads 121

Bear Call Spread 121
Bear Put Spread 127

CHAPTER 9 Butterfly Spreads 135

Introduction to Butterfly Spreads 136
Long Call Butterfly 136
Long Put Butterfly 139
Iron Butterfly 142
Short Straddle Comparison 146
Short Call Butterfly 149

Short Put Butterfly   152
Reverse Iron Butterfly   154
Reverse Iron Butterfly versus Straddle   156

CHAPTER 10   Condor Spreads   **159**

Introduction to Condor Spreads   159
Long Call Condor   160
Long Put Condor   163
Iron Condor   166
Iron Condor versus Short Strangle   170
Short Condor Spreads   172
Reverse Iron Condor   176
Reverse Iron Condor versus Long Strangle   179

CHAPTER 11   Ratio Spreads   **183**

Call Ratio Spread   184
Put Ratio Spread   189
Ratio Spread Comparisons   192

CHAPTER 12   Backspreads   **199**

Call Backspread   199
Put Backspread   203
Backspread Comparisons   207

CHAPTER 13   The Stock Repair Strategy   **213**

Doubling Down on a Position   214
The Stock Repair Trade   215

CHAPTER 14   Calendar Spreads   **219**

Time Value Effect   220
Long Call Calendar   221
Long Put Calendar   224
Combined Calendar Spread   227

CHAPTER 15 Diagonal Spreads   231

Call Diagonal Spread   231
LEAPS Call Diagonal Spread   234
Put Diagonal Spread   237
LEAPS Put Diagonal Spread   239
Double Diagonal Spread   241

CHAPTER 16 Delta Neutral Trading   245

Delta Review   245
Delta-Neutral Positions   246
Gamma   250
Market Maker Trading   251

CHAPTER 17 Executing a Spread Trade   255

Executing a Stock or Option Trade   256
A Single Option Spread   258
A Spread with Two Options   260
A Spread with Multiple Legs   261
Legging into a Spread Trade   265

About the Author   269

Index   271

Preface

I n 1973, a smoking break room at the Chicago Board of Trade was transformed into the first listed equity options market in the United States. Call options on 16 stocks were listed for trading. On April 26, 1973 the Chicago Board Options Exchange rang the opening bell for the first time and 911 contracts traded on these 16 stocks. The individuals involved in that first day of trading could never have imagined what the options market has grown to. Doing some quick math, it can be estimated the CBOE now trades 911 contracts in just a few seconds each trading day.

In 2009 the options industry experienced a record volume year, with a streak of seven years of growth and increased growth 16 of the last 17 years. With multiple exchanges now vying for orders from the public, the speed of execution has increased and the cost of trading options has decreased tremendously. The playing field has been leveled to the point where trading for individuals and institutions can compete and win in the options arena.

As an instructor for the Options Institute at the CBOE I have the privilege of interacting with a wide variety of market participants. Since each option trade is at minimum a two-step process and we pack a lot of information into a very short period of time, I often reassure students that trading options is not like riding a bike. When some time has been taken away from option trading, there is always a learning curve that is involved in getting back up to speed. My hope is if a strategy has not been implemented in some time that this book may act as a resource to allow a trader to quickly regain the knowledge to comfortably put on an option spread trade.

This book is written in a modular format, where if a reader would like to explore the mechanics of a condor spread they may turn directly to Chapter 10 and quickly explore what is involved in a condor spread. Each chapter is laid out in a similar format, with several tables and usually at least a couple of examples of how each spread would be constructed, along with the key levels to focus on for each spread.

Before delving fully into spread trades there are a few chapters that cover the basics of option trading that will be useful to refer to while reading spread related chapters. Chapter 1 is a quick overview of essential option knowledge that is focused toward those who understand options, but may need a quick refresher before tackling spread trades. Chapter 2 then covers some very basic spread strategies that involve the underlying instrument as part of the spread. This chapter lays out the mechanics of putting on a very basic position that involves two trading instruments. In Chapter 3 the ability to create similar payoffs using two different approaches is explored. The Greeks are introduced in Chapter 1, but covered extensively in Chapter 4.

The following 10 chapters individually cover a variety of spread strategies. As the book moves along, the more complex strategies become. However, the concept behind each trade is basically the same, combining a variety of positions to create a custom payout.

Toward the end of this book, there are a couple of specialized chapters laying out some useful information for all option traders. First, in Chapter 16, the concept of Delta neutral trading is introduced, along with an example of how market makers basically use isolating price risk when providing liquidity to the market place. Finally, Chapter 17 discusses the issues involved in executing a spread trade.

Acknowledgments

There are many people throughout my life that have allowed me to reach the point where I look forward to going to work each day. I am fortunate that I truly enjoy what I get to do on a professional basis day in and day out.

The primary person is my wife Merribeth Rhoads. Her patience and understanding has been a key contribution to the completion of this book in a timely manner. Also, as I write this after just completing this manuscript I am embarking on another book. Her patience is never ending.

My daughters Margaret and Emerson are a constant inspiration to work hard and accomplish as much as I can to set a proper example for them. My first friend and little pal are the driving force behind all I do.

My parents Bobbie (who would have loved to see this on a bookshelf) and Dusty Rhoads were always supportive when I needed it most. Closer to home, my wife's parents John and Arlene Rose have endured a few curve balls thrown at them by this son in law. I appreciate them treating me as one of their own.

Professionally, the staff of the Options Institute at the Chicago Board Options Exchange is probably the best group of people I have worked with in my life. Alphabetically, I want to thank Taja Beane, Jim Bittman, Barbara Kalicki, Peter Lusk, Michelle Kaufman, Marty Kearney, Laura Johnson, Debra Peters, Pam Quintero, and Felecia Tatum. Also, special thanks to Patricia Hoffmann of the CBOE for having the good judgment to hire me for this position.

Finally, Meg Freeborn and Kevin Commins of Wiley have been wonderful to work with. I hope to collaborate on more projects with them in the future.

As a note, in the time I have been at the Options Institute I have instructed several thousand individuals that are interested in options trading and strategies. Many of you have challenged me with your questions and inspired me with your enthusiasm. I really do appreciate the time you give me.

CHAPTER 1

Essential Option Knowledge

A lthough many readers will have an understanding of the basics of options, it is always a worthwhile exercise to refresh the basics for those who have not traded options in some time. Option trading is not like riding a bike, when not utilized for a while, some of the knowledge that has been second nature tends to fade from a trader's mind. A well worn text book of strategies can usually be found nearby for many infrequent option traders who use it to get some reassurance when putting on a complex strategy. This first chapter will briefly cover the absolute basics of options as a refresher or an introduction, depending on the reader's experience level.

This chapter is a basic level coverage of options and spreads. For the intermediate trader, the majority of the information in this chapter should at minimum be a review. Several readers may just scan through the text to make sure they are up to speed with essential option concepts before moving forward with this book. After the first few chapters, several chapters specifically focus on individual strategies. Having a good base of knowledge to work from is the key to getting the most of out the rest of this book.

THE OPTION BASICS

There are two types of options, call options and put options. A call option is the right to own a security at a certain price. The put option is the right to sell a security at a certain price. As owners of options purchase a right,

TABLE 1.1 Call and Put Option Rights and Obligations

	Buyer	**Seller**
Call	Right to Buy	Obligation to Sell
Put	Right to Sell	Obligation to Buy

the seller of an option contract actually takes on an obligation. A call seller is obligated to sell a security at a certain price and a put seller is obligated to purchase a security at a certain price. If this is a little unclear, Table 1.1 might clear it up.

For example, if Trader A buys a XYZ 30 Call and Trader B is the seller of this option they now have a right and an obligation respectively. Trader A would now be long 1 XYZ 30 Call and has the right to buy shares of XYZ at 30. Trader B as the seller of the XYZ 30 Call would be short 1 of the option contracts and would have the obligation to sell shares of XYZ at 30 if the option is exercised.

If instead Trader A bought 1 XYZ 30 Put and once again Trader B is the seller of this option, Trader A would now be long 1 XYZ 30 Put. As the holder of this put option, Trader A now has the right to sell shares of XYZ at 30. Trader B would now be short 1 XYZ 30 Put and would have the obligation to buy shares of XYZ at 30 if the option is exercised. Basically, the owner of an option holds all the cards as they have the choice of when and whether to exercise the option, while the seller of the option takes on an obligation and has no control over the exercise of the option.

Each option, put or call, represents the right or obligation to sell or buy a security depending on the position a trader holds. This security is what is known as the underlying for a particular option. For instance a call option on XYZ would be the right to buy XYZ, and XYZ would represent the underlying security. This holds true for put options as well. The underlying for an option contract may be a futures contract, some sort of index, an exchange traded fund, or shares of stock. This book concentrates mainly on index, exchange traded fund, and stock options. As exchange traded funds trade in a very similar fashion to stocks, this book treats them as stocks. Also, another term for stock is equity and these terms will be used interchangeably throughout the book

An option contract will relate to a standard number of shares when related to a stock or exchange traded fund. The standard number of shares in the United States is 100 shares. Due to stock splits, mergers, and corporate actions this number varies from time to time, but in general a stock option represents 100 shares. For instance, a call option on XYZ would represent the right to buy 100 shares of XYZ. If exercised, the holder of a call option would purchase 100 shares of XYZ at a certain price and the trader with a short position in the option contract would be forced to sell 100 shares of XYZ at the exercise price. A put option on XYZ would represent the right to sell 100 shares of XYZ, and the holder of a XYZ put option would sell 100 shares of XYZ upon exercising that option.

There are a wide variety of indexes that have options trading on them. They may represent anything from the stocks in an index to the volatility level of a certain index. Along with there being a variety of underlying indexes that have listed options trading, there are a variety of contract specifications. Throughout this book, an index option will be assumed to be an equity index option. Theoretically, an equity index option is the right to buy or sell a basket of the stocks that comprise a certain index. For example, a call option on the S&P 500 Index would be the right to buy a basket of S&P 500 Index components at a certain index level. However, instead of purchasing shares of stock, these index options are settled in a cash transfer or cash settled.

A cash settled index results in a transfer from the seller of an option to the buyer of an option if that option has value upon exercise. As there are a number of shares involved in the underlying for stock options, there is a dollar amount assigned to each point of an underlying index. To stick with the S&P 500 Index example, 1 S&P 500 Index point = $100. So for each point of value in an S&P 500 Index option, there is a $100 transfer from the seller of an option to a buyer of an option.

Options are contracts that have a finite life. Although there are some exceptions, equity and the majority of index options expire on the third Saturday following the third Friday of their expiration month. Being that the option market is not open on the third Saturday, the actual day options cease trading is the Friday before the third Saturday of the month. For instance a Call on XYZ expiring in August would trade in the option market until the Friday before the third Saturday of August.

Although options expire on the Friday prior to the third Saturday of the month, many options may be exercised any time until this expiration date. An option that may be exercised any time until expiration is referred to as an American-style option. The term American has nothing to do with geography, only exercise rights. All stock options and some index options traded in the United States are American-style options.

European-style options are options that may only be exercised on their expiration date. These type of options are typical of index options, with the best known being the S&P 500 Index options. Also, options that trade on the CBOE Volatility Index® (VIX®) are European style options.

Another component of both call and put options is the strike price. This strike price is the level where the holder of a call would be able to purchase the underlying security or the holder of a put would have the right to sell the underlying security. The strike price of a XYZ August 30 Call would be 30. If XYZ is a stock and an American-style option, the holder of this option would hold the right to buy 100 shares of XYZ at 30 any time until the third Friday before the third Saturday in August. In the case that this option is European style, the holder of this call would have the right to buy XYZ only on the expiration day of the option at 30. The strike price for a put option is the level at which the holder of a put option has the right to sell a security. The holder of a XYZ August 30 Put would have the right to sell 100 shares XYZ at 30.

Equity Call Option and Put Option Settlement

Expiration Day–XYZ at 35
Holder of Long 1 XYZ 30 Call–Buys 100 Shares of XYZ at 30
Holder of Short 1 XYZ 30 Call–Sells 100 Shares of XYZ at 30

Equity Put Option Settlement

Expiration Day–XYZ at 25
Holder of Long 1 XYZ 30 Put–Sells 100 Shares of XYZ at 30
Holder of Short 1 XYZ 30 Put–Buys 100 Shares of XYZ at 30

As previously mentioned, index options are settled by a method known as cash settlement. If, for example, a S&P 500 (SPX) 950 Call Option is exercised, on expiration, when the SPX is trading at 955, the holder of the SPX 950 Call would receive a credit of $500 to their account. A seller, holding a short position in the same SPX 950 Call option would be obligated to pay $500 and have their account debited by this amount. The following illustrates the math behind this settlement process.

SPX Call Settlement

$$\text{Settlement} - \text{Strike} = \text{Option Value}$$

$$\text{Option Value} \times \text{Multiplier} = \text{Profit}$$

$$955 - 950 = 5.00$$

$$5.00 * \$100 = \$500$$

Holder of Long 1 SPX 950 Call–Receives $500.
Holder of Short 1 SPX 950 Call–Pays $500.

There is a slight difference when determining the settlement for an index put option. If a SPX 950 Put is held on expiration date and the SPX is trading at 945 the holder of the SPX 950 Put would receive $500 and the short seller of the SPX 950 Put would have to pay $500. However, the

TABLE 1.2 Components of an Option Contract

Underlying	Expiration	Strike	Type	Premium
XYZ	February	55	Call	1.50

formula for this is a little different. Instead of the strike price being subtracted from the settlement price, the formula is reversed with the settlement price being subtracted from the strike price.

SPX Put Settlement

$$\text{Strike} - \text{Settlement} = \text{Option Value}$$

$$\text{Option Value} \times \text{Multiplier} = \text{Profit}$$

$$950 - 945 = 5.00$$

$$5.00 * \$100 = \$500$$

Holder of Long 1 SPX 950 Put–Receives $500.
Holder of Short 1 SPX 950 Put–Pays $500.

The final piece of an option is the premium or price of an option contract. If a XYZ August 30 Put is quoted at 1.50 and this is an equity contract with a standard $100 multiplier, the premium is 1.50 or $150. The contract would cost $150 to purchase. The multiplier for an index option would be based on the multiplier also. Again, S&P 500 Index options have a multiplier of $100 so a July SPX 1200 Call quoted at 7.50 would have a cost of $750. Table 1.2 is a quick summary of all of the components of an option.

IN-AT-OUT OF THE MONEY

An option may be what is referred to as in the money, at the money, or out of the money. This reference relates to where the underlying security is relative to the type and strike of the option. Being in the money means that an option has some sort of value if the option was exercised at that very moment. For example, if a trader owns a call option with a 30 strike price and the underlying security is trading at 35, this option would be referred to as being in the money. If a stock is trading higher than the strike of a call option, that call option is in the money.

In the case of a put option, an equity put option is in the money when a stock is trading lower than a put option's strike price. For example, if a

TABLE 1.3 Summary of In-At-Out Of The Money

	In The Money	At The Money	Out Of The Money
Call Option	Underlying greater than strike	Underlying equal to strike	Underlying less than strike
Put Option	Underlying lower than strike	Underlying equal to strike	Underlying greater than strike

stock is trading at 25 and the strike price of the put option is 30, the holder of this put option has the right to sell the stock at 30 while the stock is at 25, then there is value in this option as the right to sell a stock at 30 when it is trading at 25 is immediately worth $5 of profit.

At the money is exactly what it sounds like. An option is at the money when the underlying security has the same price as the strike price of the option. This holds true for both put and call options. So if a stock is trading at 30, both the 30 Call and 30 Put would be at the money. To slightly confuse this term, some traders will refer to the closest strike to the underlying price as being the at the money option. If a stock is trading at 31 and the closest strike prices are 30 and 35, the 30 Call and 30 Put options may be called the at the money options.

Finally, an out of the money option is an option that has no value if exercised. If a stock is trading at 35 and a trader holds the 40 Call, there is no value in exercising the 40 Call and purchasing shares at 40. In fact, there is negative value by exercising this call option and this transaction would automatically be a $5 loss. For call options, if the underlying stock price is lower than the strike price of the option, it would be considered out of the money.

With a put option, when the price of the underlying security is higher than the option's strike price, the option is considered out of the money. There is no value in exercising a put option with a strike price of 35 if the underlying stock is trading at 40. Once again, there is actually negative value in exercising this option. Table 1.3 is a quick review of the three states of an option; in, at, or out of the money.

INTRINSIC AND TIME VALUE

The value of an option is determined first by market forces. The price for an option is the level where a buyer and seller have come together to trade the option. At times the value of an option is depicted by a bid and ask, the bid being a price that a trader is a willing buyer of the option and the ask being a price that another trader is a willing seller of the option. In either case the value of the option is determined by the market. Once this value has been determined, the price of the option indicates how much time value and how much intrinsic value the market is giving to this option.

The value of an option is divided into two components. The first is the intrinsic value, which is the value of the option if it is exercised. As in the previous section this is also the amount an option is in the money. If a call option with a 30 strike is owned and the underlying security is trading at 35, the intrinsic value of this option would be 5, or 35 – 30. However, it is very possible this call option would be trading at a level higher than 5. The trading price of this option that is greater than the intrinsic value is called the time value of the option.

For instance, in the previous paragraph where an option had an intrinsic value of 5, if the trading price of this option were 6, the time value of this option would be 1, or 6–5. Any value above the intrinsic value of an option is known as the time value. In cases where an option is out of the money and has no intrinsic value, 100 percent of the value of the option is time value. In the case of a stock trading at 30 and the 35 strike call option trading at 1.50, the 1.50 represents time value and no intrinsic value. Table 1.4 is a more extensive example of intrinsic and time value for both call and put options.

In the examples in Table 1.4, the only options with intrinsic value are the 30 Call and the 40 Put. The underlying stock is trading at 35, so both the 35 Call and 35 Put options have no intrinsic value, but all time value. The far out of the money 30 Put and 40 Call both have no intrinsic value and are made up of all time value.

TABLE 1.4 Breakdown of Intrinsic and Time Value with Stock Trading at 35

Option	Market Price	Intrinsic Value	Time Value
30 Call	5.65	5.00	0.65
30 Put	0.60	0.00	0.60
35 Call	2.45	0.00	2.45
35 Put	2.40	0.00	2.40
40 Call	0.85	0.00	0.85
40 Put	5.75	5.00	0.75

SPREAD BASICS

A spread trade, either with options or another type of trading vehicle, involves taking two or more positions that should be considered by the trader as a single position. There are numerous methods of putting on spreads, possibly buying and selling two stocks that usually trade in a similar fashion or in commodities such as long corn and short soybeans. This book will focus on spread trades involving options and their underlying securities.

Spreads using options may be classified in a few different ways. An option may be traded against the underlying security, two similar options may be traded against each other, two different options may be combined together, and then two options with different types and expirations may be combined.

Using an option in combination with an underlying security is one of the more common methods of using options. These types of spreads are discussed in Chapters 2 and 3, but for example one is discussed here. Probably one of the best trades to use as an initiation to trading options is called the covered call. A covered call is when a short position is taken in a call option while a long position exists in the underlying security, usually a stock. Selling this call option would obligate the trader to sell the underlying security at the strike price of the call option. A holder of the underlying stock is now obligated to sell their shares at the strike price. If this is a level they would be a willing seller, then this would be a smart method to take in a little more income for selling this stock at that strike price.

In a case where both puts and calls are used together, a variety of potential payouts may result. A call and similar put may be bought in a case where a trader expects a large move up or down, but is uncertain what direction that move may be. More similar puts and calls may be combined for an unlimited number of payouts. These types of trades are covered in a simple fashion in Chapters 5 and 6, then more exotic spreads are covered in Chapters 9 and 10.

Another common spread method is using options of the same type, call or put, and same expiration, but with different strike prices. A call would be sold with a call being purchased, both on the same security. These types of spreads that use just a pair of options are covered extensively in Chapters 7 and 8. The idea behind one of these spreads, that just uses a pair of options, is that by having a long and short position in similar options, the potential loss is limited as well as the potential gain. Chapters 9 through 12 cover spreads that use all calls or all puts and have the same expiration, but use more than just a pair of options.

Finally, some spreads may involve options that have the same underlying security, but have different expiration dates. For example, a call option that expires in 30 days may be sold and a call option that expires in 90 days, on the same underlying security, may be purchased. Chapters 14 and 15 extensively cover how traders use different expiration dates.

THE GREEKS

Chapter 4 will comprehensively cover the option Greeks and how they apply to individual and spread trades. Also, throughout this book, the Greeks will come in to play when discussing a variety of spread trades. There are five of the Greeks that option traders focus on when initiating trades. In general the Greeks, along with the price action of the underlying security, influence the value of options. These five Greeks are: Delta, Gamma, Theta, Vega, and Rho.

Delta is the most commonly referred to Greek and probably the easiest to understand. The Delta of an option indicates how much the price of an option should change in response to a one dollar change in the underlying security. Since a call option benefits when the underlying rises in price, the Delta for a call is positive. Conversely, since a put option loses value when the underlying rises in price, the Delta for a put option is negative.

Gamma is directly related to Delta. As a stock moves around, the Delta will move higher or lower. Gamma indicates how much Delta changes with a one dollar change in the underlying security. Unlike Delta, Gamma is positive for both call options and put options. This is function of a rise in the underlying forcing the Delta of both calls higher, and puts or a decrease in the underlying to push Delta lower for both call and put options. When a put option Delta is pushed higher, it becomes less negative and when it goes lower it is more negative. Therefore the sign of Gamma is always positive.

Theta relates to the effect that the passage of time will have on the value of an option. Theta has a negative impact for both call and put options due to the passage of time decreasing the value of an option, be it a call or put. The value of Theta indicates how much value an option will lose from day to day or sometimes over a number of days. In the case of Theta, the unit to change could be based on something other than one day.

Vega focuses on the effect a change in implied volatility has on the value of an option. Option prices reflect many factors and one is the implied volatility the market price of options projects onto the underlying security. Implied volatility is determined by an option pricing model and is measured as a percent. Based on buying and selling pressure on options, the implied volatility of options varies from day to day.

Vega indicates how much the price of an option will increase or decrease with a one percent increase or one percent decrease in the implied volatility of the option contract. Vega works the same for both call options and put options, with an increase in implied volatility increasing the value of a call or put option or a decrease in implied volatility having a negative impact on the value of calls and puts. A final note on Vega: It is considered a Greek, but is not an actual Greek letter. Vega in some academic circles and textbooks may be referred to as Kappa, which is a Greek letter.

Finally, Rho indicates how much an option will increase or decrease in value based on a one percent change in the risk-free interest rate. Rho is the least discussed of the five option Greeks mainly because it usually has a very minimal impact on the value of options, especially options that have a shorter time to expiration. Long Term Equity Anticipation Securities (LEAPS), and longer dated options will see more influence from the change in interest rates. The influence of interest rate changes is more pronounced on options that have a longer life due to the increased impact of the cost of money over the life of this option.

Call options increase in value based on an increase in interest rates and put options decrease in value with an increase in interest rates, so Rho is positive for calls and negative for put options. Do keep in mind that Rho indicates the change in an option based on a full percent change in interest rates. Usually interest rates move up or down in quarter or half point increments, so Rho really does not have much of an impact of the life of most options.

PAYOFF TABLES AND DIAGRAMS

A payoff table is basically a spreadsheet that depicts the payoff of a position at expiration or possibly any time in the future. To keep things simple, each component of the option trade or spread trade is broken out in the table, from the price paid to enter the whole position to the payoff of each individual component of the trade at expiration. By keeping things this simple, it is easier to tell where the profit or loss from a potential trade comes from, especially in cases where the plan is to exit a trade before expiration.

Table 1.5 shows the payoff for a simple long call transaction. For example, a trader buys a XYZ 30 Call for 1.50. At expiration, this option would have no value with XYZ at or below 30. The first column represents the closing price for XYZ stock in five-point increments. Moving to the right, the second column is the value of the XYZ 30 Call at each price to the left. Premium represents the 1.50 paid for the position. This −1.50 is the same at all levels of expiration. Finally the Profit/Loss column is the sum of the value of the option and the premium paid at expiration. This final column represents the payoff for the entire position at expiration.

TABLE 1.5 Call Payoff at Expiration

XYZ	XYZ 30 Call	Premium	Profit/Loss
20	0.00	−1.50	−1.50
25	0.00	−1.50	−1.50
30	0.00	−1.50	−1.50
35	5.00	−1.50	3.50
40	10.00	−1.50	8.50
45	15.00	−1.50	13.50

For a summary of the trade at any level from 30 higher, the XYZ 30 Call would have some value. At expiration, if XYZ is at 30 or lower, the buyer of this option would realize a loss of 1.50. Any level above 30, the XYZ 30 Call option would have value and the result of this trade would be the value of that option minus the price paid for this option.

A payoff diagram is a graphical depiction of the payoff of an option position at expiration. The exercise of taking the numbers from the payoff table and graphing them either with a program or even by hand is worthwhile when considering an option trade, regardless of how basic or complex. Figure 1.1 is a payoff diagram for the trade from the previous table.

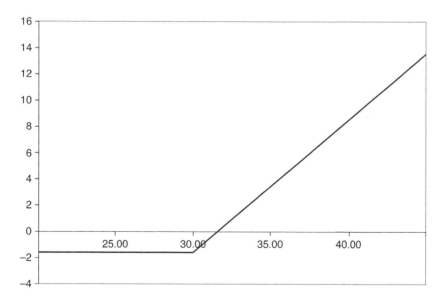

FIGURE 1.1 Payoff Diagram at Expiration

OPTION PRICING CALCULATORS

An option pricing calculator is an essential tool for any option trader. An option pricing calculator takes the variables that constitute an option's value; style (American or European), underlying price, strike price, type of option, days to expiration, volatility, and cost of money (dividends and interest rates), and determines the fair value for an option contract. In addition to the fair value for the option price, the Greeks are also determined and displayed.

Many brokerage firms include a free option calculator with their software and the CBOE offers a free pricing calculator at www.cboe.com. Table 1.6 is a demonstration of what an option calculator may look like with inputs and the outputs.

The variables on the left side of this example are all determined by the underlying security, the market, or the specifics of the option contract, with the exception of implied volatility. Implied volatility of options is a reflection of the buying and selling pressure on option contracts. As it varies and is based on the market price of an option, the price of an option may also be a variable to determine implied volatility. For instance, in the above example, if the quoted price of the option was .50 and all other variables are the same, the implied volatility may be determined. In Table 1.7, all the variables are entered including the option price and the output is the level of implied volatility being priced by the option market.

TABLE 1.6 Option Pricing Calculator Determines Option Price and Greeks

Input	
Type	American
Call/Put	Call
Underlying Price	29.00
Strike Price	30.00
Days to Expiration	15
Implied Volatility %	35.00%
Interest Rate %	1.00%
Dividends	0.15
Output	
Price	0.4292
Delta	0.3296
Gamma	0.1759
Theta	−0.0249
Vega	0.0213
Rho	0.0060

TABLE 1.7 Option Pricing Calculator Determines Implied Volatility

Input	
Type	American
Call/Put	Call
Underlying Price	29.00
Strike Price	30.00
Option Price	0.50
Days to Expiration	15
Interest Rate	1.00%
Dividends	0.15
Output	
Volatility	38.29%

As the call price is a little higher than the call fair value determined in Table 1.7, implied volatility increases a bit also. Using a pricing calculator to determine the future value of an option based on expected changes in the underlying price, time, or implied volatility will come in handy when deciding on what spread to put on when considering a trade. Using the calculator also may lead a trader to consider passing on a trade. The impact of changes in implied volatility as well as all variables will be discussed further in the chapter on evaluating potential trades.

That covers some of the basic knowledge needed to move on with this book and start mastering a variety of spread trades. Each of the topics covered in this chapter will be discussed more extensively as they apply to spreads in each chapter. However, for now, having a basic understanding is sufficient.

CHAPTER 2

Spreads Using an Underlying Security

One of the first things that comes to mind and scares people away from option spreads is the thought that a spread with options is some abstract, difficult trade that only the professional traders engage in. This is far from the truth, as many individual traders focus on a small number of spread strategies and attempt to be masters of these strategies. Some traders take this a step further and just focus on one strategy.

There are some simple spreads, with very limited risk, that are a good way to get your feet wet trading options. This chapter will introduce you to a few spreads that combine an underlying security with an option position. Although not the exotic spread that takes into account a variety of strikes and expirations, some of the spreads in this chapter are excellent introductions for inexperienced option traders. Just to keep things interesting, toward the end of the chapter, an option spread is demonstrated that involves two option positions and an underlying security. We then focus on the collar, which involves using a put and call position combined. Also, included with the discussion of a covered call, there is a spread that covers different times and strikes.

COVERED CALL

Many traders' first experience with a spread trade that involves options is through what is referred to as a covered call. The covered call is a method that allows an owner of a stock to get paid for taking on the obligation of

selling their shares at a certain price in the future. If the stock is not over
the level set by the option contract, then the income taken in for selling that
option is kept and the shares are not sold. Otherwise, if the stock is over
this level, the shares are sold. This sale of shares is an action the trader
would have done with or without entering into the option trade.

Specifically, a covered call is a position where a trader has sold a call
option against shares of an underlying stock they are currently long. For
example, if a trader owns 100 shares of XYZ, they may sell 1 call option
against the 100 shares of XYZ. This short call is 'covered' by the long position in the underlying stock. Hence the name covered call.

When an option is sold short, whether it is a call or a put, the seller has
taken on an obligation. If a trader is short a call, they have the obligation
to sell a stock at a certain price (the strike price) any time up until the
option expires. With a put, if a trader has a short put position, they have the
obligation to buy a stock at a certain price any time until the option expires.
As a seller of a call against stock a trader owns, the trader has taken on the
obligation to sell the stock they own at a set price. For example, if a trader
owns 100 shares of XYZ and has sold 1 October 50 Call against 100 shares,
they are obligated to sell 100 shares of XYZ at 50, upon exercise of this
option by an option holder.

Generally, when there is a level where a trader would be a definite
seller of a stock, they would initiate a limit order to sell the stock with the
stipulation that it is good until canceled, or open over the course of many
trading days. Eventually, this limit order would result in one of two things.
If the stock reaches this limit, the order should be executed and the stock
sold. The other alternative is the stock does not reach this level and the
order would be canceled with no transaction occurring.

For a covered call, a trader writes a call against the stock they own,
taking on the obligation to sell their shares at a certain price until the option expires. A covered call is written against long holdings of a stock or
exchange traded fund (ETF). Both options on stocks and ETFs are considered equity options. All equity options in the United States are American-
style options. American-style options are options that may be exercised
anytime until and on the expiration date. For all covered call positions this
is a possibility, however, a holder of the stock or ETF who has sold a call
option against the security does so with the hope of selling this security at
that level. Since the option seller is a willing and comfortable seller of their
shares at the level dictated by the call option, early exercise would actually
be a welcome occurrence.

Many option strategies are known by more than one name and this
holds true for the covered call. It is possible to buy a stock and sell a call
option simultaneously in one transaction. This is referred to as a buy-write.
The name stems from this being a case where a trader buys the stock and

writes an option against that long stock position, as opposed to previously owning a stock and then selling a call against that stock. Placing an order to buy 100 shares of XYZ at 37.50 and sell 1 XYZ January 40 Call at 1.00 at the same time would be called a buy-write.

As an example of a covered call, a trader owns 100 shares of XYZ and the stock is trading at 76.75. He is considering placing an order to sell his shares at 80, but also takes a look at call options to decide if selling calls might be a viable alternative. In this case, December options are 30 days to expiration and the December 80 Call is bid at 1.05. He decides to take in 1.05 by selling 1 of the December 80 Call options and take on the obligation to sell his 100 shares at 80. By selling the call options he is just being paid to take on an obligation to do something he was planning on doing in the first place.

Before going forward, a review of some key levels that exist for this trade is in order. This is actually an exercise that should be undertaken every time a new trade is initiated or considered. The levels are determined at expiration, although a more sophisticated trader may use a pricing calculator to determine potential outcomes.

For this trade, a single break-even point, level of maximum profit, and potential maximum loss should be determined.

The break-even point is calculated by taking the current price of the underlying stock and subtracting the premium received for selling the call option. In this case the break-even point is 75.70 or 76.75 (stock price) − 1.05 (premium received).

The maximum loss would be incurred on this trade if the stock were to go to zero. With XYZ at 0, the total loss on this trade would be the same as the break-even point, or 75.70. The 1.05 premium received would be nice, but not much of a buffer if the stock were to go to zero. Although in the case of this covered call, the potential of realizing a maximum loss this extreme is very low, many spread trades have limited potential loss and this exercise applies more appropriately to those trades.

Finally, the potential maximum profit of this trade should be calculated. In the case of a covered call, the maximum profit is at the call strike of 80.00. At any level above 80.00, the stock would be called away at expiration and the account would receive 80.00 per share. Combining this with the 1.05 received for selling the option gives the account 81.05 in cash, subtracting 76.75 would be a profit of 4.30. This 4.30 is the maximum potential profit from having written a call on XYZ. Table 2.1 is a summary of the key levels from this trade.

In addition to determining the key levels before a trade is initiated, a payoff diagram is useful to have an idea of where the potential profit or loss of a strategy will be. A profit and loss diagram is a good depiction of what the potential outcome of a trade will be at expiration. In addition to

TABLE 2.1   Covered Call Key Levels

Key Level	Level	Explanation
Break-even Price	75.70	Price minus Option Premium
Maximum Loss Price	0.00	Stock Goes To 0
Maximum Dollar Loss	75.70	Break-even level to 0
Maximum Profit Price	80.00	Call Strike
Maximum Dollar Profit	4.30	Max Profit Level minus Current Price plus Call Premium

at expiration, the software used at the Options Institute to indicate this outcome has the choice to include the potential profit or loss halfway to expiration.

Figure 2.1 is a profit and loss diagram created to depict the potential outcome of selling the December 80 Call at 1.05 versus being long XYZ from 76.75. There are three lines on this chart, representing different pay-offs. The simplest line, the one moving at a nice up slope from left to right represents the payoff of just being long XYZ from the closing price of 76.75. The second line, the non-curved line that looks like a hockey stick, is a de-piction of the covered call position at expiration. Starting at the left, it is a parallel line to the stock payoff. When it reaches 80, the option strike price takes a turn and continues flat for any price above 80.

Finally, the curved line represents the potential profit or loss of this strategy at certain levels halfway to expiration. As the covered call on XYZ was initiated with 30 days to expiration, the curved line depicts the profit

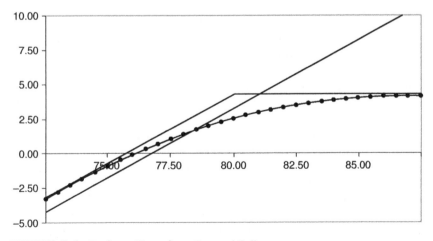

FIGURE 2.1   Profit and Loss for a Covered Call

or loss on this position when the December options have 15 days until expiration. The curved nature of this line represents the time value left on the option at different price levels. Time takes on different values at different prices for options until expiration.

Something of note from the payoff diagram for the covered call is the level where the line representing the long position in XYZ crosses the payoff of the covered call position. This is 81.05, the level from Table 2.1 of maximum profit for the covered call. There is another term for this level, the point of indifference, where a stock holder would rather hold the long position in the stock as opposed to have written a call on the stock. Above 81.05 a stock holder would have been happier having not written a call on their shares. For this reason, it should be emphasized once again that when writing a call on shares owned, an investor should be willing and happy to sell shares above the strike price of the call.

There are a handful of factors to take into account when choosing which expiration and strike to use with a covered call position. As with all option trades, a price projection of the underlying is a key component to deciding which expiration and strike to use. A second key component is the time frame of any expected move. However, with a covered call there is another piece to the puzzle that should be taken into consideration. This would be how time works, or specifically the theta of the option chosen.

Theta is a measure of, all else staying the same, how much value an option loses for a single unit of time. What is unique regarding Theta is it is not constant over the life of an option. Specifically for options with a strike price close to the price of the underlying, the time value of an option is lost at a greater rate the closer to expiration. Figure 2.2 is a chart of how time value would deteriorate for an at-the-money put or call over the last 90 days of the life of an option.

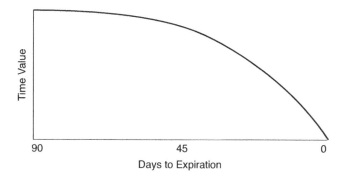

FIGURE 2.2 Time Value Deterioration

Notice in Figure 2.2 that between 90 and 45 days there is not much loss in time value. After 45 days the loss of time value really starts to accelerate, with the majority of time value being lost in the last 30 days. A goal when selling options should be to maximize the benefit from the option losing time value. When short an option, the loss of time value is working in your favor.

Here is an example of choosing strikes based on theta using a hypothetical stock and a pricing calculator to determine the value of the options. The idea here is to show a 30, 60, and 90 day call option that have all pricing factors the same except the time to expiration. January expiration is 30 days away, February is 60 days off, and March is 90 days away. The stock is XYZ, which is trading at 38.50 and the 40 strike calls are being analyzed. Using similar inputs across the board the Jan 40 Call is trading at .95, the Feb 40 Call is at 1.40, and the Mar 40 Call is at 2.05.

The first thing to notice about the individual option prices is that the Jan 40 Call is not trading at half the price of the Feb 40 Call, nor is it trading at one third the value of the Mar 40 Call. This is another illustration of the non-linear nature of the time value of options.

If a trader was considering a covered call on shares of XYZ for the next 90 days, what would be his best alternative? The first thought may be selling the Mar 40 Call, which has 90 days to expiration. However, there is a more active, flexible, and potentially profitable method to consider.

Table 2.2 depicts the difference between selling the Mar 40 Call option once for 2.05 (Trade 1) or selling an option three times with 30 days left to

TABLE 2.2 Comparison of Selling a 90-Day Call One Time or a 30-Day Call Three Times

Options	Pricing
Jan 40 Call	0.95
Feb 40 Call	1.55
Mar 40 Call	2.05
Trade 1	
Sell 1 Mar Call	2.05
Total Income =	**2.05**
Trade 2	
Sell 1 Jan 40 Call	0.95
30 Days Later:	
Sell 1 Feb 40 Call	0.95
30 Days Later:	
Sell 1 Mar 40 Call	0.95
Total Income =	**2.85**

expiration over the next 90 days for a total income of 2.85 (Trade 2). For Trade 2, the assumption is in place that all pricing factors, including the underlying stock price, will be the same when each transaction takes place. Although this is far from reality, it is a good illustration of why options expiring in around 30 days may be a preferred choice when selling calls.

Selling an option with less time to expiration is a more active strategy, but it also gives a trader more flexibility. For example, if the XYZ were to trade down to 33.50 in 30 days, a trader may choose the 35 strike call option for the next covered call. If a January call option with only 30 days to expiration was the original transaction, then it will expire with no value and another trade may be entered. In the case of selling the March option with 90 days to expiration, if a decision is made to sell a 35 strike call, then the original short option will need to be covered first.

As with all option trades, the expirations and strikes chosen have a multitude of factors, such as the price projection of the underlying or the time expectation of an event. However, when selling options, the way time works for a trader should always be a consideration and in the case of time deterioration or Theta, the last 30 days usually gives a seller the most bang for their buck.

There is a unique risk involved in the covered call strategy. The risk is that the stock will trade above the strike price during the life of the call, not be exercised, and then close under the strike price on expiration. The call would expire worthless even though the stock traded above a level where the stockholder would have hoped to sell it. This would not have occurred in case of having a limit order. With a limit order, shares would have been sold at the limit price. However, using a limit order as opposed to selling an option would also not provide any income to the trader.

If shares do trade up to a level where the holder would be a seller and there is a call written against the shares, there is always the alternative to buy back the option and sell the shares. The option market makers post markets throughout the trading day and the ability to reverse or exit positions always exists. In some cases, if enough time has passed and the amount of time value left in the option has diminished enough, the option may actually be bought back at a profit.

Table 2.3 depicts a case where a decision might need to be made regarding exiting a covered call position before expiration. This example uses the hypothetical XYZ trade from the previous example. The trader is long 100 shares of XYZ at 38.50 and has sold the XYZ 30 Day 40 Call at 0.95. In this example, the stock is trading at 40.15 which is slightly over the desired selling price of XYZ with a certain number of days left to expiration. Using a pricing calculator, the value of the XYZ 40 Call is determined. If the stock trades up very quickly and the decision is made to exit the trade, there is a little bit of a negative impact from the short option. As

TABLE 2.3 Covered Call Profit or Loss at Various Days to Expiration

Days	Stock	40 Call	Stock P/L	Opt P/L	Tot P/L
30	38.50	0.95	N/A	N/A	N/A
25	40.15	1.55	1.65	−0.60	1.05
20	40.15	1.40	1.65	−0.45	1.20
15	40.15	1.20	1.65	−0.25	1.40
10	40.15	1.00	1.65	−0.05	1.60
5	40.15	0.70	1.65	0.25	1.90
0	40.15	0.15	1.65	0.80	2.45

time passes, the impact of the option lessens and then the loss continues to shrink until a little less than 10 days to expiration. At less than 10 days to go, there is a slight profit in the option, as well as the benefit of selling the stock above the target price of 40.

COVERED CALL USING LEAPS®

A viable alternative to owning a stock is a LEAPS call option. Again, the term LEAPS is an acronym for Long-term Equity Anticipation Securities. A LEAPS call would be a call that has over a year to expiration. This is the simplistic explanation for a LEAPS option, as there is a bit more to them than just time. A major difference is LEAPS options do not work in the same way as shorter term options for various spread trades. Also, not all stocks with options have LEAPS on them. This number varies from time to time, but it is safe to say about 25 percent of stocks and ETFs with options also have LEAPS listed on them.

The biggest difference between shorter term options and LEAPS is the time to expiration. Due to the long time to expiration, the time value of LEAPS options deteriorates at a much slower rate than that of options with much less time to expiration. Since the time value deterioration for a LEAPS call is much less than a shorter term option, a LEAPS call can be a substituted for the underlying stock in a covered call strategy. This is also called a diagonal spread and there will be much more information about diagonal spreads in Chapter 15, but due to the similarities between this spread and a covered call, a quick example is worth discussion.

The previous example when choosing strikes based on time erosion should be considered. A call option with a strike near the underlying stock price will deteriorate at a rate very similar to what is depicted in Figure 2.2. A deep-in-the-money call, regardless of the time to expiration, will see the time value of the option deteriorate at a much slower pace.

This pace of time erosion is even slower when the time to expiration is stretched out to a much longer time to expiration. This difference in time erosion would benefit greatly the holder of the in-the-money LEAPS Call who is also short a slightly out of the money call.

Once again XYZ will be an example, but instead of being long 100 shares of XYZ stock at 76.75, the account will hold 1 of the XYZ January 60 LEAPS Calls, which is trading at 18.75. These LEAPS calls expire in over a year, or actually 425 days. As XYZ is trading at 76.75, this premium value of 18.75 represents just 2.00 of time value for the next 425 days. This 2.00 of time value is determined by subtracting the strike price from the current stock price (76.75 − 60.00 = 16.75), this results in knowing that the intrinsic value of the option is 16.75. Taking the intrinsic value of the LEAPS option and subtracting it from the call premium (18.75 − 16.75 = 2.00) results in the time value. As in the covered call example, the December 80 Calls expire in 30 days and are trading at 1.05.

For the trading example, the position is long an XYZ January 60 LEAPS Call trading at 18.75 and has sold 1 of the December 80 Calls at 1.05 against the LEAPS Call. The short December Calls are 'covered' by the long position in the LEAPS Call. The LEAPS Calls are a substitute for the long stock in the Covered Call position.

Due to the pricing factors influencing the price of an option being fluid—always changing—it is very difficult to know exactly what the profit or loss of the overall position would be at expiration of the short option. Many assumptions go into the pricing of options in the future, but for simplicity the assumption is being made that only time changes. An option calculator is essential when these assumptions may change around.

Using a pricing calculator, it is determined that all else staying the same (stock price, volatility, interest rates), the XYZ Jan 60 LEAPS Call would be priced at 18.55 for a loss of .20 over 30 days, which translates to less than .01 a day. All else being the same at expiration, the December 80 Call would expire worthless, but for a short call holder that would be a profit of 1.05. The profit of 1.05 is realized if the stock is below 80 at expiration, as the XYZ December 80 Call would expire with no value.

Although a little more difficult math is involved and most likely a pricing calculator, determining the potential upside, downside, and break-even levels for this trade is in order. The potential upside in this trade would be capped with XYZ closing exactly at 80.00 and the calls not being exercised at expiration. At 80.00, when factoring in the loss of time value in the LEAPS Calls, a profit would be 3.80. Using the pricing calculator to determine the LEAPS Call value and assuming no change in pricing factors except time and price, the LEAPS Call would be worth 21.50 for an unrealized profit of 2.75. This would be added to the premium received on the December 80 Call of 1.05.

As the stock moves above 80.00, the amount of time value in the LEAPS Call would actually start to go down and this would result in a smaller gain than 2.75. Also, over 80.00, some sort of action would need to be taken regarding the short term option that is in the money. The short option would be exercised with a resulting short position of 100 shares of XYZ appearing in the account. A trader is faced with a couple of choices, he could allow this to happen, if he desires to have a short position in XYZ, or he may just choose to buy back the short option shortly (as shortly as minutes) before expiration, possibly at a loss, but by doing so would avoid being assigned a short position.

The break-even point for this trade would be at 75.75. At this price at expiration, the LEAPS Call would be worth 17.70, which represents a loss of 1.05 on the LEAPS Call. This loss of 1.05 would be offset by the income kept from selling the December 80 Call, which would expire worthless, and the result is a break-even trade. Also, only the December call option is expiring, the LEAPS call still has 395 days to expiration. Choices include selling the LEAPS call, holding it, or even holding it and selling another shorter term option against it.

The maximum loss level is determined to be with XYZ 28.00 which would render the LEAPS Call worthless, even with 395 days to expiration. This is sort of a stretch, as even though the LEAPS Call would have no value on a calculator, there is still over a year for the stock to recover, with the result being some value for the Jan 60 LEAPS Call.

Figure 2.3 is a depiction of what the payoff would be for this time spread at December expiration along with a payoff line showing what just holding the LEAPS Call option would mean. The LEAPS Call payoff is very linear once the option is in the money, as there is very little time

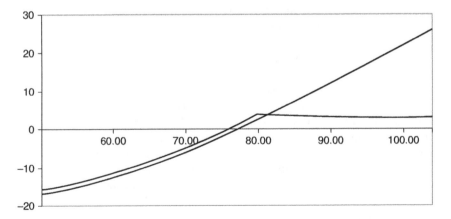

FIGURE 2.3 LEAPS Spread Payoff at Expiration

TABLE 2.4 Comparison of Covered Call and LEAPS Spread Payoffs

Key Level	Covered Call	LEAPS Spread
Break-even Price	75.70	75.75
Maximum Loss Price	0.00	28.00
Maximum Dollar Loss	75.70	17.70
Maximum Profit Price	80.00	80.00
Maximum Dollar Profit	4.30	3.80

value for the LEAPS, so the value is all intrinsic value. As the option approaches being out of the money or below 60, the payoff is more curved due to the value of the option being 100 percent time value. The payoff for the time spread is similar to the payoff at expiration for a covered call, but is a little more curved. The curved nature of this payoff relates the time value of the Jan 60 LEAPS Call at various prices on expiration of the December 80 Call.

A note regarding LEAPS versus owning an underlying stock is in order. First, although a LEAPS holder participates in the price appreciation of an underlying security, the holder does not participate in any cash dividends that may be paid out. Also, stock holders in companies have voting rights while LEAPS holders have no such voting rights. Finally, just like shorter term options, LEAPS call options are finite instruments and do expire, unlike shares of stock which do not expire.

Finally, Table 2.4 shows a quick comparison of the payoff of the Covered Call strategy and the comparable trade using the LEAPS Call as a substitute for long stock. A couple of the levels are very similar, such as the break-even level and the maximum profit level. However, there are some dramatic differences between the two strategies. The maximum loss for the LEAPS Spread is 17.70, while for the Covered Call it is 75.70. Also, the maximum profit for the LEAPS Spread is 3.80 and for the Covered Call it is a bit higher at 4.30.

When considering two spreads, this exercise of comparing the various levels of each strategy can be useful in deciding which strategy to implement. For the LEAPS Spread, the potential profit is less than for the covered call, but the potential loss in the LEAPS Spread is also lower than that of the covered call.

SYSTEMATIC COVERED CALL STRATEGIES

There is evidence that implementing a systematic program of writing calls against a long position in the S&P 500 results in superior investment results as opposed to maintaining a pure long-term long position in stocks. To gain an understanding into the potential returns of a systematic buy write strategy, the CBOE developed the CBOE S&P 500 BuyWriteIndex® (BXM) in 2002.

The BXM is a total return index based on having a portfolio that replicates the holdings in the S&P 500 index. On the third Friday each month, an S&P 500 Index call option is written against the portfolio. This covered call is held until expiration or the third Friday of the following month, when a new one-month call is written against the S&P 500. The result is an index that tracks the performance of a hypothetical covered call strategy on the S&P 500 Index.

Returns of the BXM have been impressive on a risk return basis compared to a long-only portfolio. The BXM has been calculated back to June 1, 1988 and the returns generated by this strategy have been a little superior to the performance of an investment in the S&P 500. However, the returns on a risk adjusted basis have been superior with the BXM having much less volatility or risk than a long-only investment in the S&P 500. More information on the BXM, free historical data, and updated performance can be obtained at www.cboe.com/bxm.

CASH-SECURED PUT

As previously mentioned, as a short seller of an option a trader has taken on an obligation. When short a call there is the obligation to sell at a certain price, conversely, a short put is an obligation to buy. Technically, a short put is a single position, but when combined with cash deposited to cover this obligation to buy shares it may be considered a spread between cash and a short put.

Many brokerage firms shy away from allowing clients to sell options when they do not own an underlying instrument. This is also referred to as being naked short an option. However, in the case of a cash-secured put, the short option should not be considered a naked position since the put is written against an amount of cash available to purchase the underlying stock at the level of the option's strike price.

When short an option, a trader is taking on an obligation, unlike the long option holder who has a right. In the case of being short a put, a trader is taking on the obligation to buy a security at a certain price. Much like having a short call position at a level where you would be comfortable selling a stock, it is advisable to write a cash-secured put at a level where you would be comfortable purchasing a stock.

The normal procedure for buying a stock at a certain level would be to put in a limit order to buy shares with instructions to have this order active until cancelled. This is what is known as a 'good til canceled' order. This order is out there, the hope is for the stock to trade down to the limit level and then the shares are automatically purchased through execution of the good until canceled order. Eventually one of two things will occur with this order—it will be executed or it will be canceled.

When using cash-secured puts in place of a limit order, a trader receives income for taking on the obligation of buying shares. This income is theirs to keep if the stock reaches the strike price or not. Upon expiration of the option, one of two things also happens. If the stock is lower than the strike price, it will be exercised by the put holder and the short put holder will purchase shares of the underlying stock at the strike price. Or if the stock is above the strike price at expiration the option will expire worthless. One note, which is discussed further later in this section, if the stock trades below the strike price, but does not close under the strike at expiration it is very possible the option will still expire with no value.

For example, a trader is considering buying shares of XYZ, but does not want to pay the current price of 26.45. He considers putting in a limit order to buy shares at 25 with the intention of leaving it open for the next month or two. Before placing this order, he also considers selling a put that would give him the obligation to purchase shares at 25.

The date is November 30, so the trader takes a look at the December 25 Put and January 25 Put to determine if the premium in either of these options is worth putting on a cash-secured put. The XYZ December 25 Put has just 19 days to expiration and the premium received would be 0.65, while the XYZ January 25 Put has 47 days to expiration and may be sold for 1.10.

Much like the situation with selling calls against a long position, there is more to take into account before trading than just the price a trader is willing to purchase a stock for with a cash-secured put. The time to expiration is also the time that the obligation to buy shares is in place. Also the time to expiration may come into play as far as having the option lose value as expiration is approached.

Finally, this is not just a short put, it is a cash-secured put. With a covered call, the option is covered by owning the underlying stock. With the cash-secured put, the funds to pay for shares are deposited in an account to assure the ability to buy the shares is there if the put option is assigned. The amount of funds that would need to be deposited is actually determined by subtracting the premium received for selling the put option from the price of the XYZ shares associated with the strike price. If that is a bit much to visualize, the example should hopefully clear this up.

The trader in this case decides to sell the XYZ January 25 Put as the December option's premium of 0.65 is not enticing enough to sell. Also, the time frame of the January option matches up more to his liking so he

TABLE 2.5 Cash-secured put Key Levels

	Level	Explanation
Break-even Price	23.90	Strike minus Premium
Maximum Loss Price	0.00	Stock goes to 0
Maximum Dollar Loss	23.90	Break-even level to 0
Maximum Profit Price	25 and above	Put Strike
Maximum Dollar Profit	1.10	Premium Received

chooses to sell the XYZ January 25 Put and take in 1.10 for the obligation to purchase shares of XYZ at 25. In addition to this, he will need to deposit $2,390 in his account. The cost of 100 shares of XYZ if the option is assigned would be $2,500 (100 × $25.00), the income from selling the put option was $110 (100 × $1.10) so the funds that need to be deposited comes to $2,500 − $110 or $2,390. There are key levels regarding the cash-secured put and they appear in Table 2.5.

The cash-secured put has a break-even level of 23.90, which is the strike price minus the premium received for selling the put option. This may also be thought of as the effective price for purchasing shares of XYZ if the stock is below 25 at expiration. The maximum profit for selling the option is 1.10 which would be kept by the trader if the stock is over 25 at expiration and the option expires with no value. The short put payoff appears in Figure 2.4.

The short option profit and loss from Figure 2.4 is based on the option trade only. The intention behind a cash-secured put is to improve an entry

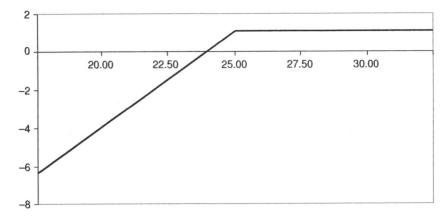

FIGURE 2.4 Short Put Payoff at Expiration

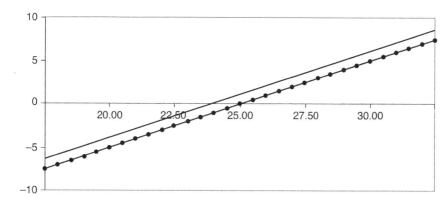

FIGURE 2.5 Stock Purchased with Cash-secured Put versus Limit Order

point into a stock that is expected to be held for some time. If that stock is to be held for longer-term appreciation, then looking at what the payoff would be upon exercise versus buying the stock with a 25 limit is in order. Figure 2.5 shows the comparison of using the short option to enter the trade as opposed to a limit order at 25.

The lines are parallel to each other, but the solid line, which represents the payoff of the stock purchased with the cash-secured put position, has a slightly lower break-even point. The breakeven is 23.90 and at any level where the stock trades, the cash-secured put will have a 1.10 advantage on the stock purchased with a limit order.

A risk to keep in mind when using a short put to enter a long position is the possibility of the stock trading under the strike price during the life of the option, but expiring out of the money. If the put option is not exercised while the stock is trading under the option strike, then it is possible shares may not be owned in a case where the option seller was hoping to purchase shares. This is exactly like the covered call example where the stock may have traded over the strike, but settled under the strike at expiration.

If the stock were to trade under the price where purchase is desirable, a trading decision would need to be made. Using a pricing calculator, Table 2.6 shows what the effective price of XYZ shares would be after buying back the put if the stock trades slightly under 25 (24.85) at certain time-to-expiration points during the life of the option.

If there is a strong desire to own shares in the 25 range, then the put option might be covered and shares purchased with the stock under 25. Using the table, with the option slightly in the money, at any time over halfway to expiration attempting to utilize the cash-secured put would actually result in a higher effective purchase price for XYZ shares.

TABLE 2.6 Effective Purchase Price at Certain Days to Expiration

Days	XYZ	25 Put	Opt P/L	Effective Price	Versus Paying 25
40	24.85	1.60	−0.50	25.35	−0.35
35	24.85	1.50	−0.40	25.25	−0.25
30	24.85	1.40	−0.30	25.15	−0.15
25	24.85	1.30	−0.20	25.05	−0.05
20	24.85	1.15	−0.15	25.00	0.00
15	24.85	1.00	0.10	24.75	0.25
10	24.85	0.85	0.25	24.60	0.40
5	24.85	0.60	0.50	24.35	0.65
0	24.85	0.15	1.10	23.90	1.10

Going into the trade, a trader should have a plan in place in case the stock reaches this point quickly. Also, if shares drop tremendously and the desire to own shares is still in place, it is possible to cover the option at a loss, and purchase shares. Table 2.7 shows the stock dropping to 23.00 and the resulting effective price paid versus having a 25 limit order sitting on the books.

Note at all time-to-expiration periods, there is a superior effective price paid relative to having an order to buy at 25. This is due to the time value nature of the put option. As the option is more in the money, the time value deteriorates. As there is a sort of reverse benefit on the intrinsic value for the cash-secured put, the shrinking time value results in adding some value to the cash-secured put position. The effective price is much higher than if the put option was never sold and shares were just purchased at 23.00. But if the original intention were to buy shares in the 25 range, odds are using that limit order would have the position as a loss when XYZ reaches 23.

TABLE 2.7 Effective Purchase Price at Certain Days to Expiration

Days	XYZ	25 Put	Opt P/L	Effective Price	Versus Paying 25
40	23.00	2.70	−1.60	24.60	0.40
35	23.00	2.63	−1.53	24.53	0.47
30	23.00	2.55	−1.45	24.45	0.55
25	23.00	2.45	−1.35	24.35	0.65
20	23.00	2.35	−1.25	24.25	0.75
15	23.00	2.25	−1.15	24.15	0.85
10	23.00	2.15	−1.05	24.05	0.95
5	23.00	2.05	−0.95	23.95	1.05
0	23.00	0.00	0.00	23.90	1.10

The cash-secured put is a method to buy a stock at a lower price or be in a position to improve the entry price of a long-term stock holding. There is some risk in using a short put to buy a stock, as if the stock trades down to the desired price to purchase and then trades up to not being in the money at expiration. In this case, shares may not be owned and the only profit would be the premium received for selling the put option.

There is some flexibility offered by the option market, where an option position may always be exited if the original intention behind a trade has changed. Using this same line of thinking, if a stock reaches a desired purchase point, the short put may be covered and the stock purchased in the open market. As shown above, the originally intended purchase price may be bettered, even if a loss is realized when the option portion of the trade is exited.

SYSTEMATIC CASH-SECURED PUT

As with a consistent program of writing covered calls, there is evidence that a continuous program of selling puts as a method to enter a market is a strategy that results in superior investment returns. With the same philosophy of the BuyWrite Index, the CBOE developed an index to track a consistent program of selling puts against the S&P 500 with the hope of purchasing the components of the S&P 500 on weakness, while being paid to take on this obligation.

The CBOE S&P 500 PutWrite Index®, which has the appropriate ticker symbol PUT, replicates a passive strategy of holding a money market account while selling put options on the S&P 500 on a monthly basis. Like the BXM, the PUT sells put options on the S&P 500 on expiration Friday or the third Friday of each month. These puts expire one month out and upon expiration a new series of put options is sold against the cash portfolio.

The specific options sold are the closest put strike to the S&P 500 that is not above the level of the S&P 500. For example if the S&P 500 is trading at 1131.20, and the strike that is less than, but closest to 1131.20 is 1130.00—then the 1130.00 puts would be sold. The goal of the PutWrite Index is to replicate a put writing strategy that would outperform in up markets, but underperform in down markets.

Like the BXM, the PUT has had very strong risk returns relative to the S&P 500, but it has also outperformed the S&P 500 over the long term. A recent study showed the PUT Index beating S&P 500 performance by over 1 percent while having about two thirds the risk using standard deviation as a risk measure. More information on the PUT may be found at www.cboe.com/put.

PROTECTIVE PUT

The option industry likes to frequently use an analogy between buying an insurance policy and using options for asset protection. Option prices are referred to as the premium, just as the cost of an insurance contract is called the premium. Probably the easiest demonstration of options as insurance is when puts are purchased to protect an asset from a drop in value. This is also known as a protective put.

If the trader is an owner of 100 shares of XYZ and is concerned about the near-term prospects for the stock, but feels it is a good long-term investment, the trader may purchase a put option to protect from a bearish move in the stock. The reason for not just selling shares could be as simple as taxes or as complex as some sort of emotional attachment to the stock. There are people that inherit a stock and are emotionally attached as in "this stock has been in my family for 100 years." For whatever the rationale, the trader would just like to protect against a bearish move in the stock and this concern is only for the next 60 days.

In this case, August expiration is 60 days off and XYZ is trading at 62.00. The August 60 Put can be purchased for 2.05. So to insure against a dramatic drop in XYZ shares for the next two months, the trader purchases a XYZ August 60 Put option for 2.05.

This protection is somewhat expensive, 2.05 represents a drop of almost 3.5 percent before the August 60 Put will have any value at expiration. A very bearish price projection over the near term is needed for this put purchase to make sense.

The key levels of this protective put appear in Table 2.8. The breakeven level for this trade is 64.05. With the stock trading at 62.00, this represents a 2.05 increase in the stock price. This price rise is needed to cover the cost of the put option that was purchased for protection. As the put option only has an effect on the position if the stock drops, the maximum potential gain is theoretically unlimited if the stock rallies to infinity. Unlikely, but that is the academic explanation. In a trader world, if the stock moves much higher, the trader participates in the rally, minus the premium paid for the put option.

TABLE 2.8 Protective Put Key Levels

	Level	Explanation
Break-even Price	64.05	Stock price plus option premium
Maximum Loss Price	60.00 and below	Put has value under 60
Maximum Dollar Loss	4.05	2.00 from stock, 2.05 option cost
Maximum Profit Price	Unlimited	Stock rallies
Maximum Dollar Profit	Unlimited	Stock rallies

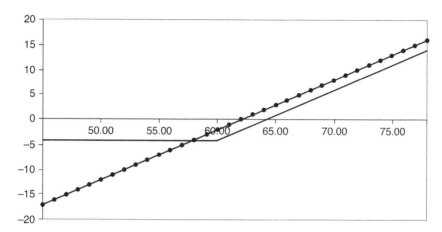

FIGURE 2.6 Protective Put Payoff

The maximum potential loss of this position is a total of 4.05. With the stock at 62.00 and a long position in the XYZ August 60 Put, any drop from 62.00 to 60.00 is not offset by the long position in the put option. However, below 60, the option starts to increase in value, but since there was a 2.05 premium paid, the protection is not fully realized until the stock is below 57.95. All of these levels are displayed in Figure 2.6.

The payoff diagram has two payoffs displayed. The hockey stick-shaped line is a combination of owning XYZ from 62 and buying the XYZ August 60 Put for 2.05. The dotted line represents owning shares of XYZ from 62 with no hedge in place. The spot where the two lines cross is 57.95, where the option actually adds value and causes the position to stop having a loss relative to a pure long position in XYZ. This point is also referred to as the point of indifference, or the point where the trader is happy they decided to purchase some protection.

Finally, this protection is only in place for the next 60 days, so if the stock is above 60 at expiration, there is no benefit from the protection and the option expires with no value. If there is still concern regarding the stock price, another put may need to be purchased to provide price protection.

THE COLLAR

The collar takes the protective put a step further. At times the insurance purchased or put option price may be a little pricey due to market conditions. There is a short-term concern about a stock, but for the long term an investor wants to hold on to the shares. At the same time, a put option may be considered expensive. When a put is expensive, the corresponding calls are probably expensive also. This is due to what is called put-call parity and is covered in Chapter 3. So to get protection, but offset the XYZ of the put, a trader may sell a call to offset the cost of the put. This strategy is called a Collar.

Using the previous example, there is some concern regarding XYZ shares and it is trading at 62.00. August expiration is once again 60 days off and the August 60 Put is trading at 2.05. The trader wants some protection on the downside, but he is not very happy with the 2.05 premium on the put option. The trader just considers this too expensive for short-term protection.

Along with being concerned with the near-term prospects of XYZ, the trader also would be a happy seller of shares over 65. The August 65 Call is trading at 1.85. To get protection to the downside, but lower the cost of this protection, the trader would put on a collar or buy 1 August 60 Put at 2.05 and sell 1 August 65 Call at 1.85. Using the collar as a strategy, the cost of protection for XYZ has gone from 2.05 to .20. However, lowering the cost of this protection has also caused the trader to take on the obligation of selling shares at 65. As there are several moving parts here, the following list shows the three positions involved in this collar:

Short 1 XYZ August 65 Call at 1.85
Long 100 XYZ at 62
Long 1 XYZ August 60 Put at 2.05

These positions are actually just a combination of two spreads that have been covered in this chapter. The short call and long stock are combined to be a covered call. Taking the stock position and then combining it with the long put results in a protective put. Another way to think of a collar is as a combination of a covered call and a protective put.

Table 2.9 summarizes the key levels for this collar. There is both limited upside and downside when a collar is used. The tradeoff for cheaper

TABLE 2.9 Collar Key Levels

	Level	Explanation
Break-even Price	62.20	Stock price plus collar cost
Maximum Loss Price	60.00	Put strike
Maximum Dollar Loss	2.20	Stock price plus collar cost minus put strike
Maximum Profit Price	65.00	Call strike
Maximum Dollar Profit	2.80	Call strike minus collar cost minus stock price

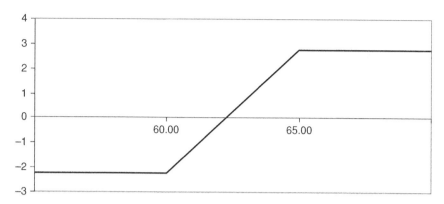

FIGURE 2.7 Collar Payoff

protection is limited upside. When using the protective put, the payment for protection was much higher, but there was also unlimited upside.

The break-even level for this trade is 62.20, which is the original value of the stock when the trade was initiated along with the 0.20 that was paid to initiate the collar. The maximum gain is realized at 65 of 2.80. Over 65 the short call would be exercised by the holder and the stock would need to be sold at 65. From 60 and lower, the position is hedged with the long put position and the maximum loss is 2.20, or 2.00 from the stock plus the 0.20 paid for the hedge.

The payoff for a collar appears in Figure 2.7. Between the two strikes, 60 and 65, there is still price exposure to the stock. From 60 on down or above 65 the hedge or limited upside due to the collar starts to take effect. The upside is limited at 65, but there is protection from 60 on down.

In cases where there is concern regarding potential downside in an underlying security, the collar is a viable alternative to buying a put option. Some upside is sacrificed, but the cost of being hedged is dramatically reduced and, at times, a premium pay may actually be received when putting on a collar.

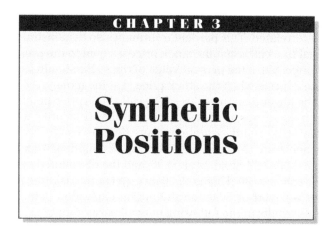

CHAPTER 3

Synthetic Positions

O ptions may be used to replicate a multitude of potential payoff strategies. This book will cover the most common payoffs designed, using a combination of calls, puts, and an underlying security. However, on a pretty basic level, there is a direct relationship between the value of calls, puts, and an underlying that holds in place due to market forces. This concept is known as put-call parity.

Put-call parity demonstrates that the value of a put is dependent on the value of the call option when they share the same expiration and strike price. Also, the price of a call will depend on the price of the corresponding put option. When the two option prices get out of line, an arbitrage opportunity may arise. This opportunity allows professional traders with sophisticated execution software and the advantage of low commission rates the chance to lock in a risk-less profit. These fast trades attempting to take advantage of any out of line pricing will push the put and call prices back in line, or parity.

The formula for put-call parity involves the time value of money and some other variables, but for this book's purposes the formula below is the basic definition for the purposes of showing how synthetic positions work.

$$P = C - S + K$$

P = Put Price
C = Call Price
S = Current Stock Price
K = Present Value of Strike Price of Put and Call

This formula shows that the relationship among a put, call, and stock price are interrelated. This particular formula also demonstrates that a put will be equal to a call when the stock price is equal to the present value of the strike price. Since the present value of the strike should usually be less than the stock price when the stock price is at the money, the value of the put would be lower than the value of the call at this price point. As the time left to expiration drops, the present value of the strike price will get closer to the actual strike, until expiration where they are equal.

To demonstrate this, use the following assumptions—an XYZ 50 Call is trading at 2.00, XYZ Stock is at 50.00, and the discounted value of strike price of the call is 49.90. That is 49.90 invested at the risk-free rate will give an investor a payoff of 50.00 on the option expiration date. Using these assumptions results in the following put-call parity formula:

$$\text{Put Value} = \text{Call Value} - \text{Stock Price} - \text{PV Strike}$$
$$P = 2.00 - 50.00 + 49.90$$
$$P = 1.90$$

So with the XYZ 50 Call trading at 2.00, through put-call parity, the corresponding fair value for an XYZ 50 Put would be 1.90. Notice that the present value of the strike price (49.90) is at a slight discount to the actual strike (50.00). This is common when there is no dividend being paid on an underlying security between the current date and option expiration. However, when there is a dividend involved the formula may be altered a bit.

As a quick example and the only time the put-call parity formula is going to get this complex, XYZ is once again trading at 50, the XYZ Call is at 2.00, the discounted value of 50 is 49.90, but there is a .50 dividend that is paid just before expiration and the discounted value of the divided is .45. Keep in mind, this is for example purposes only, the math does not add up under real circumstances. The idea here is just to demonstrate the effect of a dividend on the put-call parity formula. The following formula is an example of the put-call parity formula showing the effect of the dividend.

$$P = 2.00 - 50.00 + 49.90 + .45$$
$$P = 2.35$$

With a dividend being added to the equation, a put option may actually trade at a premium to a comparable call option. In the case from the previous figure, the put is trading at 2.35 while the call option is trading at 2.00. The reason behind this disparity is the impact of the dividend on the price of the underlying stock.

As a holder of a call option on XYZ stock the owner of the option has the right to purchase shares of XYZ at a certain price until expiration. The holder of this option is not entitled to the dividend that is paid before expiration unless he exercises the option and decides to own the stock. This is one reason call options are exercised early, so that the holder of the option may get the dividend.

Upon payment of a dividend, XYZ—or any other stock for that matter—will usually see an adjustment in the stock's price that is close to the amount of the dividend that was received by stockholders. For instance if XYZ is trading at 38 and a .50 dividend is being paid, the day after the dividend record date the shares of XYZ would be worth 37.50. This 37.50 price assumes no other market forces move the stock around. Another way to think of this is that the following day, 37.50 may be considered unchanged on the day, even though the last trade the day before was at 38.00.

In this case, as the holder of an XYZ 35 Call option, the day before XYZ pays a dividend, the option would have 3.00 of intrinsic value based on the stock price of 38.00 and the option strike price of 35.00. The following day, due to the payment of the dividend and the reduction of .50 in the price of XYZ, the intrinsic value of the 35 Call also would be reduced by .50 from 3.00 to 2.50.

Sticking with the example in the previous paragraph, with XYZ trading at 38.00, an XYZ 40 Put option would have an intrinsic value of 2.00. After the .50 dividend, with XYZ's value going from 38.00 to 37.50, the intrinsic value of the 40 put would also change. However, in the case of a put option, the intrinsic value would actually increase as the stock loses value. For this example, the new intrinsic value of the XYZ 40 Put would be 2.50, .50 higher than the day before.

Admittedly this is a very simplistic explanation of the change in the value of options. Dividend amounts and dates are well known by the marketplace. Since both the timing and amount of a dividend are well known in advance, the actual trading prices of the corresponding options discount the impending price change in the underlying stock before the actual event occurs. Basically, just because the intrinsic value of an option is going to change by a certain amount based on a dividend, this does not result in a similar trading price change of these options.

PUT-CALL PARITY

The next few sections demonstrate, in a very simplistic manner, what combination and position in options results in some sort of synthetic position. In each of the examples, a payoff table shows how the combination of two

options is equivalent to the profit or loss of the position that spread is trying
to replicate. With each payoff diagram, the synthetic payoff is represented
as a solid line. To differentiate the two positions that are combined to create the synthetic position, points are placed on the payoff diagram lines of
these positions.

To limit the formula to the three trading vehicles, the strike price is
going to be dropped from the formula for the rest of this chapter. So now
the basic put-call parity formula appears as $P = C - S$. Using this condensed
formula, the sign of each variable may also indicate a position. For instance
$P = C - S$ results in a long put that is equal to a long call and short stock.
Also, to keep things simple, the assumption that there is no cost of money
is going to be included, so when the stock is equal to the strike price the put
and call with the same expiration and same strike should be equal in value.
Once again, there is more to put-call parity in the real trading environment,
but this approach helps to isolate the three variables to an equivalent formula and hopefully make the examples more palatable.

SYNTHETIC LONG POSITIONS

Using either a put, call, or stock there are three potential trading instruments that may have a synthetic payoff created using the other two. As
each may be created at a long or short position, the result is a total of six
potential synthetics. As there are some small differences between long and
short positions, they are going to be separated, with the synthetic longs
covered first.

Synthetic Long Put

To create a long put payoff using a stock and a call, the put-call parity formula is changed around to look like the next formula. So taking the original
put-call parity formula and converting the signs of each instrument into positions creates an individual option position on one side of the formula and
a spread trade on the other side of the formula. In this case a long put is
equivalent to a spread combining a long call and short stock. The put isolated in put-call parity formula is:

$$P = C - S$$

Long Put = Long Call and Short Stock

To demonstrate, a hypothetical example is used, once again remov-
ing the time value of money issue—or discounted value of the strike

TABLE 3.1 Long Put versus Long Call and Short Stock Payoff

XYZ	Long XYZ July 50 Put	Long XYZ July 50 Call	Short XYZ	Spread P/L
40	**7.25**	−2.75	10.00	**7.25**
45	**2.25**	−2.75	5.00	**2.25**
50	**−2.75**	−2.75	0.00	**−2.75**
55	**−2.75**	2.25	−5.00	**−2.75**
60	**−2.75**	7.25	−10.00	**−2.75**

price—from the equation. With XYZ trading at 50 and July expiration 30 days off, both the XYZ July 50 Call and XYZ July 50 Put are trading at 2.75. Using these prices, the payoff tables in Table 3.1 are created.

Comparing the payoff of the long XYZ July 50 Put and the payoff of the spread demonstrates that the two strategies are equivalent. Also, when a payoff diagram is created for either, they look exactly alike. The payoff diagram for a long put or long call combined with short stock position, using the pricing from Table 3.1, appears in Figure 3.1.

As mentioned before, the payoff diagram displays the payoff of a long put, shown as the solid line on Figure 3.1. A short position in XYZ stock with a price of 50.00 is illustrated by the straight line, with points that crosses the axis at 50.00 and moves higher on a one-for-one basis based on the profit or loss. Finally, the long call is represented by the dotted line

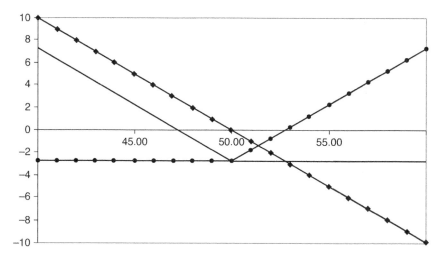

FIGURE 3.1 Payoff for Long Put or Long Call and Short Stock

that is flat from the left axis until it reaches 50.00 where it starts to move higher on a one-for-one basis with a move in the stock price.

From 50.00 and higher, the stock moves down a point for every point move higher with the XYZ 50 Call. These two moves offset each other to result in a flat loss that is similar to owning a put above a strike price. On the other side of 50.00, the short stock position starts to become profitable, while the long call has the loss capped at the premium paid for the position. This move higher in the profitability of the short stock is what results in the synthetic position to replicate the profit that occurs from a long put option when the stock is lower than the put's strike price.

Synthetic Long Call

Changing the original put-call parity formula around a bit and isolating the call results in $C = P + S$, the formula creating a long call payoff using the combination of a put and stock position. Translating the math to positions results in a long call being equivalent to the payoff of a long put combined with a long stock position. The math to position translation appears in the formula:

$$C = P + S$$

$$\text{Long Call} = \text{Long Put} + \text{Long Stock}$$

Once again, to keep things simple, XYZ will be trading right at a strike price or in this case 40. August expiration is 45 days away and both the XYZ Aug 40 Call and XYZ Aug 40 Put are trading at 3.10. To create similar payoffs, a trader could either buy the XYZ 40 Call or go long XYZ Stock and buy the Aug XYZ 40 Put. Table 3.2 shows a payoff comparison of the long call and the spread trade created with the long put and long stock position.

With the pricing used in this example, the payoff of the XYZ Aug 40 Call is equivalent to the payoff of combining a Long XYZ Aug 40 Put and

TABLE 3.2   Long Call versus Long Put and Long Stock

XYZ	Long XYZ Aug 40 Call	Long XYZ Aug 40 Put	Long XYZ	Spread P/L
30	−3.10	6.90	−10.00	−3.10
35	−3.10	1.90	−5.00	−3.10
40	−3.10	−3.10	0.00	−3.10
45	1.90	−3.10	5.00	1.90
50	6.90	−3.10	10.00	6.90

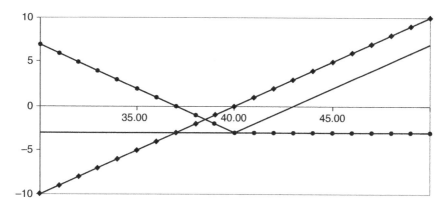

FIGURE 3.2 Payoff for Long Call or Long Put and Long Stock

also having a long position in the underlying stock. The payoff diagram in Figure 3.2 illustrates this point a bit further.

In the payoff diagram, the long stock is represented by the constantly upward sloping dotted line that crosses through 40.00 at the axis. The dotted line that is flat from 40.00 to the right side of the diagram and then starts to go up as the stock price would move under 40.00 is the long put position. The solid line represents the synthetic call that may be created by combining long stock from 40.00 and purchasing an XYZ Aug 40 Put at 3.10.

From 40.00 higher the spread position benefits from not realizing any loss beyond the premium paid for the 40 Put, but profiting from the long stock position. From 40.00 and under, the loss on the 40 Put begins to profit from the long put position while losing on a one for one basis on the long stock position. These two positions offset each other to limit losses to the put premium and results in a payoff that equates a long call.

Synthetic Long Stock

The final long example of how to create a synthetic position is creating a long stock position by combining a put and call position. Remember the put-call parity formula can be manipulated using simple math to isolate any of the three instruments. In this case the stock is isolated on the left side of the formula while the call and put are on the right side together. Altering the formula to single out the stock position results in the following formula:

$$S = C - P$$

Long Stock = Long Call and Short Put

TABLE 3.3 Long Stock versus Long Call and Short Put Payoff

XYZ	Long XYZ	Long XYZ Sep 35 Call	Short XYZ Sep 35 Put	Spread P/L
25	−10.00	−2.25	−7.75	−10.00
30	−5.00	−2.25	−2.75	−5.00
35	0.00	−2.25	2.25	0.00
40	5.00	2.75	2.25	5.00
45	10.00	7.75	2.25	10.00

To create a long stock position, a long position is taken in a call and a put is simultaneously sold short. A long stock position will naturally benefit from a higher stock price as does a long call. Being short a put is a losing proposition when a stock moves lower, as is being long a stock.

Taking a couple of options and creating a synthetic stock position may sound like a bit too much effort to replicate a payoff that can be created by just buying shares. As far as going long stock with options in this manner, that is a consideration. However, when creating a short with options comes up, there are much more legitimate purposes behind using options to create the synthetic strategy.

For a synthetic stock example, XYZ will be trading at 35.00 and September is 60 days to expiration. The XYZ September 35 Call and Put are both priced at 2.25. Table 3.3 shows the payoffs of these two strategies at a variety of price points.

The long stock position in the previous table is a perfect match for the profit and loss results created by the position that combines a long call option and short put option. The call makes money on the upside, while the gain on the put option is limited to the premium received for selling the put. On the downside, below the break-even level of 35.00, the put option realizes losses, while the call option also has a loss. The loss on the long call option is limited to the premium paid for the call.

Figure 3.3 demonstrates the payoff for the two option positions and graphically shows how they contribute to the payoff that parallels a long stock position. The dotted line that moves higher above 35.00 represents the long call, while the dotted line that moves lower with the stock under 35.00 represents the short put. The solid straight line that moves higher from end to end on the diagram is the long stock.

SYNTHETIC SHORT POSITIONS

Using the three instruments, call, put, and stock, synthetic long positions in each has been demonstrated with the other two instruments

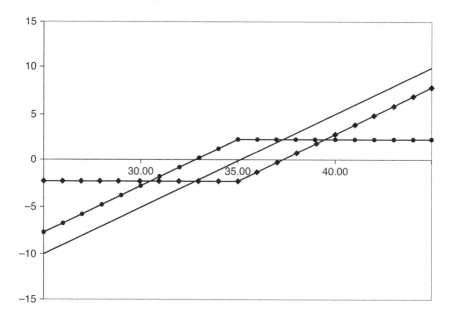

FIGURE 3.3 Payoff for Long Stock or Long Call and Short Put

appearing on the right side of the equation. Like just about all long positions, a short counterpart is always a possibility. The following three examples show how a short position in a put, call, or stock may be created using a combination of the other two instruments.

Synthetic Short Put

Returning to the original condensed put-call parity formula, but multiplying all the variables by -1 would result in isolating a short put. This method of converting the long formulas will hold true for each of the three synthetic short positions that are going to be demonstrated. To replicate the payoff of a short put, a trader would take a long position in an underlying stock and short position in the equivalent call. If this sounds like a fairly familiar position, it is, a long stock position and short call is what is commonly referred to as a covered call or buy write. This spread trade was discussed in Chapter 2.

$$-P = -C + S$$

Short Put = Short Call and Long Stock

TABLE 3.4 Short Put versus Short Call and Long Stock Payoff

XYZ	Short XYZ Oct 65 Put	Short XYZ Oct 65 Call	Long XYZ	Spread P/L
55	−7.55	2.45	−10.00	−7.55
60	−2.55	2.45	−5.00	−2.55
65	2.45	2.45	0.00	2.45
70	2.45	−2.55	5.00	2.45
75	2.45	−7.55	10.00	2.45

To replicate a short put, a long position would be taken in XYZ which is trading at 65. An at-the-money Oct expiration is 60 days off and the Oct XYZ 65 Call may be sold for 2.45. Also, due to the efficiency of the market, the Oct XYZ 65 Put is trading at 2.45. As in the long positions, the payoffs of the two positions are compared in Table 3.4.

Whenever an option is sold, the profit of the position is limited to the premium received from taking on the obligation that goes along with the short option position. In this case, a short position in the XYZ Oct 65 Put would result in a credit to the trader's account of 2.45. In the case of the synthetic short put position, the profit of the spread is also limited to 2.45. At each price level at expiration, the payoffs match for the synthetic position and a short put.

Again, the payoff diagram in Figure 3.4 should also look somewhat familiar for readers who covered the previous chapter. This is a diagram that illustrates owning an underlying security and taking a short position in a call option on the underlying stock. This is normally referred to as a covered call, but in this example is called a synthetic short put. The point here is that the payoff for a covered call and short put position are equivalent.

Many brokerage firms put restrictions on the types of option trades that may be executed by clients. Naked short option positions such as a short put are generally restricted to only very experienced or well-capitalized investors, while a covered call strategy is usually allowed by the lowest rung of traders. It is interesting that the payoffs for both strategies are approached with such different attitudes by brokers.

Synthetic Short Call

In the same manner that a synthetic short put can be demonstrated by multiplying all the long synthetic put variables by -1 the same may be done to the long synthetic call formula. Changing the sign of each of the variables in the synthetic long call example results in the next formula. In fact, all of

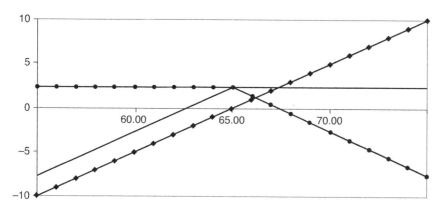

FIGURE 3.4 Payoff of Short Put or Short Call and Long Stock

the signs are now negative instead of positive.

$$-C = -P - S$$

Short Call = Short Put and Short Stock

For a trading example of how a short call payoff may be created by selling a put and selling the underlying stock, XYZ will be trading at 45.00. The November 45 options are used in Table 3.5 with both the XYZ November 45 Call and XYZ November 45 Put trading at 3.25.

A short call's profit, like all short option positions, is limited to the proceeds taken from the initiating the position. Likewise, in this synthetic equivalent, shorting a stock and the corresponding option has a limited profit. In this trade, the profit is limited to 3.25 and is realized at any price point below 45.00. As the stock moves under 45.00, there is a profit from the equity position, but this is offset on a one- for-one basis by a loss in the short put position.

TABLE 3.5 Short Call versus Short Put and Short Stock Payout

XYZ	Short XYZ Nov 45 Call	Short XYZ Nov 45 Put	Short XYZ	Spread P/L
35	**3.25**	−6.75	10.00	**3.25**
40	**3.25**	−1.75	5.00	**3.25**
45	**3.25**	3.25	0.00	**3.25**
50	**−1.75**	3.25	−5.00	**−1.75**
55	**−6.75**	3.25	−10.00	**−6.75**

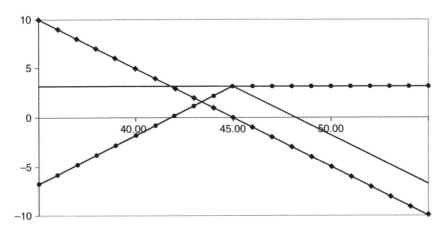

FIGURE 3.5 Payout of Short Call or Short Put and Short Stock

A short call also may incur a theoretically unlimited loss and this holds true for the synthetic position also. As the stock moves above 45 there is a loss imposed on the spread by the short stock position. This is offset a little by the proceeds from selling the put, but only by 3.25, or the max gain of the synthetic short call. Figure 3.5 shows the payout diagram for the short call or combined short put and short stock position.

Synthetic Short Stock

Finally a short stock payoff may also be created through the use of a put and a call. As a long stock payoff may be replicated through taking a long position in the underlying call option and shorting the corresponding put, a short payoff may be created by selling the call and taking a long position in the put.

Taking a short position in a stock is a more complex transaction than just clicking a mouse and entering a short sell order in XYZ. To short a stock, a trader must borrow the shares of XYZ from a trader or investor who holds a long position in XYZ. Due to a variety of circumstances, at times the ability to borrow shares of a stock when one wants to gain short exposure may not exist. A so-called "hard to borrow" stock may be costly to borrow in order to execute a short, so using options to create a synthetic short payoff is an excellent alternative.

$$-S = -C + P$$

Short Stock = Short Call and Long Put

TABLE 3.6 Short Stock versus Short Call and Long Put Payout

XYZ	Short XYZ	Short XYZ Dec 30 Call	Long XYZ Dec 30 Put	Spread P/L
20.00	**10.00**	2.25	7.75	**10.00**
25.00	**5.00**	2.25	2.75	**5.00**
30.00	**0.00**	2.25	−2.25	**0.00**
35.00	**−5.00**	−2.75	−2.25	**−5.00**
40.00	**−10.00**	−7.75	−2.25	**−10.00**

This equation shows how the payoff for short position in a stock XYZ is created using a call and a put. With the stock trading at 30, the Dec 30 Call is sold short for a credit of 2.25, while the Dec 30 Put is purchased for 2.25. The resulting position replicates a short stock position from 30 in XYZ.

The payouts from the short stock position and synthetic position created by selling a call and buying a put are displayed in Table 3.6. Above the strike price of 30, the short Dec 30 Call loses money on an equal basis with having a short position in the underlying stock. When the stock moves below the strike price of 30, the long put option position starts to gain traction and is a one-for-one profit with the move lower in the underlying stock.

The payoff diagram where a short stock position is replicated is presented in Figure 3.6. The long put position benefits from a falling price below 30.00, while the short call only maintains the income received from selling the option. Over 30.00, the short call loses value while the long put has losses that are limited to the premium paid for the option.

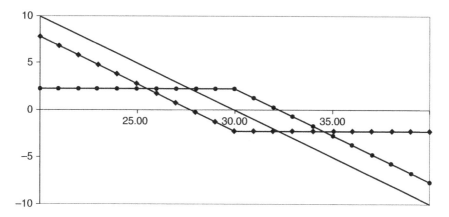

FIGURE 3.6 Short Stock or Short Call and Long Put Payout

Once again, for a variety of reasons, selling a stock short may be difficult or possibly prohibited in certain accounts. Through the use of options, a synthetic short position in an underlying security or index may be created.

ARBITRAGE IN PUT-CALL PARITY

As mentioned earlier in this chapter, put-call parity holds up due to the ability of professionals to benefit when put and call prices are not in line with each other. When this occurs, an arbitrage opportunity arises for professionals where they may purchase the cheap trade and sell an offsetting more expensive alternative, locking in an instant profit. Although beyond the trading capacity of individual traders, going through the basics of how this may work is a good exercise.

One of the best ways to demonstrate this is to find a circumstance where a synthetic long call may be created with a significantly different profit and loss profile than taking a long position in the underlying security. When professional arbitrageurs take advantage of these pricing opportunities they have the benefit of execution speed, leverage, a low cost of capital, and very low commissions. Those are just a few of the reasons to leave this type of trading to the professionals.

For this example, a very simplistic situation will be presented. Stock XYZ is trading at 49.00, with January option expiration only 15 days away. The January 50 Call is trading for 1.00, while the January 50 Put is trading for 2.00. To replicate a long stock position, the Jan 50 Call is purchased for 2.00, while the Jan 50 Put is sold for 2.00. Table 3.7 shows the payoff at expiration of the two positions.

In the table, a long position in XYZ stock outperforms the synthetic long position that is created by buying the XYZ Jan 50 Call and Short XYZ Jan 50 Put. As the long equity position outperforms the synthetic position at all price points by $1.00, the actual trade here would be to take a long

TABLE 3.7 Arbitrage between XYZ Stock and Synthetic

XYZ	Long XYZ Stock	Long XYZ Jan 50 Call	Short XYZ Jan 50 Put	Synthetic Long XYZ Stock
40	−9.00	−2.00	−8.00	−10.00
45	−4.00	−2.00	−3.00	−5.00
50	1.00	−2.00	2.00	0.00
55	6.00	3.00	2.00	5.00
60	11.00	8.00	2.00	10.00

TABLE 3.8 Arbitrage Profits

XYZ	Long XYZ Stock	Short XYZ Jan 50 Call	Long XYZ Jan 50 Put	Arbitrage Profit
40	−9.00	2.00	8.00	**1.00**
45	−4.00	2.00	3.00	**1.00**
50	1.00	2.00	−2.00	**1.00**
55	6.00	−3.00	−2.00	**1.00**
60	11.00	−8.00	−2.00	**1.00**

position in XYZ and put on a synthetic short position with the options. In order to take advantage of the arbitrage opportunity that exists due to the difference between the actual underlying stock and the synthetic position, a position should be taken in both. The position that underperforms should be shorted, while the position that outperforms should be purchased. Changing Table 3.8 around to reflect taking advantage of the arbitrage opportunity results in the positions that appear in Table 3.8.

The complete arbitrage trade involves purchasing XYZ stock at 49.00, selling the XYZ Jan 50 Call for 2.00, and paying 2.00 for the XYZ Jan 50 Put. In 15 days one of three things—XYZ over 50.00, XYZ at 50.00, or XYZ under 50.00—will occur that will result in the $1.00 profit being locked in.

The first possibility to explore is that XYZ will be below 50.00 at expiration. In this case, the XYZ Jan 50 Call will expire with no value and there will be no action taken with respect to the call. The Jan 50 Put will be in the money and the long position will result in selling shares of XYZ at 50.00. However, there are 100 shares of XYZ long in this position from a cost of $49.00. So the put is exercised and the shares are automatically sold by the broker. Monday after expiration there is no position from this trade and the account has profited by $1.00.

Next, if XYZ is over 50.00 at expiration, the XYZ Jan 50 Put would expire with no action being taken as the option is out of the money and has no value. However, since the stock is over 50.00, the XYZ Jan 50 Call is in the money. As this trade involves a short position in the XYZ 50 Call the option is actually assigned and the result is 100 shares being sold by the broker at 50. Once again, Monday after expiration there is no position remaining from this trade in the account and the profit is $1.00.

Finally, and this is a possibility, XYZ could settle exactly at 50.00 at expiration. As shown in Table 3.9, the result for this outcome is that both options expire with no value. However, sometimes these options may be exercised by individuals that want to engage in the transaction to which the right of the option entitles them. There may be some difficulty in determining exactly what occurs at this point. For one reason or another,

TABLE 3.9 Arbitrage Trade Outcome Scenario

XYZ	Result
Over 50	Short Call Exercised, Stock Sold at 50
At 50	Options Expire, Long Stock from 49
Under 50	Long Put Exercised, Stock Sold at 50

holders of the Jan 50 Call may elect to exercise those calls. If the account is assigned against one of these exercised calls, shares will again be sold at $50.00. However, if the trader chooses not to exercise the 50 Put, and the 50 Call is not assigned, Monday morning the account has no option positions, but is actually long XYZ from $49.00. Shares should be sold at the best possible price Monday morning as the intent of this trade was to make money on the arbitrage opportunity, which has now gone away. Another alternative is to exercise the Long XYZ Jan 50 Put option and sell shares at $50.00. The risk here is the XYZ Jan 50 Call could be assigned and, come Monday morning, a short position of 100 shares in XYZ could appear in the account. Unfortunately, when a stock settles right at a strike price at expiration and a trader is short this option, there is no certainty that the option will not be assigned come Monday morning.

The previous example is mostly for educational purposes. Arbitrage trading should be left to the professionals. Also, the impact of use of capital, transaction costs, and interest rates have been left out to keep things simple. Generally, when options appear to not be fairly priced, there is some sort of reason for it. Possibly the contract will not be for the standard 100 shares of stock or possibly there is a large dividend coming that is being discounted by the options. The market makers and professional traders will not last very long if they are not fairly valuing options.

INDIVIDUALS USING PUT-CALL PARITY

There are cases where individual traders may use put-call parity to their advantage when making a trading decision. When considering a trade, comparing the synthetic to the actual position can be a worthwhile exercise. There may be cases where a synthetic position will be a little less expensive than the equivalent position.

As displayed earlier in this chapter, a long call may be replicated using the combination of a long put and long stock. If a trader has a bullish opinion on a security, but wants to limit downside risk, a long call is the first strategy that may come to mind. However, checking out a long stock–long

TABLE 3.10 Payoff Comparison

XYZ	Long XYZ May 35 Call	Long XYZ	Long XYZ May 35 Put	Synthetic
25	−1.40	−7.50	6.25	−1.25
30	−1.40	−2.50	1.25	−1.25
35	−1.40	2.50	−3.75	−1.25
40	3.60	7.50	−3.75	3.75
45	8.60	12.50	−3.75	8.75

put combination, to make sure the pricing may be a little more in the traders' favor can result in a better entry point for this strategy.

For example, if a trader is expecting a very bullish move in XYZ—which is trading at 32.50—over the next 60 days, and the May options expire in 60 days the trader may consider buying the XYZ May 35 Call—priced at 1.40—to benefit from this move. The alternative here may be buying shares of XYZ and taking a long position in an XYZ May 35 Put—priced at 3.75—to limit the downside risk. Table 3.10 is a payoff comparison between a long XYZ May 35 Call position and a synthetic payoff created with a combination of long XYZ stock and long XYZ May 35 Put.

In this case, comparing the two similar strategies shows that initiating this trade as a synthetic position, as opposed to buying the XYX May 35 Call outright would result in a slightly better payoff. At each outcome at expiration, the synthetic payoff is superior by .15. Of course, there may be more commissions, cost of capital, and uses of margin issues that also would come into play by putting on the synthetic position, but as a start, there is an awareness that the synthetic could work a bit in a trader's favor.

This concludes taking a look at put-call parity and how it works in the marketplace. A trader should keep in mind that there are always alternatives to creating a payoff scenario when considering a trade. For instance, the long call example where it is nothing more than a long stock and a long put combined shows that at times a synthetic trade may be a viable alternative. Before initiating a trade, a trader should always take a look at the potential alternatives.

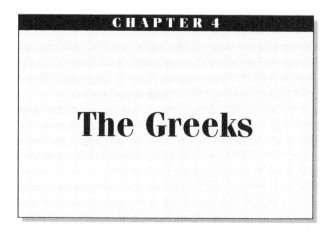

CHAPTER 4

The Greeks

M any casual option traders—those that may just buy a call when bullish or buy a put when bearish—believe the Greeks should be left to the professional traders. Yes, it is true that the Greeks come into play more for professional traders, but at least an elementary awareness of the impact the Greeks have on an option's value is essential knowledge for all levels of option traders. When considering spread trades, an awareness of how the impact of price changes, along with time and volatility, may be estimated ahead of time by using the Greeks.

In this chapter, each of the five Greeks that are commonly displayed on quote systems will be covered. Although there are five Greeks, they may be broken down into four categories: price-, time-, volatility-, and interest rate-related. This chapter will approach them in this fashion. The price-related Greeks are delta and gamma. Theta is the Greek that relates to time and vega (although not a real Greek letter) is based on volatility. Finally, rho focuses on interest rates, but in the current low interest rate environment, rho does not get a lot of focus.

PRICE-RELATED GREEKS

The most common term that comes to mind when a trader hears option Greeks is probably delta. However, there is another price-related Greek, which is gamma. If anything, delta is probably thought of first because it is the easiest to understand.

Delta

An option's delta is the amount the option's price will change based on a one-unit change in the underlying security. In the example, of a stock a unit would represent a $1.00 change in the price of the stock. For index options, this would be reflected by a 1.00 change in the index.

For a call option, the delta will always be a number between 0 and 1.00. If a call option has a delta of .50, then a $1.00 increase in the value of the underlying stock would result in a .50 increase in the value of the call option. Conversely, a $1.00 drop in the price of a stock would result in a .50 drop in the value of the call option.

The delta may also be referred to in some places as a percent between 0 percent and 100 percent. Although the math works out the same, if the delta of a call option is shown at 50 percent instead of .50, this can be taken as the call option will move 50 percent as much as the move in the underlying security. If the underlying moves up or down $1.00, then the option would increase or decrease by .50 (50 percent of $1.00). The only difference is the delta being displayed as an absolute number or a percentage.

For a put option, the delta will fall somewhere between −1.00 and 0. The inverse nature of the delta of a put option relative to a call option relates to the price action of a put relative to a move in the underlying security. When a stock rises, the put option loses value and when a stock moves lower, the put option increases in value. This relationship results in the negative sign in front of the delta for a put.

In the case of a put option that has a delta of −.50, with a $1.00 gain in the underlying stock, the put option would lose .50. A $1.00 drop in the stock would actually result in a .50 gain in the value of an option. Put options benefit from a drop in the underlying security and the level of the delta gives an indication of just how much of a price move to expect out of a put option based on a $1.00 move in the underlying.

Table 4.1 illustrates how delta relates to the change in value of an option when an underlying stock moves higher. The first two columns represent the option prices and the delta of each option. The underlying stock is trading at 50, and with a call delta of 0.50 the XYZ 50 Call moves up from 1.50 to 2.00 with a 1.00 move in the underlying stock. The 50 Put has a negative price impact from a gain in XYZ stock and this is equal to the

TABLE 4.1 Impact of $1.00 Gain in Underlying

	XYZ @ 50	Delta	XYZ @ 51
XYZ 50 Call	1.50	0.50	2.00
XYZ 50 Put	1.45	−0.50	0.95

TABLE 4.2 Impact of a $1.00 Loss in Underlying

	XYZ @ 50	Delta	XYZ @ 49
XYZ 50 Call	1.50	0.50	1.00
XYZ 50 Put	1.45	−0.50	1.95

delta of .50. With a $1.00 gain in the stock price, the XYZ 50 Put moves from 1.45 to .95.

In Table 4.2 the stock drops by a $1.00 instead of rising by $1.00. In this case the XYZ 50 Put gains by .50 from 1.45 to 1.95, the math here is −1 × −.50 and—remember from basic algebra—a negative multiplied by a negative results in a positive. As expected, the XYZ 50 Call loses value equal to the delta of .50 going from 1.50 to 1.00.

Traders may use delta to determine what sort of impact a move in the underlying will have on their position. This comes in to play more for positions with multiple legs. Spread trades will rarely move in lockstep with a move in the underlying due to the unique outcome that has been created with multiple options.

Before discussing delta in a portfolio context, it is worthwhile to point out the delta of the underlying is 1.00. A long stock position has a delta of 1.00, as each move up by $1.00 in the stock results in a 1.00 move up in the stock. If a stock moves down by $1.00, the underlying stock moves down by 1.00.

Another use of delta might be when using options to hedge a position or portfolio. When protecting an asset such as a long stock position by purchasing puts, an investor may check out the delta to determine how the hedge will work. Another way to refer to being hedged is being delta neutral. If a spread position has positive delta, when the underlying moves higher then the spread position would increase in value at the rate of the position's delta. A spread that has negative delta would increase in value as the underlying loses value. Finally, if a spread has neutral delta, then a price move in the underlying would result in no gain or loss to the spread position.

For example, an owner of XYZ is a bit concerned over the near-term prospects for the stock. He owns 100 shares which is trading at 41 and takes a look at the XYZ April 40 Put which is trading at 1.20 and has 45 days to expiration. The delta of this put option is −.40. To hedge himself he buys 1 XYZ April 40 Put at 1.10. The total spread position appears in Table 4.3.

The trader initiates this position first thing in the morning and then checks on it shortly before the market close the same afternoon. He sees XYZ has now lost 1.00 and is happy he decided to buy the put option. However, he notes that the XYZ 40 Put is now trading at 1.60, a gain of .40.

TABLE 4.3 Protected Put Position

	Price	Delta
Long 100 XYZ	41.00	1.00
Long 1 XYZ 40 Put	1.20	−0.40

Although he considered himself hedged, the position still lost some value, in this case a loss of .60.

The position lost .60 with a drop of 1.00 in the underlying. Therefore, by definition the delta of the spread is actually .60 and not delta neutral. In the case of a position being delta neutral, it would be considered fully hedged for relatively small price moves. Reducing the delta from 1.00, as it was with just a long stock position to .60 is a partial hedge. At least for the first $1.00 move down in the stock the position is only hedged to lose .40, less than if the put were not purchased.

This example isolates just the impact of delta on the price change of the option. Moving through this chapter, each of the Greeks will be isolated to display their impact on the value of options. Although in reality the Greeks all have varying impacts on the value of options and all change during the life of an option, isolating is a worthwhile academic exercise.

Some traders, mostly professional, actually have a second use for delta, other than estimating the price change of an option based on a change in the underlying. Although the math is less than perfect, the delta is considered by some as the chance that an option will finish in the money at expiration. For example, at-the-money call options have a delta very close to .50, which can be considered a 50 percent chance that the option will be in the money at expiration. An at-the-money put option should have a delta very close to −.50, taking the absolute value of this also results in the option having a 50 percent chance of being in the money at expiration.

Deep in-the-money calls have a delta that comes very close to, if not right at 1.00. When the delta of a call option is at or very close to 1.00, this could be considered a case of the market giving the option close to a 100 percent chance of being in the money at expiration. For a put option, when the option is deep in the money the delta would be very close −1.00.

TABLE 4.4 Protected Put Position

	AM Price	PM Price	Profit/Loss
Long 100 XYZ	41.00	40.00	−1.00
Long 1 XYZ 40 Put	1.20	1.60	0.40
		Total P/L	−0.60

As the delta is close to -1.00, this would also be a case of the market pricing close to a 100 percent chance that the option will finish in the money at expiration.

Call and put options that are very far out of the money would both have a delta very close to 0. With a delta near 0, the market is indicating the odds are very close to 0 percent that the option will finish in the money at expiration.

Something that is consistent between the delta for both put and call options is that the delta does not remain at a certain level. The delta will shift around as the price of the underlying security changes. The amount that a delta moves up or down based on a one-unit change in the underlying security is the other price-related Greek, known as gamma.

Gamma

Gamma indicates the expected change in delta based on a $1.00 move up or down in an underlying stock. If the delta of a call option is .50 and the gamma is .05, then after a move of $1.00 higher in the underlying security the delta would be expected to be at .55. With the delta of a call option at .50 and the gamma at .05, the expected delta after a drop of $1.00 in the underlying stock would be .45.

Although delta is a negative number for put options, gamma is actually positive for both calls and puts. This is due to the delta for a put option increasing or decreasing in the same direction as a move in the underlying. It may seem a bit counterintuitive at first, but after seen in action this actually should make complete sense.

Take a put option that has a delta of $-.50$ and a gamma of .05. A decrease of $1.00 in the underlying security would result in the delta now being at $-.55$ ($-.50 -.05$). An increase in the underlying security of $1.00 would move the delta of the put option to $-.45$ ($-.50 + .05$). Table 4.5 summarizes the impact of gamma on delta.

To return to the actual impact on price from delta, it may be noted if delta is always changing based on gamma, the impact of the Greeks on a $1.00 move in the underlying may not be exactly equal to the price move expected from the delta. For example, if the gamma for a call option is

TABLE 4.5 Gamma Impact on Delta

	Delta	Gamma	Delta Stock Up $1.00	Delta Stock Down $1.00
Call Option	0.50	0.05	0.55	0.45
Put Option	−0.50	0.05	−0.45	−0.55

TABLE 4.6 Impact of Delta and Gamma on Call Option

Stock Price	Delta	Gamma	50 Call
49 (down 1)	0.45	0.04	0.78
50	0.50	0.05	1.25
51 (up 1)	0.55	0.06	1.77

.05 and the delta is .50, a move up of .50 in the underlying would result in the delta being at .525. Realizing the delta shifts along with the underlying should lead to the awareness that if the delta of a call is .50 and there is a stock move higher by $1.00, the move in the call option will actually be just a little more than .50. For a move lower of $1.00 in the underlying, the price of the call options would actually drop a little less than .50.

Table 4.6 shows a slightly more realistic expectation of the price change of a call option that would be expected with a $1.00 move higher or lower in the underlying. Note that with a $1.00 gain in the stock price, a .50 delta, and a .05 gamma, the actual increase in the 50 call option is around .52 to 1.77. Also, with a drop of $1.00 in the underlying stock, the 50 call loses .47 to .78. Once again a slightly different result than relying on delta. The larger the move, the farther the price change in the underlying option will be from the change that is indicated by delta.

Note that as the option is more in the money, the gamma actually increases, by .01 for this example. As the option is farther out of the money, the gamma will actually decrease. Once again, this decrease was pretty slight.

Table 4.7 shows how delta and gamma work together to determine the value of a put with a price move up and down $1.00. As the stock moves lower, the delta of the put option will also move lower approaching −1.00. Also, like the call option, there is an imbalance between the impact of a similar move up or down in the underlying. In the case of the put option, with a move down by $1.00, the option gains a little more than the .50 delta and in the case of the stock moving up by $1.00, the option loses a little less than the delta. Both are reflecting the slight impact of gamma that occurs over the $1.00 move.

TABLE 4.7 Impact of Delta and Gamma on Put Option

Stock Price	Delta	Gamma	50 Put
49 (down 1)	−0.55	0.06	1.77
50	−0.50	0.05	1.25
51 (up 1)	−0.45	0.04	0.78

TIME-RELATED GREEK

Option contracts are financial instruments that have a finite life. All exchange-traded options have an expiration date and this time to expiration has an impact on the value of the option. The value of an option is divided into two pieces, intrinsic and time value.

The intrinsic value is the value of an option if it is exercised immediately. For example, a 35 Call option, with the underlying stock trading at 40, would have an intrinsic value of 5.00. If this 35 Call were exercised, the stock would be bought at 35 and could be sold in the market for 40, an instant profit of $5. Any option that is at or out of the money—that has no value if exercised—will have an intrinsic value of 0. An option cannot have a negative intrinsic value.

The other value component of an option's price is the time value of the option. The time value is the market value of an option above the intrinsic value of the option. For example, using the previous example, if the market price of the 35 Call option is 7.00 and that option has 5.00 of intrinsic value, then the option has 2.00 of time value.

In a case where an option has no intrinsic value, the total value of the option is time value. A call option with a strike price of 35 and the underlying trading at 30 would have no intrinsic value. If the market price of this option is 1.00, then the whole 1.00 premium represents time value.

Time value of an option deteriorates as the option moves closer to the date it expires. At expiration an option has no time value and is all intrinsic value. If the option has intrinsic value at expiration, it will be exercised. If an option has no intrinsic value at expiration it should not be exercised. The loss of time value as an option moves closer to expiration is indicated by the option Greek theta.

Theta is the amount of value an option will lose over a unit of time. As the loss of value over time decreases the value of an option over time, the theta is displayed on a quote line as a negative number. The unit of time used to calculate theta can be anything a trader chooses to make it, but the most common measures of theta are one day or seven days (representing one week). At different times throughout this book, either of these choices may be used depending on the time to expiration.

A straightforward example of how theta works is if a call or put option has a one-day theta of .02. All else being the same, the options will lose .02 from one day to the next. What is very interesting about theta is how it behaves over the life of an option. The loss of time value for an at-the-money option actually occurs in a very non-linear fashion. In fact, the majority of the loss of time value occurs in the last 45 days or so in the life of an option. Table 4.8 was developed using a pricing calculator to maintain the consistency of the inputs. The option value is based on a call option with

TABLE 4.8 Representation of At-the-money
Option Time Value Deterioration

Days	Option Value
180	1.75
165	1.67
150	1.59
135	1.51
120	1.42
105	1.32
90	1.22
75	1.11
60	0.99
45	0.86
30	0.70
15	0.49
0	0.00

a 30 strike price, 20 percent volatility, and the underlying stock at 30.00. The days column represents how many days to expiration.

To analyze how the option would lose value, divide the time periods into thirds. For an at-the-money option starting at 180 days to expiration, during the first third or 60 days the option would lose 0.33 of value. In the second third of the time to expiration, from 120 to 60 days, the option loses 0.43. Over the final section of time, the last 60 days, the option loses 0.99 of value. Subdividing the last 60 days even further, the majority of the value, 0.70, is lost during the last 30 days.

The value loss on Figure 4.1 for the at-the-money option accelerates until hitting 0 at expiration, as there is no intrinsic value with the stock finishing right at the money. This type of loss of value is unique to an at-the-money or near-at-the-money option. When working with deep-in-the-money or out-of-the-money options, the time loss is actually more linear. Table 4.9 takes the same parameters as Table 4.8, but represents the time loss for an in-the-money 25 strike call and an out-of-the-money 35 strike call.

Focusing on the in-the-money option first, being in the money, the option has 5.00 of intrinsic value and only .29 of time value with 180 days left to expiration. With so little time value to start with, there is very little available time value to lose from day to day. In fact the theta is less than .01 a day. The out-of-the-money option has only .33 of value with 180 days to expiration. Like the in-the-money option, since there is very little time value, it also loses time value on a miniscule basis from day to day. The theta for this option would also be very low, less than .01 per day.

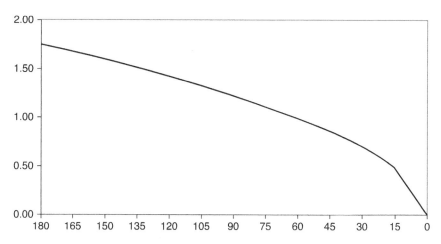

FIGURE 4.1 Time Deterioration for At-the-money Call Option

Figure 4.2 shows that the loss of time value for both out of the money and in the money is a bit more linear than it is for an at-the-money option. The line that starts a little higher than the other represents the out-of-the-money time-value change, while the other line represents the in-the-money time-value change. Both cross about halfway to expiration, but both have a similar more linear type form. This difference between the effect of time on at the money and options with strikes farther from the underlying

TABLE 4.9 Impact of Time on In-the-money and Out-of-the-money Options

Days	ITM Option Value	OTM Option Value
180	5.29	0.33
165	5.25	0.29
150	5.22	0.25
135	5.18	0.20
120	5.15	0.16
105	5.12	0.12
90	5.09	0.09
75	5.07	0.06
60	5.05	0.03
45	5.03	0.01
30	5.02	0.00
15	5.01	0.00
0	5.00	0.00

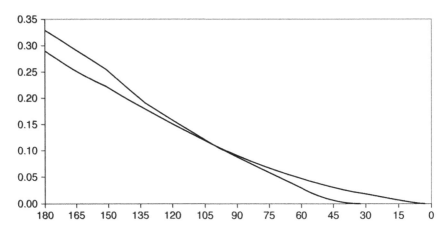

FIGURE 4.2 Out-of-the-money and In-the-money Time Value Loss

price may be taken advantage of through the use of time spreads, which are discussed further in Chapter 14. Also in Chapter 2, the impact of time-value loss is discussed in relation to a covered call position.

To owners of options, whether calls or puts, the deterioration of time value is always a concern. As an option gets closer to expiration, the time value of the option will deteriorate, having a negative impact on the price of the option. On the other hand, if short an option, the time value works in the trader's favor. Being aware of the impact the loss in time value will have on an option over the life of an option or over the life of a trade is an important aspect to trading options. If planning to sell an option, or have a net short option spread trade on, theta can indicate how time value will work in the trade's favor, or if long an option how theta is going to work against the position.

Up to this point, the examples depicting the effect of the passage of time on an option's value have used call options. The impact of time passage has the same effect on calls and puts. Table 4.10 shows the theta for both calls and puts. The underlying stock in this situation is trading at 45 and there are 30 days to expiration. In order to display the difference among the thetas, a seven-day theta is used in this example.

TABLE 4.10 Seven-day Theta

	Price	7-Day Theta		Price	7-Day Theta
40 Call	5.15	−0.07	40 Put	0.15	−0.06
45 Call	1.55	−0.20	45 Put	1.50	−0.19
50 Call	0.25	−0.09	50 Put	5.15	−0.08

As expected, the loss of value for the options, both the put and call, that are at the money experience the most dramatic loss in time value over seven days. In fact, it is more than twice the time value loss for the in-the-money and out-of-the-money options. The key piece of knowledge regarding time value and theta is: being long, time does not work for a position; being short, time erosion will benefit a position.

VOLATILITY-RELATED GREEK

There are two types of volatility that relate to a stock or index, historical and implied. Historical volatility of a stock may be calculated using historical trading prices. For example, the historical volatility for the previous 20 days trading may be determined by calculating the historical annualized standard deviation of day-to-day returns over the past 20 days.

Implied volatility is the level of volatility that is being indicated by option prices as the expectation of the range of daily returns expected over the life of the option. The implied volatility of the option is one of the pricing factors of an option that appears on a quote line. Also, when the price of an option is known, the volatility may be determined using an option calculator. This was covered in the first chapter, but as a refresher Table 4.11 shows what the inputs and output would look like for determining the implied volatility of a put and call option.

After the inputs are fed into this example the output is an implied volatility level of 38.29 percent. This indicates that the stock is expected to have an annualized move of 38.29 percent over the next 15 days (note the days to expiration input). There is a formula that can break this down

TABLE 4.11 Option Calculator Determines Implied Volatility

Input	
Type	American
Call / Put	Call
Underlying Price	29
Strike Price	30
Option Price	0.50
Days to Expiration	15
Interest Rate	1.00%
Dividends	0.15
Output	
Volatility	38.29%

to the time remaining to expiration. Figure 4.4 shows how to break the 38.29 percent from the option calculator and show what sort of price movement is being projected over the next 15 days. This calculation indicates that the options are pricing in a 9.34 percent range in movement over the next 15 days. Therefore, the formula for determining near-term price move projection would be:

(Implied Volatility/Square Root (252) × Square Root (Days to Expiration)

   (.3829/15.87) × 3.87 = .0934

Implied volatility may also be interpreted as the risk level of the underlying security. The higher the implied volatility, the higher the risk involved in owning the underlying instrument. When leading up to some sort of announcement that will result in a possible large move, up or down, in a stock, the implied volatility of the options tends to increase. In front of an announcement, such as earnings, there is more risk of owning shares. After a known announcement has occurred and the knowledge is public, the risk goes down and so should the implied volatility as indicated by option prices.

A common misperception regarding implied volatility is that it may be set by professionals or market makers. Implied volatility is set by the market action in the options markets. If there is a large amount of buying of calls and/or puts, the implied volatility of the options will increase and when there is selling pressure on calls and/or put options, the implied volatility will decrease.

Since options may be purchased to speculate on a big short term move, there does seem to be a consistent increase in implied volatility of options before an announcement. Also, as put options may be used as insurance for a long stock holding, in front of a risky period of time there can be an increase in put buying which will push the level of implied volatility higher.

The Greek that relates to implied volatility is known as vega. In some text books and academic circles the Greek letter kappa may be used in place of vega. Vega is actually not a Greek letter, but was chosen as an indicator of option price changes based on volatility because both vega and volatility start with v.

Vega, like theta, has the same impact on call and put options. However, the sign for vega is positive. An increase in volatility will have a positive price impact on a call and a put and a decrease in volatility will have a negative price impact on a call and a put option. Table 4.12 shows the impact of a drop of 1 percent in volatility and a gain of 1 percent in volatility on a call and a put option.

TABLE 4.12 Vega and Volatility

Volatility	Vega	30 Call	30 Put
29% (down 1%)	0.20	1.80	1.70
30%	0.20	2.00	1.90
31% (up 1%)	0.20	2.20	2.10

The vega of .20 is an estimate that the option will gain or lose .20 based on a 1 percent gain or loss in implied volatility. The vega is the same in this case for both the call and the put, so a 1 percent drop in volatility takes the call from 2.00 to 1.80 and the put from 1.90 to 1.70. With a gain of 1 percent in volatility the call price rises from 2.00 to 2.20 and the put price goes from 1.90 to 2.10.

A shift in implied volatility can have a dramatic impact on the value of options. Many traders have been perplexed by the move in option prices relative to the moves seen in the underlying security. This surprise at the option's price movement is usually a case of not having a full understanding of the impact that a change in volatility may have on an option's price.

INTEREST RATE-RELATED GREEK

The final Greek is related to the interest rate input that goes into an option's valuation. The interest rate used for option pricing models is the risk-free rate, which at the writing of this book is at a very low level. The Greek that indicates how much an option's value will change relative to a one unit or one percent change in interest rates is rho.

Rho does not get much attention and is not even currently taught in many courses due to the current low interest rate environment. Also, the small impact a change in interest rates has on the value of an option with only one or two months to expiration allows some option educators an excuse to leave out rho when discussing the Greeks. The longer the time to expiration, the more impact a change in interest rates may have on an option's value. LEAPS options with a year or more to expiration see much more of an impact when there is a change in interest rates, so when considering longer-dated options an interest forecast should be included in assumptions. A comparison of the impact of a change in interest rates for a 60-day option and a LEAPS option with 450 days to expiation appears in Table 4.13.

The underlying assumptions used to create Table 4.12 are a 50 stock, strike of 50, and 30 percent volatility. Using these numbers with an option pricing calculator, the various option values were determined. Looking at

TABLE 4.13 Comparison of the Impact of a Change in Interest Rates

Option	1%	2%	3%
60 day Call	2.45	2.50	2.55
450 day Call	6.85	7.15	7.45
60 day Put	2.40	2.35	2.30
450 day Put	6.25	5.95	5.65

the 60-day calls first, each 1 percent increase in the level of interest rates results in a .05 increase in the value of an option. Keep in mind, the Federal Reserve sets interest rates based on economic conditions and their moves are normally just one quarter or one half a percentage point. A full 1 percent move in the risk free rate over a 60-day period is unlikely, but that extreme case would have just a .05 impact on call prices.

The longer term call option in the table shows that the longer the expiration the more of an impact a change in interest rates will have on an option's value. Each percentage point move raises the value of the 450-day call options by .30. A change in interest rates of this magnitude over the course of more than a year is more likely than in 60 days, but the impact is still not terribly dramatic.

For put options, a rise in interest rates will actually have a negative impact on the value of options. This relates to the time value of money and the interest rate input into the option valuation and put-call parity models. With put-call parity, an input is the present value of the strike price of an option. When interest rates rise, the present value of the strike price actually is lowered. When the present value of the strike price is reduced, this results in a higher call premium and a lower put premium. Another way to approach this is that with higher interest rates, the future value of a stock is expected to be higher than in a lower interest rate environment. If the future value of the stock is expected to be higher, then the call option should be worth more and a put option should be worth less.

As far as the impact of interest rate changes on the put option in the table, the magnitude of changes is similar for put options as it is for the comparable call options. The 60-day put options lose .05 for each 1 percent increase in interest rates and the 450-day put options lose .30 for each 1 percent increase in interest rates.

The impact of interest rates on option pricing is a function of the time to expiration for an option. It is of little concern when considering shorter-term options, but may be something to take into consideration when looking at LEAPS options that may go as far as two years out for expiration. In the case of trading a LEAPS option, a coincidental interest rate forecast may be in order.

CONCLUSION

A cursory knowledge of the Greeks and their impact on option pricing is a key to trading single options or option spreads. As spreads are presented through the remainder of this book, the impact that a change in the Greeks will have on the pricing of the spread components will be discussed. One of the benefits of using spreads will be the ability of lessening the impact of price changes or a change in the underlying pricing factors of an option. Understanding the Greeks will go a long way to understanding and effectively trading options and options spreads.

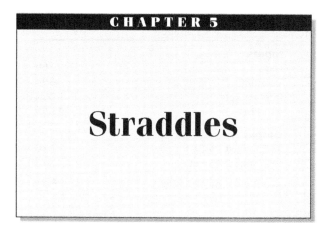

CHAPTER 5

Straddles

A long straddle can initially appear to be a very attractive position to novice option traders. The buyer of a straddle takes a long position in both a call and put with the same strike price and expiration. The idea behind this trade is that if the stock moves enough in either direction the holder of the straddle will benefit from this price move. An owner of a straddle does not care what direction a stock moves, just as long as it moves in a certain magnitude.

Like all things in life that may appear too good to be true, just buying a straddle and waiting for the big move, without anticipating the direction of that move, is not as simple as knowing a market-moving event is on the horizon. The cost of a straddle varies based on market conditions and often the market does a very good job of anticipating future stock moves and fairly prices straddles. Due to this market efficiency, straddles should be approached with a good base of knowledge on how they are priced and what sort of move in the underlying is reflected in this pricing.

Finally, as with all long trades, there is always the possibility of taking the other side, or a short straddle position. A short straddle is just the opposite of a long straddle. A call and a put with the same strike prices and expiration dates may be sold. A long straddle is put on in anticipation of the underlying security making a large move. The short straddle has the opposite goal—that is, a stock or index staying in a narrow range.

TABLE 5.1 Inputs and Output to Create XYZ 45 Straddle

Inputs	
Days	60
Volatility	30%
Interest Rate	1.00%
XYZ Price	45.00
Output	
XYZ August 45 Call	2.20
XYZ August 45 Put	2.15
XYZ August 45 Straddle	4.35

LONG STRADDLE MECHANICS

As previously stated, a straddle involves taking a long position in both a put and a call with the same expiration and strike price. For example an XYZ August 45 Straddle would consist of a long XYZ August 45 Call and a long XYZ August 45 Put. A straddle is always initiated with a debit or cost to a trader's account as there is an outflow for both legs. Table 5.1 shows the inputs and output from using a pricing calculator to create a long XYZ August 45 Straddle.

Using 60 days to August expiration, implied volatility of 30 percent, a risk-free interest rate of 1.00 percent, and XYZ trading at 45, an XYZ August 45 Call would be priced at 2.20 and an XYZ August 45 Put should be trading around 2.15. Therefore, the total cost of the August 45 Straddle would be 4.35 (2.20 + 2.15).

Assuming a valuation of 4.35 for the 45 Straddle indicates that XYZ would need to be greater than 49.35 or less than 40.65 at expiration for this trade to make money. These two levels would be the break-even points for this trade. Also, this represents a move of almost 10 percent in either direction over 60 days. Depending on the stock, a 10 percent move in 60 days might be an unusual occurrence.

The worst case scenario for this trade, if held to expiration, would be if the stock settled on expiration right at 45. Both options would expire worthless and a loss of 100 percent of both premiums would be realized. Finally, the potential profit of this trade is unlimited in the case of the stock rallying to infinity. Table 5.2 is a summary of the key levels for this trade.

The payoff diagram in Figure 5.1 shows just how much of a move XYZ needs to make in order to realize a profit from this position if held to expiration. In order to get to the upside or downside break-even point there would probably need to be some sort of news event to push the stock in

TABLE 5.2 Key Levels for the XYZ August 45 Straddle

Level	Level	Explanation
Up Break-even Price	49.35	Strike plus Straddle Cost
Down Break-even Price	40.65	Strike minus Straddle Cost
Maximum Dollar Loss	4.35	Option Premiums
Maximum Loss Price	45.00	Options Both Worthless
Maximum Dollar Profit	40.65/Unlimited	Stock Goes To 0/Stock Rallies

either direction in a dramatic fashion. This leads directly to a common motivation for putting on a straddle, expecting a market-moving event, but not sure what direction this event will push the stock.

A prime example of a price-moving event for a stock would be the company's quarterly earnings report. Although referred to as a quarterly earnings release, it is much more than what a company has earned in profits over the past three months. Four times a year a company will release a slew of financial data that represent the performance of the company's operations. In addition, projections are shared with investors and a conference call usually accompanies this release where the officers of a company field questions. Due to the impending news contained in this report the risk

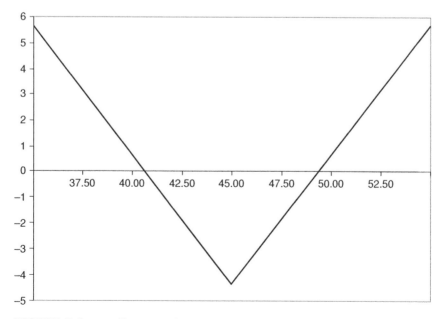

FIGURE 5.1 Payoff Diagram for August 45 Straddle

of being long or short the underlying stock has increased over the short term and with this increase in risk is an increase in the option premiums due to higher levels of implied volatility.

Long Straddle and Volatility

Therefore, one of the best uses of a straddle actually is in front of some sort of catalyst. However, when earnings or some other type price-moving event is on the horizon, option prices start to reflect an impending event. As a straddle would be entered going into an event, the proper response after an event would be to exit the trade after the event has occurred. The reason the trade was entered was the catalyst, once the catalyst has passed the trade should be exited, win or lose.

The previous payoff diagram shows the payout of a straddle based on option expiration. If the trade had been put on a day before a potential market-moving event and exited the day after, even with no big move, there should be some time value left in both the call and put. This would allow the trader to avoid a total loss of premium even in a case where there is very little movement.

Chapter 4, which covers the Greeks, discusses vega and volatility as a component of the value of an option. Generally, as earnings approach, the volatility component of the option prices expands. For some stocks it may be a dramatic change in volatility up to the day of earnings and then quite a drop off in the volatility component of the option as values return to historically normal levels. A note about earnings dates, they are well known in advance and free calendars that inform investors and traders of earnings dates for companies are widely available on the Internet. As earnings announcements affect movements in the underlying stock, as well as impact implied volatility before placing a trade, always check to see when the next earnings report or any other scheduled company events are set to occur.

For example, it is very feasible that between earnings periods the implied volatility of options on stock XYZ could normally be in the mid 20s, or 25 percent. When an earning announcement starts to approach, the volatility component of option values could regularly expand to 40 percent. In Table 5.3 below, all factors are the same for XYZ, 30 days to November expiration, stock at 35, and the risk-free interest rate at 1.00 percent. The comparison is to show the various values for the XYZ November 35 Call and XYZ November 35 Put when volatility is at 25 percent and at 40 percent.

The November 35 Straddle would be 60 percent more expensive when there is an increase in implied volatility due to the market pricing in higher volatility in front of a scheduled event. This can be significant when trading a straddle into some sort of event. If the implied volatility of options

TABLE 5.3 Comparison of November 35 Call and Put with 25 percent and 40 percent Volatility

Option	25% Volatility	40% Volatility
Call	1.00	1.60
Put	1.00	1.60
Straddle	2.00	3.20

is in the 25 percent range, when no events are on the horizon, but when a known price-moving event is imminent, and volatility is 40 percent, consideration should be given to what volatility will be after the event. Most likely, volatility will return to historical norms.

An easy example would use the comparative November 35 Straddle prices from Table 5.3. The straddle priced with 40 percent volatility was 1.20 more expensive than the straddle priced with a more historically normal 25 percent volatility. Assuming options go from 40 percent volatility before earnings to 25 percent volatility post earnings, the Long November 35 Straddle should lose about 1.20 due to a shift in volatility, regardless of what the underlying stock does based on the potential price-moving event.

The key levels for these straddles vary due to the difference in premium between the two. Table 5.4 compares the key levels for the Long November 35 Straddle. The maximum loss difference is the premium of the two straddles, or 2.00 for the lower volatility straddle and 3.20 for the higher volatility straddle. Also, the break-even levels are higher for the straddle that cost 3.20 versus the lower-priced straddle. The maximum gain levels are somewhat similar.

Figure 5.2 shows the difference at expiration between a 25 percent and 40 percent volatility straddle. The lower potential loss and closer break-even levels for the November 35 Straddle priced at 25 percent volatility is pretty apparent. With all payoff diagrams that have angular features, these two are showing holding a straddle to expiration. As mentioned before, one of the reasons to buy a straddle is the expectation of a quick move either

TABLE 5.4 Key Levels for Straddle Priced at 25 percent and 40 percent Volatility

	25% Straddle	40% Straddle
Up Break-even Price	37.00	38.20
Down Break-even Price	33.00	31.80
Maximum Dollar Loss	2.00	3.20
Maximum Loss Price	35.00	35.00
Maximum Dollar Profit	33.00/Unlimited	31.80/Unlimited

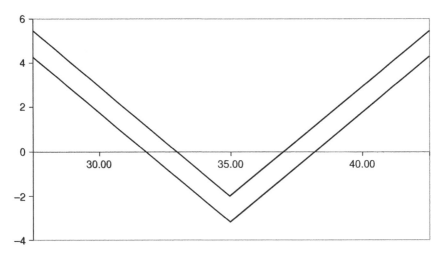

FIGURE 5.2 Comparing a Straddle Priced at 25 percent and 40 percent Volatility

up or down based on a price-moving announcement, so it is very likely that this trade would be exited before expiration.

A straddle bought for an event should be purchased very close to the event. A component that works against long options is a deterioration of time value. Buying a straddle a week before earnings may allow a trader to get ahead of the expansion of volatility before the event. However, the deterioration of time value over those few days may offset any or all of the benefit of being ahead of the expansion of volatility. All situations vary from trade to trade, so for simplicity a short-term long straddle trade in this example will involve buying the straddle just before an earnings announcement and selling the straddle very quickly after the earnings report has been disseminated to the market.

Event Trading with a Long Straddle

Earnings announcements are almost always made outside of regular market hours. This news will be released either after the closing of the stock market or just before the open of the stock market. When being done for a very short-term trade, a long straddle to benefit from an earnings move may be put on just before the stock market close before the earnings announcement. It should be exited during the trading day that occurs just after the earnings announcement.

By assuming that a return to normal implied volatility based on history will occur after an earnings announcement, reasonable payoff levels may be estimated. This is one of those exercises that definitely will involve the

TABLE 5.5 Straddle Key Levels

Level	Nov 35 Straddle	Explanation
Up Break-even Price	37.85	Nov 35 Call = 3.05
		Nov 35 Put = 0.15
Down Break-even Price	32.00	Nov 35 Call = 0.10
		Nov 35 Put = 3.10
Maximum Loss Price	35.00	Volatility Drops To 25%
		Stock Does Not Move
Maximum Dollar Loss	1.20	Nov 35 Call = 1.00
		Nov 35 Put = 1.00
Maximum Dollar Profit	31.80/Unlimited	XYZ to 0/XYZ Huge Rally

use of a pricing calculator. Take the XYZ November 35 Straddle priced at 40 percent volatility. A long position is taken in this spread a day before an earnings announcement, with the knowledge that the volatility pricing component of the spread will return to 25 percent after the earnings announcement. Using these assumptions, the key levels of this trade vary somewhat, but are closer to a realistic payoff than using the payoff at expiration. Keep in mind the assumption is made that this trade will be exited shortly after the earnings announcement.

Before the trade, November expiration is 30 days off, after the trade November option expiration is 29 days away, just a loss of one day in time value. The most significant change is the move in volatility from a pre-earnings level of 40 percent to a post earnings level of 25 percent. Due to this drop in volatility, a pretty big move is in order for this trade to become profitable.

The break-even levels involve a move of 2.85 higher or down a full 3.00. This slight difference in pricing relates to the role of interest rates in put-call parity pricing. The slight difference related to put-call parity was discussed in Chapter 3. In the case of a positive price reaction to the earnings announcement if XYZ trades up to 37.85 then the November 35 Call would be worth 3.05 with the November Put having 0.15 of value left. This would result in a value of 3.20 for the November 35 Straddle. As the stock moves beyond 37.85 on the upside, the trade becomes profitable.

In the other direction, a little more of a move would be needed in the bearish direction to get breakeven. With XYZ trading at 32.00 the November 35 Put would benefit greatly and have a value of 3.10 while the November 35 Call would be priced at 0.10. Together this results in the November 35 Straddle having a value of 3.20, which covers the cost of entering the position. At these levels a trader would be able to sell both options and exit the trade with no loss or gain.

Even though there will be just a loss of one day in time value, the expected loss of value due to a decrease in volatility will have a dramatic effect on the value of the XYZ November 35 Straddle. A move of more than 8 percent in either direction would be needed just to break even on this trade. Going into earnings, sometimes market forecasters may project how big of a move is being expected out of a stock. These projections of how much of a move may occur will also have no direction, bullish or bearish, associated with them. Usually this prediction is determined by what sort of move option valuations and volatility levels are indicating. Also, some of what has happened in history will be taken into account, but usually the option market is a pretty clear indicator of the expected magnitude of a price move. In the case of this previous example, the options were pricing in a quick move of just over 8 percent, either up or down, in XYZ based on the break-even levels.

As far as the worst case scenario for this trade, this would be if the stock does not react at all, that is stays right at 35.00 and volatility returns to a normal level of 25 percent. With these inputs, both the November 35 Call and Put would be priced at 1.00, so the straddle would be priced at 2.00. Upon exit of the November 35 Straddle a loss of 1.20 would and should be taken.

If a straddle is purchased for an event, this event was the reason for the trade. Regardless of winning or losing, if a trade is entered for a reason and that reason is over, the trade should be exited. If earnings come out, the stock uncharacteristically does not move at all and a straddle has lost some value, take the loss. Taking losses is never a pleasant experience, but the willingness to take a loss and move on to the next trade is exactly how professionals stay in the trading game.

Long Straddle Leading Up to a Catalyst

A final way to approach a long straddle is worth discussion. The previous example involved buying a straddle into an announcement and then selling it after the news has been disseminated. Before the news, volatility is high and afterward it has returned to a more normal level. This drop has a very negative impact on the long straddle. How about situations where volatility expands? A long straddle will benefit greatly from an expansion in volatility.

Volatility expansions can be expected or unexpected. An example of an expected expansion in volatility would relate to the previous earnings example. As far as an unexpected volatility expansion, any sort of unscheduled announcement that greatly moves a market or stock would also have an impact on the volatility of the underlying options. This impact would probably be very short lived, but the impact on a long option position, call or put, would provide a nice opportunity to realize a quick profit.

As the unexpected volatility expansion is pretty difficult to anticipate since it is *unexpected*, a sample of how to trade an expected volatility increase is in order. Like the previous example where a straddle is bought in order to attempt to benefit from a big move on an earnings announcement. This example takes advantage of the volatility expansion that occurs over 10 trading days leading up to an earnings announcement. Then, just before the close before the earnings announcement is made, the straddle is sold.

In this example, XYZ is trading at 65.00 and an earnings announcement will be after the close in 10 days. As a reminder, all examples in this book use calendar days to expiration. Historically, the implied volatility for XYZ options has gone from 30 percent to 45 percent from 10 days before earnings to the day of earnings. Although there is also some loss in time value due to the passage of time, this loss of time value is more than offset by an expansion of implied volatility.

With XYZ earnings coming up, the nearest option expiration just after the announcement would be October expiration. October options expire 20 days after the earnings announcement. Therefore, 30 days before expiration and 10 days before the earnings announcement an XYZ October 65 Straddle is purchased. Using a pricing calculator and volatility at 30 percent, the 65 Call would be valued at 2.25 and the 65 Put would have a value of 2.20. The XYZ October 65 Straddle would be bought for a cost of 4.45.

Fast forward 10 days to the trading day before earnings. All pricing factors are kept the same for this straddle except days to expiration (now 20) and volatility, which has expanded to 45 percent. Although time has worked some against the two legs of this position, the increase of volatility has had an impact on the option values that offsets this loss in time value.

With 20 days to expiration, the XYZ October 65 Call is now valued at 2.75 and the XYZ October 65 Put is at 2.70, so the straddle now has a value of 5.45 or a profit of 1.00. This represents a profit of over 20 percent in just 10 days. Table 5.6 is a breakdown of the change in the value of the straddle due to a decrease in time and an increase in volatility.

TABLE 5.6 Straddle Valuation Change with a Decrease in days and Increase in Volatility

Position	30 days/ 30% Volatility	20 days/ 45% Volatility
XYZ Oct 65 Call	2.25	2.75
XYZ Oct 65 Put	2.20	2.70
XYZ Oct 65 Straddle	4.45	5.45

TABLE 5.7   Straddle Value at a Variety of Prices with Volatility Expanding

XYZ	Oct 65 Call	Oct 65 Put	Oct 65 Straddle	P/L
55.00	0.15	10.10	10.25	5.80
57.50	0.40	7.85	8.25	3.80
60.00	0.85	5.80	6.65	2.20
62.50	1.60	4.10	5.70	1.25
65.00	2.75	2.70	5.45	1.00
67.50	4.20	1.70	5.90	1.45
70.00	6.00	1.00	7.00	2.55
72.50	8.10	0.55	8.65	4.20
75.00	10.30	0.30	10.60	6.15

Another factor to consider is the underlying price of the options. XYZ will most likely not just sit at 65.00 for the next 10 days until earnings. So in addition to the possibility that volatility will not expand as in the past, the price of the underlying stock may move in a way that causes this attempt to benefit from an expansion of volatility to be a profitable trade. A pricing calculator comes in handy when estimating what sort of outcome this straddle would have at expiration. Table 5.7 on the next page shows what the value of the XYZ October 65 Straddle would be at a variety of prices just before earnings and with volatility priced at 45 percent

Table 5.7 shows that the expansion of volatility trumps all other factors. Dramatic moves in volatility definitely can make or break any option trade, regardless of what happens relative to the price of an underlying security. As touched on in Chapter 4, a shift in volatility can cause an option's price to move opposite of expectations, such as a call losing value while the correspondent stock moves higher. Volatility has the same impact, positive or negative, on a variety of option trades.

So in this case, it appears buying a straddle before the volatility starts to rise into an earnings release is a winning proposition. Things can always go wrong with trades and a long straddle into a volatility expansion may encounter unexpected problems. The main issue could be that, although historically volatility in a certain stock has expanded into their earnings report, it may not occur that way in this instance. Table 5.8 shows what might happen to the XYZ October 65 Straddle if there is no volatility expansion into this earnings announcement. In this table, the October 65 Straddle would have been purchased at 4.45 for a variety of prices just before earnings, but no expansion in volatility.

Although not a terrible outcome, if no expansion in volatility occurs and the price of the stock stays in a range until just before earnings this

TABLE 5.8 Straddle with No Expansion in Volatility

XYZ	Oct 65 Call	Oct 65 Put	Oct 65 Straddle	P/L
55.00	0.00	10.05	10.05	5.60
57.50	0.05	7.55	7.60	3.15
60.00	0.25	5.25	5.50	1.05
62.50	0.80	3.25	4.05	−0.40
65.00	1.85	1.80	3.65	−0.80
67.50	3.35	0.85	4.20	−0.25
70.00	5.35	0.35	5.70	1.25
72.50	7.65	0.10	7.75	3.30
75.00	10.05	0.00	10.05	5.60

trade may not work out as planned. Historically stock reactions to earnings tend to repeat themselves. However, in the stock market, there are always occurrences of the market not repeating itself and the consistent thing to remember about all types of investing is that past performance is no indication of future results.

To summarize the long straddle, it is a position taken to speculate on a dramatic move, up or down, in an underlying instrument. The direction of the move is not the key, just that the magnitude of this move is sufficient to cover the cost of the two legs of the straddle. As a big move is needed to create a profitable situation for the owner of a straddle, straddles are often considered in front of known market-moving events.

Volatility, a large factor in many types of option trades, takes on more significance related to a straddle. Since a straddle is taking on two long positions, one call and one put, any increase in volatility should have positive impact on both legs of the long straddle. Conversely, a decrease in volatility would have a negative impact on both legs of a long straddle. Due to the potential impact of volatility on a long straddle, positive or negative, investigating if current implied volatility is cheap or expensive relative to history is in order when considering a long straddle.

SHORT STRADDLE

As a long straddle is the purchase of a call and a put with the same expiration and same strike prices, a short straddle is exactly the opposite. A short straddle involves selling (or shorting) a call and a put with the same expiration and same strike price. For example selling both an XYZ April

25 Call and an XYZ April 25 Put would be selling or short an XYZ April 25 Straddle.

A short straddle is implemented for opposite of many reasons that a long straddle would be traded. Initially, the main reason a short straddle would be traded is if there is the anticipation that a stock is going to settle exactly at a certain price on expiration. For example, with the short April 25 Straddle from the previous paragraph, if on April expiration XYZ were to close right at 25 both the April 25 Call and April 25 Put would expire worthless. Any premium received for selling this straddle would be kept by the seller.

For a short straddle example some assumptions are made to create a Short XYZ April 25 Straddle. Assuming XYZ is trading at 25, with 40 days to April expiration, 35 percent volatility, and a risk-free interest rate of 1.00 percent, the XYZ April 25 Call would be trading at 1.20 and the XYZ April 25 Put would be priced at 1.15. For selling the XYZ April 25 Straddle the trader would take in a credit of 2.35 (1.20 + 1.15).

As always, key levels should be determined when considering this trade. The maximum gain for this trade would be the premium received of 2.35, which would occur if XYZ is at 25 at expiration. The two break-even levels are determined by taking the strike price of the straddle and adding to and subtracting from the premium received for the short position. In this case, the two break-even levels are 22.65 on the downside and 27.35 on the upside. Finally, the maximum loss at expiration for this trade is either 22.65 if the stock is at 0 on expiration or unlimited if there is a large rally in shares. Table 5.9 covers the key levels for this position.

The payoff diagram for this position is a mirror image of a long straddle. It depicts that single point where a maximum profit may be realized and then as the price of XYZ moves in either direction, the profit of this position diminishes until the two break-even points are reached. At these two levels the losses start to increase 1 for 1 with a drop or rise in the stock. The payoff diagram for the Short April 25 Straddle is in Figure 5.3.

A note is in order regarding a short straddle and individual investors. Many brokerage firms are reluctant to allow individuals the ability to sell

TABLE 5.9 Key Levels for Short XYZ April 25 Straddle

	Level	Explanation
Up Break-even Price	27.35	Strike + Premium Received
Down Break-even Price	22.65	Strike − Premium Received
Maximum Dollar Gain	2.35	Both Options Expire Worthless
Maximum Gain Price	25.00	Options Both Worthless
Maximum Dollar Loss	22.65/Unlimited	Stock Goes To 0/Stock Rallies

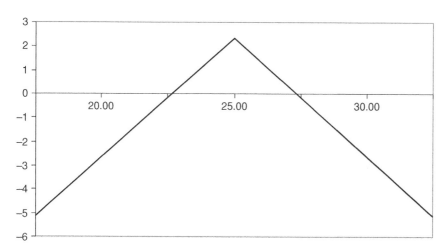

FIGURE 5.3 Payoff Diagram for Short XYZ April 25 Straddle

options naked or without a matching underlying security to offset potential losses. For example, in Chapter 2 selling a covered call or a call against a long position in an underlying stock was discussed. If this call had been sold with no position in the underlying stock it would have been considered a naked short position and may not have been permitted by some brokers based on an individual's trading permissions. Before trying to put on a short naked option position for the first time a trader should always consult their broker to make sure they have the proper trading permission.

Relative to volatility, the short straddle is a position that would benefit from a reduction in volatility. Many professional traders often refer to positions where they hope to benefit from an expansion or contraction in volatility as being long or short volatility. When discussing the long straddle in the previous section, a long straddle would benefit from an increase in volatility. Owning a straddle is a method of being long volatility, being short a straddle is a method of being short volatility.

Short Straddle and Volatility

For example, sticking with the short XYZ April 25 Straddle, the volatility input to price the call and put for this position used a volatility input of 35 percent. A trader may consider this high for a variety of reasons. Possibly the historical range has been 25 percent to 30 percent and due to unwarranted option activity there has been an increase in volatility. Maybe there is an unfounded rumor going around about shares. Whatever the

TABLE 5.10 XYZ April 25 Straddle Values at Lower Volatility Levels

	Percent Implied Volatility		
	25%	**30%**	**35%**
Call	0.85	1.00	1.20
Put	0.80	0.95	1.15
Straddle	1.65	1.95	2.35

reason, a trader believes the volatility should quickly return to the historical norm of 25 percent to 30 percent.

The trader in this instance would need to use a pricing calculator to get a good idea what the value of the XYZ April 25 Straddle would be if the volatility were to come in quickly. Based on all other inputs staying consistent, the XYZ April 25 Straddle would be valued at 1.65 if volatility were reduced 25 percent and 1.95 if volatility dropped to 30 percent. Table 5.10 illustrates the lower straddle values.

Although the expectation of lower volatility is not the only motivating factor when considering selling a straddle, it is a nice benefit to find options with relatively high implied volatilities when choosing to sell these options. The potential profit on selling the XYZ April 25 Straddle may not have made much sense to a trader at 25 percent volatility, but at a higher level like 35 percent this may have been a more attractive trade.

Figure 5.4 is a payoff diagram comparing all three of the straddles. It may be seen that the lower the volatility going into the trade, the less attractive the key levels are for a short straddle.

Just by looking at the payoff comparison diagram, it is pretty apparent that there is more likelihood of success when selling a straddle that has a higher level of volatility. The higher and wider payoff in Figure 5.4 represents the 35 percent volatility straddle, the middle straddle shows the payoff for a straddle priced at 30 percent volatility, and the lowest straddle is priced with implied volatility at 25 percent. Once again, although not the primary reason to take a long or short position in a straddle, current implied volatility and where it is relative to historical volatility is something to be aware of before trading a straddle.

Short Straddle Alternative

As mentioned earlier in this section, a short straddle involves taking two naked option positions. Many brokerage firms do not allow most customers to take naked option positions. Also, the margin requirements involved in these uncovered option positions may reduce the desirability of putting on

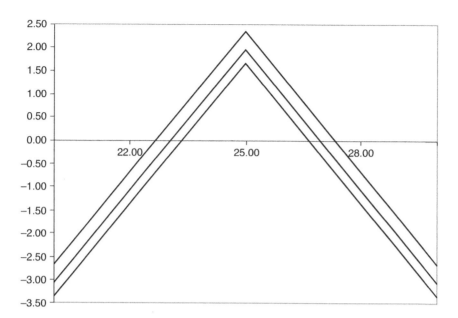

FIGURE 5.4 Comparison of Short Straddles Priced at 25 percent, 30 percent, and 35 percent Volatility

one of these trades. However, by adding a couple of long options to a short straddle, a trader may put on a position that would be similar in structure to a short straddle, but not have the unlimited risk characteristics of a short straddle.

For instance if a trader had a neutral opinion on shares of XYZ over the next 30 days and July option expiration happened to be 30 days off, they may choose to sell an at-the-money call and an at-the-money put. With XYZ trading at 55.00, this would involve shorting an XYZ July 55 Call and an XYZ July 55 Put. In addition to those positions, they would buy slightly out-of-the-money options to cover these two short positions. In this case, they may purchase the XYZ July 50 Put and the XYZ July 60 Call.

An astute and experienced trader may recognize the position that has been created by purchasing these out-of-the-money options. It is commonly referred to as an iron butterfly. The iron butterfly consists of a short straddle and then purchasing an out-of-the-money put and call for protection. This may also be called buying the wings to create the butterfly. Butterfly spreads are covered much more extensively in Chapter 9.

Using a pricing calculator, the following prices are determined for the options in this iron butterfly: XYZ July 50 Put at .60, XYZ July 55 Put at 2.30, XYZ July 55 Call at 2.35, and July XYZ 60 Call at .75. A short straddle would

TABLE 5.11 Short Straddle and Iron Butterfly Comparison

Option	Price
XYZ July 50 Put	0.60
XYZ July 55 Put	2.30
XYZ July 55 Call	2.35
XYZ July 60 Call	0.75

Straddle	Price
Sell 1 55 Put	2.30
Sell 1 55 Call	2.35
Income	4.65

Iron Butterfly	Price
Buy 1 50 Put	0.60
Sell 1 55 Put	2.30
Sell 1 55 Call	2.35
Buy 1 60 Call	0.75
Income	3.30

be entered by just selling the XYZ July 55 Put and XYZ July 55 Call, while the iron butterfly would be created by also buying the XYZ July 50 Put and XYZ July 60 Call. Table 5.11 depicts a breakdown of the trades used to create an iron butterfly, as well as a comparable short straddle.

The income or credit received for putting on a short straddle is greater than the credit received for the iron butterfly. This difference is due to the insurance being purchased to assure limited downside. A quick comparison of the key levels for the short straddle and iron butterfly is depicted in Table 5.12.

There is a little difference between the key levels for this short straddle and iron butterfly. The straddle has superior potential gain and break-even levels. However, as far as risk goes, for a risk adverse trader, the iron butterfly is a much better choice with potential downside of only 1.70 versus potentially unlimited downside for the short straddle. This unlimited risk

TABLE 5.12 Key Levels for the Short Straddle and Iron Butterfly

Level	Short Straddle	Iron Butterfly
Up Breakeven	59.65	58.30
Down Breakeven	50.35	51.70
Maximum Gain	4.65	3.30
Maximum Loss	Unlimited	1.70

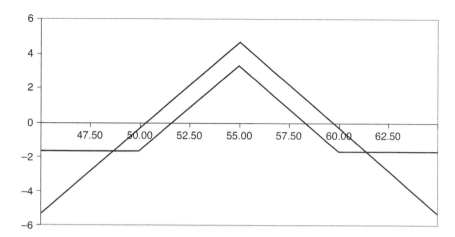

FIGURE 5.5 Short Straddle versus Iron Butterfly Payoff

that goes along with a naked short option is exactly why many brokers are reluctant to allow naked option selling by many investors. It is also why many traders choose to use an iron butterfly or other strategy with limited downside when taking a neutral position on a stock or index. A payoff diagram comparing the unlimited downside of this short straddle and the iron butterfly appears in Figure 5.5.

Although covered much more extensively in Chapter 9, a final note regarding the iron butterfly is in order. When trading an iron butterfly compared to a short straddle, the level of volatility does not have nearly the impact on the value of the iron butterfly. This has two implications, first when evaluating the trade beforehand, the level of implied volatility relative to historical implied volatility is not as much a consideration as it would be with a short straddle. Also, during the life of a trade, the iron butterfly does not have the same exposure to implied volatility risk as a short straddle.

One consideration regarding volatility and these two trades is the level of volatility compared to history may push a trader to consider one spread over the other. A key to trading is buying cheap (low) and selling expensive (high). If implied volatility is low compared to history and a trader is considering a short straddle, they would be selling low. Since traders are in the business of buying low, they may consider buying the wings of a short straddle to protect against an upward move in volatility.

In the previous XYZ trade, a volatility level of 37.50 percent was used with a pricing calculator to create the short straddle and iron butterfly. In order to display the effect of a move in volatility (up and down) for both

TABLE 5.13 Short Straddle and Iron Butterfly value with 25 percent, 37.50 percent, and 50 percent Volatility

	Percent Implied Volatility		
Option	25%	37.50%	50%
XYZ 50 Put	0.15	0.60	1.15
XYZ 55 Put	1.55	2.30	3.10
XYZ 55 Call	1.60	2.35	3.15
XYZ 60 Call	0.20	0.75	1.40
Short Straddle	3.15	4.65	6.25
Iron Butterfly	2.80	3.30	3.70

positions, the volatility level for all options in each spread was changed to 25 percent and 50 percent. Table 5.13 on the following page depicts the impact of these changed in volatility.

When comparing the effect of volatility on the short straddle and iron butterfly, the difference is pretty dramatic. Shorting a straddle with 25 percent volatility and then seeing a spike to 50 percent volatility would result in almost a 100 percent rise in the value of the straddle. A similar volatility move would have the iron butterfly moving up about 32 percent. If volatility is low or there is a fear it may rise during the life of a trade, the iron butterfly would be the preferred trade. On the other hand, if a dramatic drop in volatility is expected, also called a volatility crush, the short straddle may be the better trade.

A long straddle would be initiated in front of some sort of large move in the underlying, while a short straddle anticipates that an underlying would have very little price move. Implied volatility is a major factor to take into account when considering a straddle. The level of implied volatility, with respect to the two options that will comprise the straddle, may result in a straddle being expensive or cheap. Also, if a position is going to be exited before expiration, making some assumptions of future implied volatility is a worthwhile exercise.

Strangles

A very close association exists between straddles—covered in the previous chapter—and strangles. The motivation for a long or short strangle is the same as for a straddle. Like the long straddle, a long strangle expects a large price move or an expansion in volatility. The short strangle, just like a short straddle, is put on in order to benefit from a reduction in volatility or a stock price that stays in a range. They are usually considered interchangeable as the trading motivations behind both strategies are very similar. The decision to trade a straddle or strangle usually comes down to just a couple of factors which will be covered in this chapter.

Also, as a short strangle, just like the short straddle, will consist of two naked options, there is an alternative that may be utilized by traders who are restricted from putting on an uncovered or naked short option position. With the short straddle, wings were purchased to protect against unlimited risk. Wings are also purchased with a short strangle to protect the position from an unbearable loss.

LONG STRANGLE MECHANICS

A long strangle consists of a long call and a long put position. Both have the same expiration date, but have different strike prices. Specifically the call has a higher strike price than a put. For instance, being long a 35 Put and long a 40 Call would be considered a Long 35/40 Strangle. The real major difference between a strangle and a straddle is that the options involved in

TABLE 6.1 Inputs and Output Used to Create an XYZ May 30/35 Strangle

Inputs	
Days	30
Volatility	35%
Interest Rate	1.00%
XYZ Price	32.5
Output	
XYZ May 30 Put	0.35
XYZ May 35 Call	0.40
XYZ May 30/35 Strangle	0.75

creating strangles have different strike prices, while the options used for a straddle consist of a put and call with the same strike price.

To illustrate a long XYZ May 30/35 strangle, the inputs and output from a pricing calculator were used. These figures appear in Table 6.1.

Now that the cost of the XYZ May 30/35 Strangle has been determined, key levels should also be investigated before actually putting on the trade. Before initiating the trade, these key levels should match up to a price projection for the underlying, in this case XYZ stock. Also, the trader's risk tolerance factor should be taken into account. Table 6.2 lays out the key levels for the XYZ May 30/35 Strangle.

The first noticeable factor regarding the XYZ May 30/35 Strangle is how inexpensive it appears to be with a cost of only 0.75. With XYZ trading at 32.50, both the XYZ May 30 Put and XYZ May 35 Call are out of the money. When options are out of the money the results will be cheaper options compared to at-the-money and in-the-money options. In Table 6.2 the key levels depict just how large of a move is involved in this straddle becoming profitable. XYZ would need to move up or down 3.25 or right at 10 percent, in 30 days, to reach the break-even point on this trade.

TABLE 6.2 Key Levels for the XYZ May 30/35 Strangle

	Level	Explanation
Up Break-even Price	35.75	Higher Strike plus Straddle Cost
Down Break-even Price	29.25	Lower Strike minus Straddle Cost
Maximum Dollar Loss	0.75	Option Premiums
Maximum Loss Prices	30 to 35	Options Both Worthless
Maximum Dollar Profit	29.25/Unlimited	Stock Goes To 0/Stock Rallies

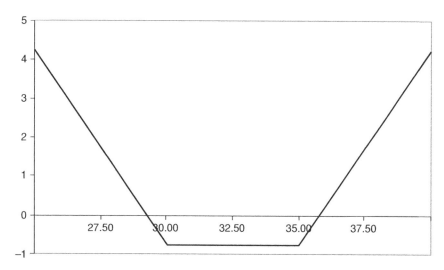

FIGURE 6.1 XYZ May 30/35 Strangle Payoff at Expiration

Figure 6.1 is a profit and loss diagram at expiration for the XYZ May 30/35 Strangle. Graphically the needed move for this position to become a profitable one is pretty apparent. As a large move—in a relatively short period of time—would be needed in order for this trade to work out, like the straddle in the previous chapter this is another type of trade that would be considered before some sort of market catalyst or price-moving event such as earnings or another corporate announcement.

Strangle Compared to Straddle

Due to their similarities, there will be a handful of contrasts and comparisons between straddles and strangles throughout this chapter. The 30/35 Strangle comes at a very cheap price, just 0.75. What would a comparable straddle cost? Using a pricing calculator and consistent inputs with the 30/35 Strangle, using an XYZ May 32.50 Call and XYZ May 32.50 Put an XYZ May 32.50 Straddle is created. Table 6.3 shows the inputs and output to create this spread.

Even though the XYZ May 32.50 Straddle is more expensive than the XYZ May 30/35 Strangle, it does have some advantages over the strangle. A key level comparison is shown in Table 6.4, which highlights the payoff differences between the straddle and strangle.

When comparing the key levels of the XYZ May 30/35 Strangle and XYZ May 32.50 Straddle, the break-even levels favor the straddle. A price move of 2.60, either higher or lower, is needed to get to breakeven, less than the

TABLE 6.3 Inputs and Output Used to Create an XYZ May 32.50 Straddle

Inputs	
Days	30
Volatility	35%
Interest Rate	1.00%
XYZ Price	32.5
Output	
XYZ May 32.50 Put	1.30
XYZ May 32.50 Call	1.30
XYZ May 32.50 Straddle	2.60

up or down move of 3.25 needed for the strangle. On a percentage basis, the strangle has to move higher or lower by 10 percent while the straddle needs a price move of 8 percent. Both are substantial moves, but this key level does favor the straddle.

However, the straddle is more expensive than the strangle, and the maximum loss for both a long straddle and strangle is limited to the premium paid for the options that make up the spread. As the maximum loss is limited to this premium paid, the strangle has the advantage with an outlay of 0.75 versus the cost of 2.60 for the straddle.

As far as maximum profit for either spread, this is dependent on the amount of price move seen in XYZ. For instance, if this spread is held to expiration and the stock closes at 36.50, this would be a profit of 0.75 for the strangle and 1.40 for the straddle. On a dollar basis the straddle has the superior profit. However, on a use of capital basis the strangle is actually more profitable.

With an outlay of 0.75 and XYZ settling at 36.50 the XYZ May 30/35 Strangle would have a profit 0.75. A 0.75 profit on a 0.75 capital investment is a return of 100 percent. The straddle cost 2.60 to implement and with

TABLE 6.4 Key Levels Compared for the XYZ May 30/35 Strangle and XYZ May 32.50 Straddle

	XYZ May 30/35 Strangle	XYZ May 32.50 Straddle
Up Break-even Price	35.75	35.10
Down Break-even Price	29.25	29.90
Maximum Dollar Loss	0.75	2.60
Maximum Loss Prices	30 to 35	32.50
Maximum Dollar Profit	29.25/Unlimited	29.90/Unlimited

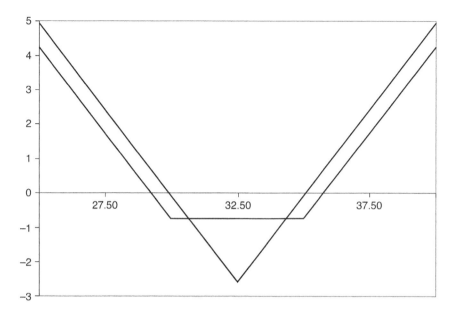

FIGURE 6.2 Payoff Comparison Between Straddle and Strangle

XYZ at 36.50 had a profit of 1.40. A 1.40 profit on 2.60 would be a return of about 54 percent. Still a nice return, but inferior to the percent return on the strangle. A payoff diagram that compares these two strategies is in Figure 6.2.

This use of capital leads to another point about considering a straddle versus a strangle. As both strategies involve the same underlying reasoning, that is, a price projection that the underlying security is going to have a big move in one direction or another, use of capital is something to analyze when deciding between a straddle or strangle. Take the case of the previous XYZ situation. At 32.50, the trader is expecting a large move in the underlying over the next 30 days. His initial thought is the XYZ May 32.50 Straddle trading at 2.60, but before moving on the trade he takes a look at the XYZ May 30/35 Strangle also.

Straddle, Strangle, and Leverage

The XYZ May 30/35 Strangle is trading at 0.75 and the trader considers this spread due to the extra leverage he can get with only putting up 75 dollars. However, he has another thought; for the cost of one XYZ May 32.50 Straddle he could buy three XYZ May 30/35 Strangles. One XYZ May 32.50 Straddle costs 2.60 while buying three XYZ May 30/35 Strangles would cost 2.25.

TABLE 6.5 Payoff Comparing One XYZ 32.50 Straddle
versus Owning Three XYZ 30/35 Strangles

XYZ	1 32.50 Straddle	3 30/35 Strangles
27.50	2.40	5.25
30.00	(0.10)	(2.25)
32.50	(2.60)	(2.25)
35.00	(0.10)	(2.25)
37.50	2.40	5.25

So the trader could put on three of the strangles and still have a little money
left over relative to trading one of the straddles. Table 6.5 compares the
profit or loss of these two spreads based on owning one straddle versus
buying three strangles at a variety of levels.

After comparing the potential payout for one straddle versus three
strangles the trader can make a decision on how he would like to approach
this trade. If the trader's price projection is for the stock to move up or
down $3.00, the trader would be better off trading the single straddle ver-
sus three strangles. At up or down 3.00, the strangle is not yet profitable,
while the straddle has made a small profit of 0.40. However, if the trader
expects a 5.00 move out of XYZ, the superior choice would be the strangle.
A 5.00 move results in a profit of 5.25 or about 233 percent for the strangle
while the straddle would have a profit of 2.40 which is a return on capital
of 92 percent. Figure 6.3 shows the payoff difference between these two
trades. Note that the three strangle position is a single line that shows the
results from trading three of the spreads.

As far as choosing either a straddle or strangle, at times this may be
based purely on where the underlying stock is trading when the position
is entered. For instance if XYZ is trading at 37.50 and the only available
strike prices close to 37.50 are 35 and 40, there may be no choice but to use
a strangle to benefit from a market move. On the other hand, if a stock is
trading at 45 and only the 40, 45, and 50 strikes are available, only a straddle
would make sense, as with a strangle both the strike prices would be more
than 10 percent from where the underlying stock is trading. However, there
continues to be an expansion of the number of strike prices available, so in
the future the level of flexibility will expand with this increase in available
strike prices.

So far in this chapter, all payoff comparisons have been at expiration.
As mentioned earlier, a strangle benefits more from a big move in either
price direction by an underlying security. Once a big move has occurred or
the event has passed and the desired price move did not occur, the trade

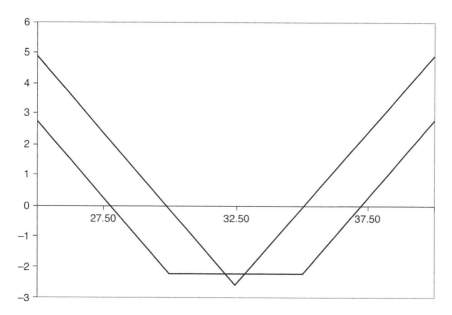

FIGURE 6.3 One Straddle versus Three Strangles

should be considered over. When purchased to benefit from an expected event or announcement, a strangle should then be sold after this announcement. The reason for the trade was the announcement, and when this event has passed, win or lose, the strangle should be sold.

Finally, as a strangle is a strategy that may be used in front of some sort of catalyst or announcement, there should be some consideration as to how much options are pricing in terms of implied volatility. That is, there should be some consideration given to how much anticipation is being priced into options. As mentioned in the previous chapter, when there is a potential market-moving announcement, options become expensive with an expansion in implied volatility. Also once an announcement has passed, there is usually a contraction in implied volatility. This change in implied volatility can have a dramatic impact on the value of a strangle, even more so than with a straddle. This is due to the use of out-of-the-money options when trading a strangle in this fashion.

For instance, XYZ is trading at 47.50 and earnings are scheduled to be released today after the market close. There is a lot of uncertainty regarding how XYZ will react to this earnings report, so options are being priced with an implied volatility of 50 percent, compared to a historical norm of 30 percent. November options expire in 20 days and the risk-free interest rate is 1.00 percent. Table 6.6 shows the inputs and outputs used to

TABLE 6.6 Inputs and Output Used to Create an XYZ November 45/50 Strangle

Inputs	
Days	20
Volatility	50%
Interest Rate	1.00%
XYZ Price	47.50
Output	
November 45.00 Put	1.15
November 50.00 Call	1.25
November 45/50 Strangle	2.40

create the November 45/50 Strangle to take advantage of a potential large move in XYZ stock.

Normal implied volatility for XYZ options is usually in the 30 percent range, but implied volatility has inflated to 50 percent due to the impending earnings announcement. Combined with the other pricing factors, a November 45/50 Strangle would cost 2.40 to implement. On first glance it appears a move of 4.90, up or down, would be needed in order to reach breakeven on expiration. However, the intention behind this trade is not to hold the strangle until expiration in 20 days. The intention is to benefit from a large move in XYZ based on earnings, exit this trade, and move on to the next trade. Another factor that comes into play here is what the expectation for volatility is after the earnings announcement has been released. That is, after the earnings release where would a trader expect the implied volatility of the options owned in the strangle to be. Probably the most reasonable level would be the historical norm of 30 percent implied volatility. Table 6.7 shows a quick comparison of the options involved in creating the 45/50 Strangle with volatility priced at a historical normal level of 30 percent and a close-to-the-earnings announcement inflated level of 50 percent.

TABLE 6.7 Comparison of Options with 30 percent and 50 percent Volatility

Option	Volatility	
	30%	50%
Nov XYZ 45 Put	0.40	1.15
Nov XYZ 50 Call	0.45	1.25
Nov XYZ 45/50 Strangle	0.85	2.40

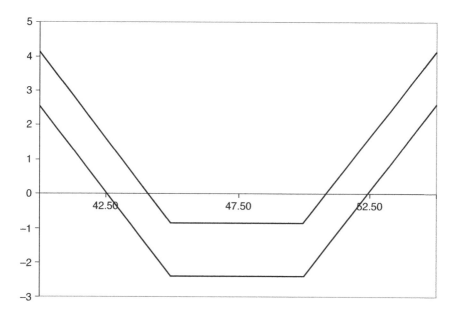

FIGURE 6.4 Strangles with 30 percent Implied Volatility and 50 percent Implied Volatility

These numbers are pretty dramatic, with both options losing two-thirds of their value when reducing implied volatility back down to normal levels. A similar impact on these options should result when a reduction in volatility occurs post earnings. A payoff diagram that compares these two strangles at expiration appears in Figure 6.4. The lower of the two strangles represents the more expensive strangle created with options that have 50 percent implied volatility. The upper one on the graph represents the less expensive strangle created with options pricing in 30 percent implied volatility.

Although the motivation behind this trade is a catalyst and then to exit, it is interesting to compare the dramatic difference between these two strangles. With options trading at a lower volatility break-even levels are not too far outside the two strike prices. When having to pay higher premiums due to expanded volatility levels, the move in the underlying required is much more dramatic. Luckily, the motivation with this trade is to exit after a price-moving announcement.

Using 30 percent implied volatility and 19 days to expiration, XYZ would need to be priced at 43.05 for the 45/50 Straddle to have 2.40 of value. On the upside, XYZ would need to be priced at 51.70. This means with a return to normal volatility, a move of 4.45 to the downside or an upside move of 4.20 would be needed to reach the break-even point just one day later. A move of either of these magnitudes would represent about a 9 percent move. Price changes like this are not uncommon when company earnings are released, but are usually somewhat anticipated. It is for this reason that volatility expands to high levels in the option markets in front of potential market-moving events. Also, this is why a decrease in implied volatility occurs after an announcement has been released and is priced into the market.

In summary, a long strangle is a position initiated in order to benefit from a very large move, either up or down, in the price of an underlying security. A long strangle position would be a common method to play some sort of company announcement or other upcoming market event to benefit from a dramatic move. Before initiating a long strangle, a price projection should be in place along with analysis of the implied volatility of the underlying options that make up the strangle. As always, a pricing calculator comes in handy when estimating the value of options after a market-moving event.

From the previous chapter, the straddle is very similar to the strangle as far as the motivating factors behind the trade. Both the straddle and the strangle should be taken into consideration when anticipating a large price move in an underlying stock. Many factors come into play, such as timing of the announcement, available strike prices, what implied volatility is pricing in for a move, and an estimate of what the magnitude of the price move will be.

SHORT STRANGLE MECHANICS

As there may be a long strangle position taken by buying a put with a lower strike price and selling a call with a higher strike, a short strangle may be created by doing the opposite or taking a short position in both options. Therefore, a short strangle involves selling a put with a lower strike and selling a call with a higher strike price. For instance, if a trader were to sell an XYZ August XYZ 25 Put and an XYZ August 30 Call, they would be short an XYZ August 25/30 Strangle.

The previous chapter discussed the lack of ability for many individual traders to sell uncovered or naked options. As with a short straddle, the short strangle does involve having two uncovered short option positions. Due to broker restrictions, this type of trade may not be implemented in many accounts, however, toward the end of this chapter an alternative to a short strangle that requires lower broker approval will be discussed.

To create a short XYZ August 25/30 Strangle the following inputs are used with a pricing calculator, 45 days to expiration, 35 percent volatility,

TABLE 6.8 Inputs and Output Used to Create an XYZ August 25/30 Strangle

Inputs	
Days	45
Volatility	35%
Interest Rate	1.00%
XYZ Price	27.5
Output	
XYZ August 25.00 Put	0.40
XYZ August 30.00 Call	0.50
XYZ August 25/30 Strangle	0.90

and an interest rate input of 1.00 percent. The inputs and output are shown in Table 6.8.

By selling options, a trader takes on an obligation and is being paid to take on this obligation. Through selling a strangle a trader is obligated to buy stock at a lower price or sell it at a higher price or buy at the strike price of the put option or sell at the strike price of the call option. In the case of the XYZ August 25/30 Strangle, the seller of this spread would be obligated to buy XYZ at 25 or sell XYZ at 30 at expiration. As long as the stock settles between 25 and 30, this obligation will not need to be fulfilled and the profit will be equal to the income produced from selling this strangle. In this range of 25 to 30 both premiums are kept by the seller and both options sold would expire with no value. All key levels for this strangle appear in Table 6.9.

Key levels for the XYZ August 25/30 Strangle depict a high level of risk for a small amount of premium income. The maximum potential loss for this strangle is theoretically unlimited while the maximum gain is just 0.90. However, this maximum gain of 0.90 would be achieved as long as XYZ does not settle up or down more than 2.50 or just a bit over 9 percent in

TABLE 6.9 Key Levels for the XYZ August 25/30 Strangle

	Level	Explanation
Up Break-even Price	30.90	Higher Strike plus Strangle Income
Down Break-even Price	24.10	Lower Strike minus Strangle Income
Maximum Dollar Gain	0.90	Option Premiums
Maximum Gain Prices	25 to 30	Options Both Worthless
Maximum Dollar Loss	24.10/Unlimited	Stock Goes To 0/Stock Rallies

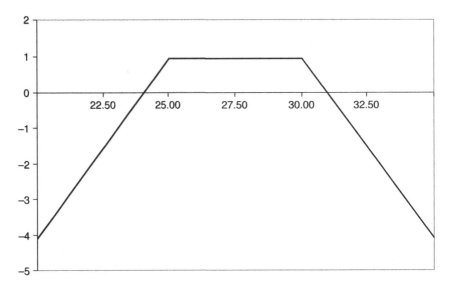

FIGURE 6.5 Payoff Diagram for the Short XYZ August 25/30 Strangle

either direction upon expiration. Nine percent is admittedly a pretty large move over the course of 45 days.

The payoff diagram in Figure 6.5 shows just how much of a move is needed before this short strangle begins to be a losing trade. Also, note that the potential loss is substantial to the downside or specifically 24.10 if the stock goes to 0.00 at expiration. On the upside the loss is potentially unlimited.

A point should be made regarding a position like this short strangle when the plan is to hold the position to expiration. If a position requires that a stock or market settles in a range at expiration, check to be certain no company announcements are expected between initiating the trade and option expiration. For instance, if selling a strangle on XYZ, check to make sure the company is not reporting earnings before expiration of the options sold is a must.

Always keep in mind that volatility of options usually expands when an event starts to become imminent. This expansion of volatility occurs as traders buy put or call options to speculate on the stock movement that will result from an announcement. Also, some put buying may be attributed to investors protecting their holdings in front of some sort of announcement. There should always be reluctance to sell options in front of a market-moving announcement due to the increase in risk perceived by the market. This caution from option sellers is another contributing factor to the increase in implied volatility that usually happens around known company

TABLE 6.10 Volatility Comparison for XYZ August 25/30 Strangle

Option	Volatility		
	25%	35%	45%
XYZ Aug 25 Put	0.15	0.40	0.70
XYZ Aug 30 Call	0.25	0.50	0.85
XYZ Aug 25/30 Strangle	0.40	0.90	1.55

announcements. On the other hand, whatever the motivation for options being purchased, increased buying pressure for both puts and calls results in an expansion in volatility.

As volatility increasing has a negative impact on short option positions, a short strangle would lose value when there is an increase in volatility. If a short strangle position is entered with the expectation of exiting this trade before expiration, volatility takes on more importance. Different levels of volatility, higher and lower, can influence the value of options very dramatically. For instance, for the XYZ August 25/30 Strangle, the volatility assumption of the options used to create this spread was priced at 35 percent. To illustrate exactly what effect a shift in volatility may have on this position, Table 6.10 shows the value of the two options and the XYZ August 25/30 Strangle when volatility rises to 45 percent and drops to 25 percent.

If volatility were to contract 10 percentage points immediately after an XYZ August 25/30 Strangle were sold, the spread seller would have an instant profit of .50. This scenario is highly unlikely, but is a good illustration of the impact of volatility on option prices. On the other hand, a 10 percent increase in volatility would result in a .65 increase in the value of the strangle. Not exactly what a strangle seller is looking for from this spread, and definitely not a good way to start off the trade.

Short Strangle Alternative

Many traders who would like to take a neutral position such as a short strangle are not permitted to sell naked options in their accounts. Since the short strangle is a combination of two naked option positions, a trader wanting to take a neutral position may not be permitted to use a short strangle due to their broker's account restrictions. However, there is a spread that does not require the ability to sell naked options that has a very similar payoff structure. Through selling a strangle, but then buying a put and a call that are both farther out of the money than the short options, a trader creates what is commonly called an iron condor. Chapter 10

TABLE 6.11 Construction of the July 40/45/50/55 Iron Condor and 45/50 Short Strangle

Inputs	
Days	40
Volatility	35%
Interest Rate	1.00%
XYZ Price	47.50
Output	
XYZ July 40 Put	0.15
XYZ July 45 Put	1.10
XYZ July 50 Call	1.25
XYZ July 55 Call	0.30
Short XYZ 45/50 Strangle	2.35
XYZ 40/45/50/55 Iron Condor	1.90

addresses all types condors more extensively, but for comparison purpose, an iron condor will be covered briefly here.

An iron condor consists of being short a strangle, but then purchasing the wings for protection. Through purchasing the wings of the spread, there are no naked option positions. For example, if XYZ were trading at 47.50 an iron condor could consist of selling a 45 put, buying a 40 put, selling a 50 call, and buying a 55 call. Using July options with 40 days to expiration, 30 percent volatility, and an interest rate of 1.00 percent, a July 40/45/50/55 Iron Condor is created. Also, for comparison, a short XYZ July 45/50 Strangle is created. Table 6.11 shows the inputs and pricing of this iron condor.

By selling the 45 Put and 50 Call, then buying the less expensive out-of-the-money 40 Put and 55 Call the Iron Condor is created. This iron condor is created with a credit of 1.90 going into the account of the trader that creates it. If a short strangle were created by selling the 45 Put and 50 Call, a credit of 2.35 would be received by the seller. Although not a large difference between the two credits, the potential downside of a short strangle versus an iron condor is pretty dramatic. A short strangle has potentially unlimited downside, but the potential loss of an iron condor is actually limited. Table 6.12 shows a comparison of the key levels of this short strangle and iron condor.

The maximum potential loss level is the most dramatic difference between the two spreads. For the XYZ July 40/45/50/55 Iron Condor, the maximum potential loss is 3.10. This maximum potential loss occurs at either of the long option strikes. For instance if XYZ is at 40 on expiration, there would be a loss of 5.00 on the XYZ July 45 Put while the XYZ Jul

TABLE 6.12 Key Levels Comparison for Iron Condor and Short Strangle

	XYZ July 40/45/50/55 Iron Condor	XYZ July 45/50 Short Strangle
Up Break-even Level	51.90	52.35
Down Break-even Level	43.10	42.65
Maximum Gain	1.90	2.35
Maximum Gain Levels	45 to 50	45 to 50
Maximum Loss	3.10	42.65/Unlimited

40 Put would expire worthless. By subtracting the credit received on the spread of 1.90 from the loss of 5.00, a maximum loss of 3.10 is determined. If the stock is at 35 at expiration, the short 45 Put would be a loss of 10.00, but this would be offset by a gain of 5.00 for the 40 Put, a loss of 5.00. Once again, taking the 1.90 credit received for the spread into account results in a loss of 3.10.

Other levels for the two spreads are fairly comparable. The credit received for implementing either spread is not too different. The break-even levels do not vary too much either. Because the only substantial difference between the two strategies is the maximum potential loss, many traders choose to use iron condors in place of short strangles when putting on a market neutral position.

Even traders allowed to place short option positions that are uncovered often use an iron condor in place of a short strangle. The motivating factor is the limited downside loss. Any trader that has been short an option in a situation where the market moves dramatically against them will consider some cheap protection such as buying the wings of an iron condor to lessen their potential downside risk if things do not play out as they anticipate.

There is a payoff diagram in Figure 6.6 that illustrates the different payouts at expiration between the iron condor and short strangle created in this example. The lines almost overlap until the outer strike prices that are used for the long options on the iron condor are reached. At that point, the benefit of owning these options takes over and losses are limited. With the short strangle, however, losses continue to mount as XYZ moves higher or lower.

Finally, with respect to comparing a short strangle and the iron condor the relative effect of changes in volatility is explored. Due to holding long option positions, the iron condor sees a smaller impact by a shift in volatility than a short strangle would. This may be a positive or negative depending on a trader's market outlook.

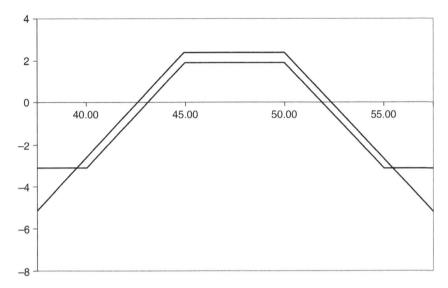

FIGURE 6.6 Payoff Diagram Comparing a Short Strangle and Iron Condor

To demonstrate the impact of volatility on both spreads a pricing calculator was used, and in addition to pricing the individual options at 35 percent volatility, option values were calculated using both 25 percent and 45 percent volatility. Table 6.13 shows the impact of these various levels of volatility on both spreads.

Comparing the impact of volatility is an interesting exercise. All options that make up both of the spreads in the previous table are out of the money. As a reminder, there are two components to the value of an option. There is intrinsic value, which is the value of an option if it is exercised

TABLE 6.13 Iron Condor and Short Strangle Prices at Various Volatility Levels

	Volatility		
Option	**25%**	**35%**	**45%**
XYZ July 40 Put	0.05	0.15	0.40
XYZ July 45 Put	0.60	1.10	1.65
XYZ July 50 Call	0.65	1.25	1.80
XYZ July 55 Call	0.05	0.30	0.65
XYZ July 40/45/50/55 Iron Condor	1.15	1.90	2.40
XYZ July 45/50 Strangle	1.25	2.35	3.45

today, and time value, which represents the value of an option above the intrinsic value. Since they are out of the money, all of their value is based on time since there is no intrinsic value to the options. Shifts in implied volatility can have a big impact on time value and have no impact on the intrinsic value of an option. These options are out of the money and 100 percent time value so the move in these options is pretty dramatic based on a 10 percent shift in volatility.

As far as volatility projections prior to a trade, if volatility is relatively high or a trader believes that volatility will contract, both spreads have a similar reaction to a contraction in volatility, with the short strangle having a slight advantage. Using the XYZ spreads, the iron condor goes from 1.90 to 1.15 while the value of the short strangle contracts from 2.35 to 1.25.

However, if there is a concern that volatility will expand, the iron condor would be a superior choice as the long options provide some protection against a rise in volatility just as they provide protection against a large price move. A .50 move would occur with the iron condor versus a move of 1.10 for the short strangle.

For accounts that may not be allowed naked short option positions an iron condor is a good alternative to a short strangle. Also, in cases where a trader wants to limit risk on a trade, purchasing out-of-the-money options for protection would allow a trader to benefit from a neutral market with limited risk. The payout can be very similar with a short strangle and iron condor, with the exception of the limited downside from an iron condor.

On the long side, the strangle can be a low risk, high reward way to play a potentially volatile move in an underlying stock or market. However, the required move to profit from a strangle may be pretty dramatic. Consideration should be given to just how much of a move in an underlying security is needed before placing one of these trades. Shorting a strangle is a low reward strategy that may pay off as long as the underlying security settles at expiration or trade exit in a certain range. This may be a pretty wide range, so the potential for a winning trade may be high. Although the winning potential is likely for one of these trades, when an unexpected move occurs, the loss may be pretty substantial. To offset this, an iron condor is a viable alternative with limited risk.

CHAPTER 7

Bull Spreads

A bull spread is a subcategory of what is commonly referred to as a vertical spread. Vertical spreads may be bearish or bullish. A vertical spread that would be considered bullish is covered in this chapter, while bear spreads will be introduced in the following chapter. Any vertical spread consists of two options, both are the same type (call or put), have the same underlying security, and share a common expiration date, but the strikes of the two options are different.

A vertical spread initiated with bullish intent can be created with all calls or all puts. When created with put options, the higher strike is sold and the lower strike option is purchased. If call options are used to create a bullish payoff, the lower strike is purchased and the higher strike option is sold. The major difference between the two is a bull spread created with puts will be done at a credit or with income generated for a trader's account. When created with call options, a bull spread will result in an account debit or cost to the trader.

BULL PUT SPREAD

Taking the bull put spread first, the option that is purchased would be at a lower strike than the option sold. Put options that have a lower strike price will always be less expensive than put options with a high strike price. A quick intuitive example to illustrate this: The right to sell something at 30 will always be more expensive than the right to sell the same security at 25. In this case, since the less expensive option is being purchased, the result will be a credit. The mechanics behind creating a basic bull put spread are:

> Long 1 45 Put at 0.60
> Short 1 50 Put at 2.40
> Net Credit = 1.80

This bull put spread takes a short position in the 50 strike option and a long position in the 45 strike option. Through selling the higher-priced option, the position is initiated with a net credit. The position is initiated with the expectation that the underlying stock will be higher than 50.00 at expiration. With the stock over 50.00 at expiration, both options expire with no value and the credit received for the position is kept.

For a bull put spread, the maximum gain is limited to the credit received for initiating the position. In the case of the example above, the credit of 1.80 received is the maximum potential gain from this position. This gain is realized if the stock is over the higher strike price at expiration. When a stock settles above the strike price of the option, the option expires with no value and in this case, the profit for the spread is maximized. For this bull put spread that would require the underlying stock to settle above 50.00 at expiration.

The maximum loss for a bull put spread is calculated as the maximum potential gain subtracted from the difference between the two strike prices. The maximum loss in the previous example is 3.20, calculated by subtracting 45 from 50, then subtracting 1.80 from that result.

Finally, to determine the break-even level for a bull put spread subtract the credit received from the higher strike price. For the example, this would come to 48.20 which is the strike of 50 minus the credit received of 1.80. The key levels and the methods used to determine them appear in Table 7.1.

TABLE 7.1 Key Levels for Bull Put Spread

	Level	Explanation
Maximum Loss	3.20	High Strike minus Low Strike minus Credit
Maximum Loss Level	45 and under	Short 50 Put worth $5 more than Long 45 Put
Maximum Gain	1.80	Credit Received—Both options expire worthless
Maximum Gain Level	50 and over	Both options expire worthless
Breakeven	48.20	Upper Strike minus Credit Received

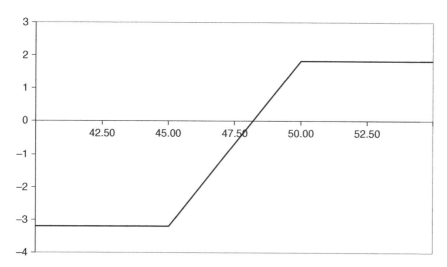

FIGURE 7.1 Bull Put Spread Payoff Diagram

As with all option positions, spread or not, there is a corresponding payoff diagram that may be created to highlight these key levels or the profit or loss at any other level. Figure 7.1 is a payoff diagram for the bull put spread. The shape is similar to all bull vertical spreads with an up sloping line between the strikes. Above the upper strike, the profit is locked in regardless of how high the stock goes. Under the lower strike, the potential loss of the position is also certain. The unchanged nature of the profit or loss outside these strikes graphically demonstrates that the maximum gain and loss are limited with this type of spread.

There are two circumstances where a bull spread would be a desired trade. First, if a trader is neutral to bullish on a stock—that is, expects the stock to stay flat or move slightly higher—a bull put spread that actually pays off with no movement might be used. In this case, the stock should already be trading at a level higher than the upper strike price of the spread. Another possible motivation behind a bull put spread would be an actual bullish move, the expectation that a stock is going to trade higher than the upper strike price in the spread. In this case, the stock should be trading lower than the upper strike and may even be trading below the lower strike price.

For the first case, where the expectation is that a stock will be neutral at worst, but hopefully work higher, involves XYZ trading at 35.50 and the October options with 45 days left to expiration. The implied volatility for XYZ is 40 percent, which is a high level and another motivation behind selling options. The concept here is when the volatility is at a historically high level, a trader may consider selling an option to offset the relatively high expense. This concept will be covered more toward the end of this chapter.

The bull put spread used to benefit from a neutral to bullish stock price outlook would short the XYZ October 35 Put at 1.70 and take a long position in the XYZ October 30 Put at .25. The net credit for this position is 1.45. The trades involved in the creation of this bull put spread are:

Long 1 XYZ Oct 30 Put at 0.25
Short 1 XYZ Oct 35 Put at 1.70
Net Credit = 1.45

The intention with this trade is to hold until expiration. The breakeven at expiration is calculated as 33.55, subtracting the credit received of 1.45 from the upper strike price of 35.00. This is a move lower of almost 2.00 from the current XYZ level of 35.50. The maximum gain of this position is, like all bull put spreads, the credit received of 1.45 which will be kept by the trader if XYZ is over 35.00 at expiration. XYZ above 35.00 results in both put options expiring worthless. Finally, the maximum potential loss of this spread would be 3.55, which is the difference between the two strike prices minus the credit received or 35 − 30 − 1.45.

Another way to look at the maximum potential loss with this spread is to consider what transactions would occur based on the option positions at expiration. At expiration, with the 35 Put in the money and a short position in that option, the short 35 Put would result in a purchase of XYZ at 35. When short a put option, the short position has the obligation to purchase shares at the strike price. In this case there would be a purchase of XYZ at 35.

Table 7.2 is an overview of the key levels for this spread. The worst case results in the long 30 Put being in the money. The long put is a right to sell shares at the strike and this right would be exercised with a sell of

TABLE 7.2   Key Levels for XYZ Oct 30/35 Bull Put Spread

	Level	Explanation
Maximum Loss	3.55	High Strike minus Low Strike minus Credit
Maximum Loss Level	30 and under	Short 35 Put worth $5 more than Long 30 Put
Maximum Gain	1.45	Credit Received—Both options expire worthless
Maximum Gain Level	35 and over	Both options expire worthless
Breakeven	33.55	Upper Strike minus Credit Received

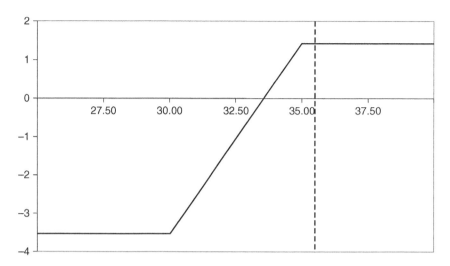

FIGURE 7.2 Payoff Diagram for XYZ Oct 30/35 Bull Put Spread

shares of XYZ at 30. So the two transactions are a buy at 35 and a sell at 30, a loss of 5.00 a share. The credit for this position was 1.45. The transaction results in a cost of 5.00 at expiration, but a credit of 1.45 at the beginning of the transaction, resulting in a trade loss of 3.55.

Figure 7.2 is a payoff diagram for the XYZ Oct 30/35 Bull Put Spread. Notice that in addition to the normal payoff diagram there is a broken line that running from the bottom to the top of the chart. This represents the price of XYZ when the spread was implemented. The significance here is that the spread will result in maximum profit if the stock stays neutral and even goes a little lower, even though this is referred to as a bull spread. The bull spread could pay off with a small bearish move. This trade may be initiated when the stock is between the strike prices when the trade is initiated as well as when the stock is below both strikes. In either of those cases the original payoff diagram looks the same, but the trades are slightly different.

The ability of this spread to make money when the underlying is neutral is not unique. There are several neutral spreads that may be implemented and several more will be presented throughout this book. In the case of this spread, a trader may just consider selling the XYZ October 35 Put and not purchasing the 30 Put. Although the potential profit is a little higher than the bull put spread, 1.70 versus 1.45, there are a couple of reasons that selling the 35 Put alone might be avoided by some traders.

First, many traders do not have the ability to short options—puts or calls—naked. That is many traders must have an offsetting position such as a position in the underlying or a long position in a comparable option. If a trader was considering taking a position that involved selling the 35 Put as in the previous trade, they would need to have it covered in some fashion. Purchasing the XYZ October 30 Put would satisfy this requirement as the short 35 Put is covered by the long 30 Put.

Another reason that the 30 Put may have been purchased is just to protect against a substantial loss. Proper risk management is a trading concept that keeps most professionals in the game. Purchasing a cheap option to limit losses is a common form of risk management. In the case of being naked short the XYZ October 35 Put, the trader has tremendous downside exposure, while a trader who initiates the bull put spread has a limit on their potential loss from this trade. Even traders who have the ability to trade naked option positions often consider protection in the form of owning an out-of-the-money option that will limit their downside in the case things do not go the way the they expect.

As mentioned earlier in this section, a bull put spread may be initiated in both neutral and bullish situations. The more bullish a trader is, the farther away the higher put strike price will be from the price of an underlying. In a very bullish situation, a trader may choose to buy and sell put options that are both in the money.

Take XYZ, trading at 64 with January options having 30 days to go to expiration. The expectation is that XYZ will trade more than 10 percent higher and settle at just over 70.00 at expiration. With an implied volatility of 30 percent, the XYZ Jan 70 Put is trading at 6.40 and the XYZ Jan 65 Put is trading at 2.75. This trade may be put on for a credit of 3.65, through selling the 70 Put at 6.40 and paying 2.75 for the 65 strike put option. This is a very bullish outlook, but there is also a nice risk/reward involved in this trade.

In Table 7.3 the first key level for this trade is the maximum potential profit which is realized if XYZ reaches 70.00 or better at expiration. The maximum loss is 1.35 or 70 – 65 – 3.65, and occurs if the stock is not above 65.00 at expiration. This includes if it stays at the current level of 64.00.

TABLE 7.3 Key Levels for XYZ January 65/70 Bull Put Spread

	Level	Explanation
Maximum Loss	1.35	High Strike minus Low Strike minus Credit
Maximum Loss Level	65 and Under	Short 70 Put worth $5 more than Long 65 Put
Maximum Gain	3.65	Credit Received—Both options expire worthless
Maximum Gain Level	70 and Over	Both options expire worthless
Breakeven	66.35	Upper Strike minus Credit Received

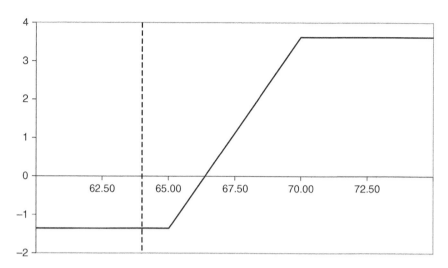

FIGURE 7.3 Payoff Diagram for XYZ Jan 65/70 Bull Put Spread

Finally at 66.35 (70.00 − 3.65) the trade has reached a point where it would be breakeven at expiration. Therefore a minimum move higher of 2.35 is needed for the trade to become profitable.

In addition to the key levels, in Figure 7.3 a payoff diagram is produced for this more bullish of bull put spreads. Like the more neutral version in the previous example the stock price when the spread is initiated is highlighted on the diagram. The broken line this time is in an area of maximum loss instead of at a price level where there would be a maximum gain.

As with the first bull put spread example that involved a neutral outlook, there are alternatives to attempting to benefit from a bullish move like the one that was expected in the previous example. The most common potential alternative would be the purchase of a call option. In the case of the previous example, the call option that would have the closest payout would be realized through buying the XYZ January 65 Call.

Using the same pricing inputs as the put options in the bull put spread, the XYZ January 65 Call would have a premium of 1.80. Like the bull put spread, owning the slightly out of the money call option would require a bullish move to realize a profit. The key levels for this long call option versus the previous spread appear in Table 7.4.

On two of the three key levels, the bull put spread appears preferable to the long call. Unlike the long call which has unlimited profit upside, there is limited upside to the bull put spread. The bull put spread has a lower maximum potential loss and a slightly better break-even level. The key for a trader deciding between the two might come down to their price target.

TABLE 7.4 Bull Put Spread versus Long Call

	Bull Put Spread	Long Call
Maximum Loss	1.35	1.80
Maximum Loss Level	65 and Under	65 and Under
Maximum Gain	3.65	Unlimited
Maximum Gain Level	70 and Over	Unlimited
Breakeven	66.35	66.80

In a case of expecting XYZ to settle very close to 70.00, the bull put spread would be the better choice, if there is an expectation that the stock may run way past the 70.00 level, the call option may be the better choice.

The bull put spread may be used either in a neutral to bullish or bullish circumstance, depending on price projection, time to expiration, and the risk and reward of the position. Regardless of the circumstances behind the position, when a bull spread is created with put options, it will be done so at a credit and with limited downside. In return for initiating a position like this for a credit, the potential upside is also limited. For many traders, that assurance of knowing the worst and best case scenario when entering a trade is nice peace of mind to have.

BULL CALL SPREAD

Referring to the very first spread example in the chapter, a bull call spread may be created using similar strikes and expirations as the trade in Table 7.1. With the same price projection of the underlying closing higher than 50.00 at expiration, a bull call spread would involve buying the lower strike and selling the higher strike call. The mechanics of entering a bull call spread using the same parameters that were used for the bull put spread are:

Long 45 Call at 5.65
Short 50 Call at 2.45
Net Debit = 3.20

The bull call spread involves purchasing the more expensive 45 strike option while selling the less expensive 50 strike call. This position is initiated at a debit, as the more expensive call is a purchase. The payout parameters for this spread are actually the same as the bull put spread, the only significant difference between the two is that the call spread involves a debit to enter the trade while the put spread involves taking a credit. A broken line in the two payoff diagrams shows the difference between the two. Without these lines, the payoffs look very similar even through one is very bullish and the other is neutral to bullish.

The payout levels for both spreads are the same; however, the formula to determine these payouts is different. The maximum profit for each spread is 1.80. If the underlying stock is at or above 50 at expiration, both put options expire with no value and the credit received for the position is retained by the trader.

In the case of the call spread, there is a little math involved in determining the maximum profit for the position. If the stock is above 50 at expiration, both options in the spread are in the money and have value. The 45 call will have 5.00 more value than the 50 call. As the 45 call is long and the 50 call is short, the result is a value of 5.00 for the spread. Since 3.20 was paid to enter the spread, the maximum profit for the trade turns out to be 5.00 – 3.20 or 1.80, or the value of the spread minus the premium paid. Table 7.5 reviews the key levels for this trade; these key levels match the key levels in Table 7.1, but the methods of determining a couple of levels are slightly different.

For a bull call spread, the maximum loss is the debit paid to enter the spread. If the underlying stock is below the lower strike price at expiration, both call options expire with no value. With this, the debit paid to enter the spread is lost. The debit paid for the 45/50 Bull Call Spread was 3.20 which is also the maximum potential loss in this position.

The break-even level for the bull call spread may be calculated by adding the cost of the spread to the lower strike price. With the 45/50 Bull Call spread, the lower strike is 45 and the price paid was 3.20. The result is a break-even level of 48.20.

Like the bull spread created with put options, a bull call spread may be entered into with the consideration that a stock may have neutral price action until expiration. The first example creating a bull spread with calls

TABLE 7.5 Five Key Levels for Bull Put Spread

	Level	Explanation
Maximum Loss	3.20	Debit Paid
Maximum Loss Level	45 and under	Both Options Expire Worthless
Maximum Gain	1.80	High Strike minus Low Strike minus Debit Paid
Maximum Gain Level	50 and over	Long Call worth $5 more value than Short Call
Breakeven	48.20	Lower Strike plus Debit Paid

is a case of a neutral expectation for XYZ. XYZ is trading at 31.00, the May options have 60 days remaining, and volatility is at 35 percent. Creating a bull call spread that would profit from a neutral stock price over the life of the options would involve a long position in the XYZ May 25 Call at 6.30 and a short position in the XYZ May 30 Call at 2.70. This trade would be initiated for a cost or debit of 3.60.

> Long XYZ May 25 Call at 6.30
> Short XYZ May 30 Call at 2.70
> Net Debit = 3.60

The position is entered for a debit of 3.60, but if the stock does not move at all, at expiration the position will be worth 5.00. The result will be a profit of 1.40 on the bull call spread with no price movement. In fact, there is a little downside that may occur in the stock price before the maximum gain of the spread is not realized any more. Anywhere above 30.00, the spread has a value of 5.00 and the trader's profit is 1.40. The value of the spread is determined by subtracting the lower strike from the higher strike. The lower strike will have more value than the higher strike at expiration as this option is farther in the money. In the case of this trade it would be 30 − 25 or 5.00. All of these key levels are displayed in Table 7.6.

The break-even point for this trade is determined by adding the cost of the spread to the lower strike price. At that point, the May XYZ 25 Call would have the same value as the debit paid and the trade would be right at no profit or loss. At 28.60 the long 25 Call is worth 3.60, the debit paid was 3.60, so the cost is equal to the value of the spread at this level. Under the lower strike of 25, the trade would realize a maximum loss of 3.60, the debit paid. At this point, neither of the options have any value and they would both expire with no value.

As with the bull put examples, the bull call payoffs also highlight the level where the stock is when the trade is initiated. A payoff diagram for the

TABLE 7.6 Key Levels for the XYZ May 25/30 Bull Call Spread

	Level	Explanation
Maximum Loss	3.60	Debit Paid
Maximum Loss Level	25 and Under	Both options expire worthless
Maximum Gain	1.40	High Strike minus Low Strike minus Debit Paid
Maximum Gain Level	30 and Over	Long Call has $5 more value than Short Call
Breakeven	28.60	Lower Strike plus Debit Paid

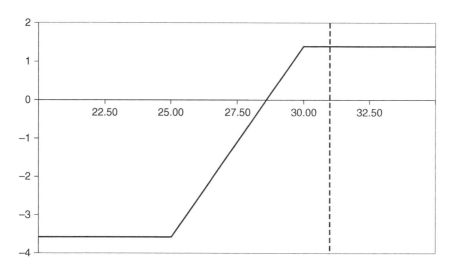

FIGURE 7.4 Payoff Diagram for XYZ May 25/30 Bull Call Spread

XYZ May 25/30 Bull Call Spread appears in Figure 7.4. At 31.00, the stock can drop to 28.60 at expiration before the trade becomes a loser. This is a pretty good cushion, but the tradeoff is the potential profit versus the potential loss in this position. The maximum potential gain is about half of the potential loss.

The bull call spread, as its name implies, may also be purchased when expecting a bullish move from an underlying security. If XYZ was trading at 54.00 and the expectation was that the stock would be over 60.00 at expiration, a bull call spread is a viable choice. For this case, the expectation is that the stock will trade to 60.00 in the next 90 days and February expiration is 90 days off. The implied volatility for XYZ February options is at 45 percent, a high level, but a bull call spread is usually a good strategy in high volatility situations. This point will be covered more fully after this example.

The XYZ Feb 55 Call is purchased for 4.40 and the XYZ Feb 60 Call is sold for 2.70. The cost of this position comes to a debit of 1.70. With a debit of 1.70 and the strike prices of this bull call spread, the key levels are determined in Table 7.7.

This spread would be entered with bullish expectations, specifically that the stock reaches 60.00 by expiration. If over 60.00, the spread has 5.00 of value which results in a trade profit of 3.30—1.70 debit to enter the spread and 5.00 of value at expiration. The break-even level is 56.70 which would require a move of 2.70 in XYZ to reach profitability.

Figure 7.5 shows how much of an up move XYZ needs in order to realize the full profit of 3.30 from this spread. The expectation is a full

TABLE 7.7 Key Levels for the XYZ Feb 55/60 Bull Call Spread

	Level	Explanation
Maximum Loss	1.70	Debit Paid
Maximum Loss Level	55 and Under	Both options expire worthless
Maximum Gain	3.30	High Strike minus Low Strike minus Debit Paid
Maximum Gain Level	60 and Over	Long Call has $5 more value than Short Call
Breakeven	56.70	Lower Strike plus Debit Paid

6.00 move over the next 90 days, so the spread matches the expectation perfectly, regardless of how aggressive that expectation is.

A common question is why would a trader consider a bull call spread instead of just buying a call option to benefit from an upside move in a stock. A call option has limited downside, as does a bull call spread, but does benefit from an upside move. One reason to consider a bull spread as opposed to a long call position relates to implied volatility.

If an option has a higher implied volatility level than is considered normal for that option or high relative to historical volatility, it may be considered expensive by option traders. High implied volatility will generally have the same impact on options that have strike prices in the same range and the same expiration date. If the option a trader considers purchasing has

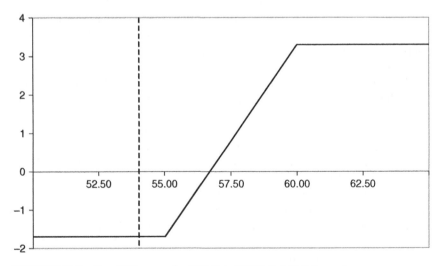

FIGURE 7.5 Payoff Diagram for XYZ Feb 55/60 Bull Call Spread

TABLE 7.8 55/60 Bull Call Spread versus a Long 55 Call

	Bull Call Spread		Long Call	
XYZ	P/L	% Profit	P/L	% Profit
50	−1.70	−100%	−4.40	−100%
55	−1.70	−100%	−4.40	−100%
60	3.30	194%	0.60	14%
65	3.30	194%	5.60	127%
70	3.30	194%	10.60	241%

high implied volatility, then other options with the same expiration would also probably have higher implied volatility.

In the previous example, XYZ options were pricing in 45 percent implied volatility. Assuming that historical implied volatility is much lower than this, maybe in the mid 20 percent range, the premium of the call options would be considered expensive. When options are expensive, it is possible to take advantage of this and sell some options to bring the cost of a trade down a bit. Basically buy an expensive option and help pay for it by selling an expensive option.

Using the previous example, if a trader wanted to just purchase a call option to benefit from the prediction that the price of XYZ would move from 54.00 to 60.00, a logical choice would be the XYZ Feb 55 Call. This call would be trading at 4.40, due mostly to the high implied volatility of 45 percent. If the price projection is correct and XYZ is at 60 at February expiration, the Feb 55 Call would have a value of 5.00 at expiration, a profit of .60 after subtracting the 4.40 premium paid for the option. A side-by-side comparison of the two strategies appears in Table 7.8.

It is in cases like this, where the premium for an option is expensive due to high implied volatility, that traders give consideration to selling an option to offset the cost of the expensive option. Buy cheap (low), sell expensive (high) is a constant motto of traders. In cases where cheap options are not available, selling an expensive option to offset an expensive option's premium is the next best thing to finding an inexpensive option to purchase.

A bull spread, credit or debit, may be used with an extremely bullish, slightly bullish, or even neutral-to-bullish outlook on an underlying security. When considering one of these spreads or any directional trade, analyze the potential payoff over the time frame of the trade and compare to the potential payout using similar strategies. At times using a spread that lowers the cost of a trade may be superior to pure long option positions on a cost and risk reward basis.

CHAPTER 8

Bear Spreads

I n the previous chapter vertical spreads created with a neutral to bullish or bullish bias were covered. This chapter takes the other side and looks at vertical spreads created with a bearish intent. A vertical bear spread may be created with a combination of call or put options. Both are the same type of option, have the same expiration, but have different strike prices.

To initiate a bear spread and take in a credit, all calls would be used. The lower strike call would be sold, while the upper strike call would be purchased. As a higher strike call option should always have less value than a lower strike one, the result would be a credit to a trader's account.

Using put options, once again, the lower strike option would be sold and the higher strike option would be purchased. However, as a higher strike put option will have more value than a lower strike put option, a vertical bear spread done in this manner would result in a debit to a trader's account. This is opposed to the credit that is received when call options are used to create a bearish spread.

BEAR CALL SPREAD

The vertical bear spread created with calls is a preference for many traders when considering a bear spread. This is due to the ability to take in a credit when putting the position on. Being paid for a position is nice, but in reality it is better to focus on the payoff structure upon exit.

A bear call spread would be initiated as:

Short 1 35 Call at 3.40
Long 1 40 Call at 0.80
Net Credit = 2.60

In this case a call option with a 35 strike is sold, while a call with a 40 strike is purchased. This spread would be put on with the intention of both options expiring with no value. A close at expiration under 35.00 would achieve this goal. As a credit was received for entering this trade, the credit would be kept by the trader when both options expire with no value. The maximum potential profit is the credit received of 2.60.

If the stock were over 40.00 at expiration, both options would be in the money and have value. The lower strike option would have more value than the higher strike option. The exact amount of this difference is determined by subtracting the lower strike from the upper strike. The difference between the two strikes if 5, so the spread would have a value of 5.00 at expiration. As a credit of 2.60 was received upon entry into this trade, the loss would be 2.40, or the high strike minus the low strike minus the credit received.

Breakeven for a bear call spread would be achieved if the stock is at 37.60 at expiration. In this case the long option has no value, but the short call has 2.60 of value. This offsets the 2.60 credit received when entering the trade. All of these key levels are summarized in Table 8.1.

The payoff diagram for a vertical bear spread (see Figure 8.1), created with puts or calls, is a mirror image of the payoff for a vertical bull spread. Above the higher strike price, the maximum loss is incurred for a vertical put spread. From the example, this is 2.40. Between the strikes, there is a partial loss or gain, which replicates a short position in the underlying security between the strikes. Finally the profit and loss line reaches the lower strike price, where the maximum potential gain in the trade is realized.

TABLE 8.1   Key Levels for Bear Call Spread

	Level	Explanation
Maximum Loss	2.40	High Strike minus Low Strike minus Credit
Maximum Loss Level	40 and over	Short Call has 5.00 more value than Long Call
Maximum Gain	2.60	Credit Received—Both options expire worthless
Maximum Gain Level	35 and under	Both options expire worthless
Breakeven	37.60	Lower Strike plus Credit Received

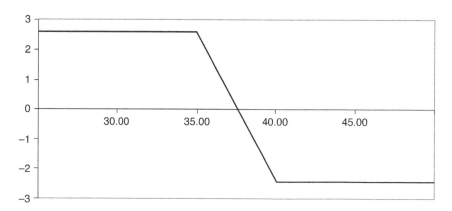

FIGURE 8.1 Bear Call Spread Payoff Diagram

The trading motivation for a bear spread may not necessarily be due to a bearish outlook on the underlying stock. In Chapter 7 a bull spread that was motivated through a neutral stock outlook was introduced. That trade worked out as a profit if the stock closed at a price level that was equal to the price it was trading at when the trade was initiated. It was possible for the stock to trade a little lower and still result in a maximum profit for this trade.

Once again, there are three potential directions for a stock to move; up, down, and neutral. If the correct strike prices are chosen relative to the price of the underlying security, a bear spread may profit from no stock movement in the underlying.

With XYZ trading at 43.50, a trader believes that the stock is going to be stuck in a range and, if anything, the stock is going to move lower. With this sort of outlook a bear spread would be a good trading choice. At least it would be something to take a look at. Through the trader's analysis, he believes the stock will not trade over 45.00 over the next 60 days and July option expiration is 60 days out. He decides to take a look at the July 45 and July 50 Call options on XYZ.

The implied volatility for these July Calls is at 35 percent which results in the July 45 Call trading at 1.85 and the July 50 Call trading for 0.55. He sells the July 45 Call and purchases the July 50 Call with the result being a credit of 1.30:

Short 1 XYZ Jul 45 Call at 1.85
Long 1 XYZ Jul 50 Call at 0.55
Net Credit = 1.30

TABLE 8.2 Key Levels for XYZ Jul 45/50 Bear Call Spread

	Level	Explanation
Maximum Loss	3.70	High Strike minus Low Strike minus Credit
Maximum Loss Level	50 and Over	Short 45 Call worth $5 more than Long 50 Call
Maximum Gain	1.30	Credit Received—Both options expire worthless
Maximum Gain Level	45 and Under	Both options expire worthless
Breakeven	46.30	Lower Strike plus Credit Received

The maximum profit for this trade, like any vertical spread created for a credit, is the credit taken when entering the trade, or 1.30. The maximum potential loss at expiration in 60 days is 3.70, or the difference between the option strikes minus the credit received. At any price below 45.00, the options will both expire with no value, which is the goal of this trade. Above the higher strike price of 50.00, both options will have intrinsic value with the short call being worth 5.00 more than the long call. Finally, the break-even level for this trade comes to 46.30. At 46.30, the long option has no value, but the short option has 1.30 of value, which offsets the 1.30 credit that was taken. For a summary of all the key levels for this trade, see Table 8.2.

This trade was entered with the stock trading at 43.50. A maximum profit is gained as long as XYZ closes under the lower strike price of 45.00 at expiration or a buffer of 1.50 before the trade results in less than the maximum profit. Also, the break-even point for this trade is at 46.30, a move of 2.80 before the trade becomes a losing transaction at expiration.

The payoff diagram in Figure 8.2 shows the potential results based on the closing price of XYZ at expiration. The broken line running vertically on the payoff diagram shows where XYZ was trading when the bull call spread was entered. In this case, if XYZ is steady at 43.50 or trades lower, the credit received is kept with no other actions taken at option expiration. Even if the stock moves a little higher, as long as it does not close at a level higher than 45.00, the maximum profit is kept. Above 45.00, the short option begins to have value and a negative implication for the spread holder. With the stock at any level above 50.00, the maximum potential loss will be realized.

A bear call spread may also be used in cases where a trader is truly bearish. The stock may be between the two strikes or even at a level greater

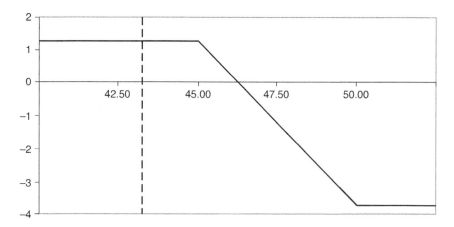

FIGURE 8.2 Payoff Diagram for XYZ Jul 45/50 Bear Call Spread

than both strikes. In the latter case, a very bearish outlook would need to play out for the trade to be successful.

For a bearish bear call spread example, XYZ is trading at 47.00 and the trader believes a down move of 15 percent may occur in the next three months. This would result in the stock being just under 40 at the end of this time period. With March expiration 90 days away, the trader takes a look at the March 40 and March 45 Calls. At an implied volatility of 30 percent the March 40 Call would be trading at 7.55 and the March 45 Call would be trading at 3.90. To initiate the bear call spread with this bearish opinion, the trader would sell the March 40 Call and purchase the March 45 Call taking in a credit of 3.65:

Short 1 XYZ Mar 40 Call at 7.55
Long 1 XYZ Mar 50 Call at 3.90
Net Credit = 3.65

Table 8.3 is a summary of all the key levels for the Mar 40/45 Bear Call Spread. The potential maximum loss is less than half of the potential gain for this trade, 1.35 versus 3.65. The very low maximum loss is a result of the move that XYZ will need to make to the downside over 90 days to reach breakeven or the maximum profit level. A 15 percent move lower comes to about 7.00 which would put the stock just below the lower strike price of this bear spread. Just to breakeven a move of over 3.00, or exactly 3.35 is needed, which is a loss of more than loss of 7 percent in the value of shares. As with all trades, there are tradeoffs or choices to be made. The

TABLE 8.3 Key Levels for XYZ Mar 40/45 Bear Call Spread

	Level	Explanation
Maximum Loss	1.35	High Strike minus Low Strike minus Credit
Maximum Loss Level	45 and Over	Short 40 Call worth $5 more than Long 45 Call
Maximum Gain	3.65	Credit Received—Both options expire worthless
Maximum Gain Level	40 and Under	Both options expire worthless
Breakeven	43.65	Lower Strike plus Credit Received

dollar risk of this trade related to the reward is a direct function of what the stock would need to do in order to have a profitable result.

Figure 8.3 is a payoff diagram showing the profit or loss of the spread at expiration at various price levels. Note the vertical broken line on the far right of the diagram. This is where XYZ is trading up entry into the position. The line is also in an area where the maximum loss of 1.35 would be taken if XYZ closes at 47.00 at expiration.

For all trades using options, there are alternative potential choices. In the case of expecting a bearish move in a stock, the first option trade that comes to mind is buying a put option. In the previous trade, if XYZ is trading at 47.00, the most logical 90 day put option would be the 45 strike put. Using the same parameters that were used for bear spread, the XYZ Mar 45 Put would be trading at 1.80.

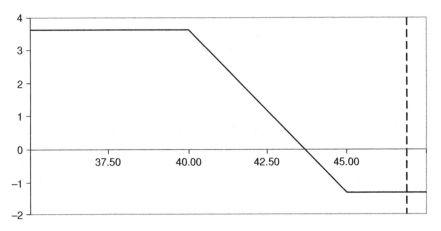

FIGURE 8.3 Payoff Diagram for XYZ Mar 40/45 Bear Call Spread

TABLE 8.4   Bull Put Spread versus Long Call

	Bull Put Spread	Long Put
Maximum Loss	1.35	1.80
Maximum Loss Level	45 and Over	45 and Over
Maximum Gain	3.65	Substantial
Maximum Gain Level	40 and Under	Substantial
Breakeven	43.65	43.20

The capital required for the bear call spread is 1.35 versus 1.80 for the put purchase. With a 15 percent price drop projection, the stock would be just under 40.00 at expiration. At 40.00, the put is worth 5.00 for a profit of 3.20, while the bear call spread has no value, but the credit of 3.65 is retained by the trader resulting in a little more profit at this level for a little less capital. Finally, the long put position has a slightly lower break-even level at 43.20 versus the break-even stock price of 43.65. All key levels for this spread are displayed in Table 8.4.

The benefit from purchasing the put would occur if the stock traded much lower than the price target of 40.00. In that case, the long put would continue to work for the trader as the stock traded lower. However, as the price estimation on this trade is that the stock will trade right to the 40.00 level at expiration, the bear call spread is a better choice in this case.

BEAR PUT SPREAD

The same bear spread payoff that would be created using call options may also be implemented using put options. At the beginning of this chapter a very basic example of how the bear spread is implemented with call

TABLE 8.5   Key Levels for Bear Put Spread

	Level	Explanation
Maximum Loss	2.40	Debit Paid
Maximum Loss Level	40 and over	Both options expire worthless
Maximum Gain	2.60	Upper Strike minus Lower Strike minus Debit Paid
Maximum Gain Level	35 and under	Both options in the money
Breakeven	37.60	Upper Strike minus Debit Paid

options was introduced. Using the same pricing parameters a bear put spread may also be implemented:

Short 1 35 Put at 0.80
Long 1 40 Put at 3.20
Net Debit = 2.40

The spread is created by selling a put option with a lower strike and purchasing a put option with a higher strike. The higher strike put will have more value than the lower strike put so the bear put spread would be implemented at a cost or debit to the trader's account. In the example case in Table 8.8, the 35 Put is sold for 0.80 and the 40 Put is purchased for 3.20. The result is a net cost of 2.40.

The key levels for the bear put spread are the same as the key levels for the bear call spread in Table 8.1. However, they are determined in a slightly different way. The debit paid for the spread is the maximum potential loss and this is incurred at any level over the higher strike. At this level and higher, neither put option has any value. The resulting loss will be the price paid for the spread.

The break-even level for this spread is the same as the prior example, but the level is calculated in a slightly different way. Taking the price paid for the spread and subtracting the cost of the spread results in the break-even level. At 37.60, the 40 Put will be worth 2.40 and the 35 Put which is out of the money would expire worthless. As the cost of the position was 2.40 and the spread's value is 2.40 at expiration, the value of the spread would be equal to the cost of the position or breakeven.

Figure 8.4 is a typical bear put spread payoff diagram. The maximum profit for this trade occurs with both options being in the money, or with the stock under 35.00 at expiration. At this level, the higher strike option would be worth more than the lower strike option. This difference is determined by subtracting the lower strike from the higher strike. For this spread that would result in a value of 5.00 at expiration and subtracting the cost of the spread, 2.40 from 5.00 would result in a profit of 2.60.

A neutral outlook for a stock may also be traded using a bear put spread. There is a cost to this spread, as opposed to taking in a credit when using calls to create a bear spread. However, the payout of this spread will have a similar profile to the spread initiated with calls.

For example, if XYZ were trading at 24.25 and a trader feels the stock has strong resistance at 25.00. The trader also thinks that there is more of a possibility of the stock trading lower instead of breaking this resistance over the next 75 days and trading higher. With this outlook, the trader may choose to initiate a bear spread using put options. With April expiration 75 days out and an implied volatility of 40 percent, the April 30 Put would

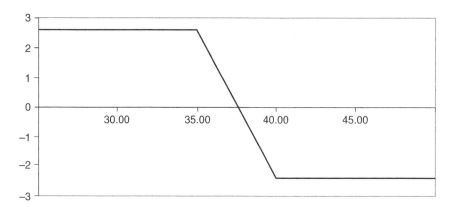

FIGURE 8.4 Bear Put Spread Payoff Diagram

be trading at 5.95 and the April 25 Put would be at 2.15. To put on a vertical bear spread with these two options, a trader would have to pay 3.80:

Short 1 Apr 25 Put at 2.15
Long 1 Apr 30 Put at 5.95
Net Debit = 3.80

The debit of 3.80 for a potential profit of 1.20 may appear to be a pretty high price. However, the stock is already trading at a level where, on expiration day, the trade reaches the maximum potential gain. In fact, the stock can move up .75 before the trade is out of this maximum profitability area. A move of 75 cents on a stock trading at 24.25 is a move of just over 3 percent.

Also, the break-even level for this trade results in a little bit of a price-move buffer. The break-even level is 26.20, or 1.95 above where the stock is trading when the trade is put on. This is a move of just over 8 percent to the upside with 75 days before this becomes a losing trade. Refer to Table 8.6 for a summary of all key levels.

The upper strike option on the spread represents where a maximum loss of 3.80 would be incurred due to the trade. This is a pretty substantial move over the life of the options. The sort of price move that would be required to cause this trade to be a 100 percent loser is directly related to the cost of the spread relative to the potential profit received at expiration. The potential risk of 3.80 versus the reward of 1.20 may initially seem unattractive. Unattractive, that is, until assessing what sort of price action would be involved in the breakeven and maximum loss out of this trade.

TABLE 8.6 Key Levels for 25/30 Apr Bear Put Spread

	Level	Explanation
Maximum Loss	3.80	Debit Paid
Maximum Loss Level	30 and over	Both options expire worthless
Maximum Gain	1.20	Upper Strike minus Lower Strike minus Debit Paid
Maximum Gain Level	25 and under	Both options in the money
Breakeven	26.20	Upper Strike minus Debit Paid

Figure 8.5 is a payoff diagram of this neutral to bearish bear put spread. The broken line represents the price level of 24.25, which is where the stock was trading when the position was entered. If the stock stays right at that level, trades slightly higher, or moves lower the full profit is realized.

A bear put spread may also be used to take advantage of an anticipated bearish move in a stock. Many times, based on the price projection and implied volatility of the options involved in the trade, this may be a preferable method to taking a bearish position than a directional long put purchase.

In the case of XYZ trading at 56.25, with a relatively high 45 percent implied volatility and May expiration 60 days out, a bear put spread is a method of trading a bearish outlook on XYZ. The feeling is that XYZ should trade down to just below the 50.00 level in the next 60 days. To take advantage of this move a trader might use a May 50/55 Bear Put Spread. With the parameters laid out, a May 50 Put would be priced at 1.50 and the May 55

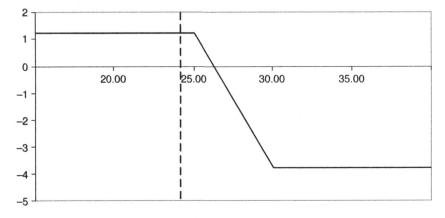

FIGURE 8.5 Payoff Diagram for XYZ Apr 25/30 Bear Put Spread

TABLE 8.7 Key Levels for 25/30 Apr Bear Put Spread

	Level	Explanation
Maximum Loss	1.90	Debit Paid
Maximum Loss Level	55 and over	Both options expire worthless
Maximum Gain	3.10	Upper Strike minus Lower Strike minus Debit Paid
Maximum Gain Level	50 and under	Long 55 Put worth $5 more than Short 50 Put
Breakeven	53.10	Upper Strike minus Debit Paid

Put would be trading at 3.40. The debit or cost to enter this spread comes to 1.90 as shown:

Short 1 XYZ May 50 Put at 1.50
Long 1 XYZ May 55 Put at 3.40
Net Debit = 1.90

The payoff for this spread may initially appear pretty attractive—that is potentially 3.10 for initially paying 1.90 to enter the spread. However, in this case, the stock must move a bit to reach profitability and an even larger move is needed to get the stock to a level where maximum profitability is reached. The key levels for this trade appear in Table 8.7.

The goal of this trade is for XYZ to be below 50.00 at expiration. Anywhere under 50.00 both options will be in the money with the long option having 5.00 more value than the lower strike option. At this point the trade will have a profit of 3.10, based on the 5.00 value of the spread and subtracting the 1.90 cost to enter the trade.

The bearish move needed from XYZ to reach breakeven, a partial profit, or even the maximum profit of 3.10 is represented by the payoff diagram in Figure 8.6. The stock is slightly higher than the upper strike price of 55.00 when the trade is initiated. Again, this does not necessarily need to be the case. The stock could have just as easily been a little under the upper strike with the projected target price below the lower strike.

As the stock moves closer to 50.00 the break-even point of 53.10 would be passed and eventually the maximum profit zone that begins at 50.00 might be reached. Keep in mind that more than a six-point move to the downside is required to make it to maximum profitability at expiration.

Of course there is a more directional alternative to the previous bear put spread. With a target of 50.00 at expiration, a trade might consider just purchasing a put option with the expectation of the stock going lower. The

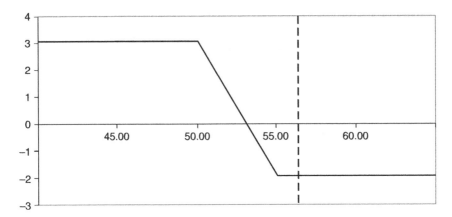

FIGURE 8.6 Payoff Diagram for XYZ May 50/55 Bear Put Spread

most likely choice with the same price outlook would probably be the May 55 Put from the previous example. Using the 55 Put would involve paying a premium of 3.40. This would be the cost of the position as there is no option being sold to offset this cost as there was in the bear put spread.

Table 8.8 compares the payoff at expiration for a long position in the XYZ May 55 Put and the XYZ May 50/55 Bear Put spread. At the target price of 50.00 from the spread example, the spread outperforms the long put position on both a dollar and use of capital basis. Between 50.00 and 45.00 there is a point where the preferred trade would have been the long put on both a dollar and percentage of capital basis.

Figure 8.7 compares the payoff for a long position in the XYZ May 55 Put and the XYZ May 50/55 Bear Put spread. The most significant thing to note about this payoff diagram is that the put outperforms dramatically if a catastrophic bear move occurs in XYZ that results in a much lower stock price at expiration. Once again, the target of the spread was 50.00 and with

TABLE 8.8　50/55 Bull Put Spread versus a 55 Long Call

	50/55 Bear Call Spread		55 Long Put Call	
XYZ	P/L	% Profit	P/L	% Profit
40	3.10	163%	11.60	341%
45	3.10	163%	6.60	194%
50	3.10	163%	1.60	47%
55	−1.90	−100%	−3.40	−100%
60	−1.90	−100%	−3.40	−100%

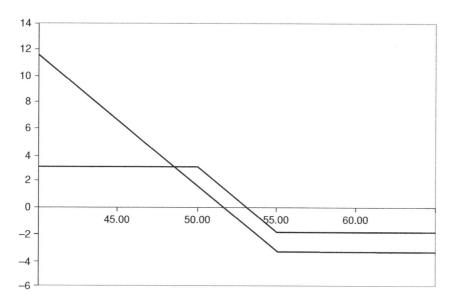

FIGURE 8.7 Payoff Diagram for XYZ May 50/55 Bear Put Spread

that target in mind it was the preferred trade. However, in the case that level is greatly surpassed, the long put position would have been a better alternative.

Bear spreads may be traded with a debit or credit and the focus should be on which provides the most favorable profit or loss scenario based on a trader's outlook. In some, but not all cases, if a bearish scenario is forecast, a bearish vertical spread may provide the best potential payout. If anything, a vertical spread should be considered when considering a directional or neutral trade with options.

CHAPTER 9

Butterfly Spreads

T his is the first chapter in which some of the more intimidating spreads start to come into play. This intimidation generally stems from multiple legs or a unique payout structure being the motivation behind a trade. Many traders and investors shy away from using options in their portfolios because even a single option position requires two-step thinking. This is further compounded when looking at a spread that takes multiple options into account. Another factor that may contribute to traders shying away from these spreads is that professional traders like to label these spreads exotic. That label alone might steer some traders away from taking the time to master and trade these types of spreads.

In fact, there is very little that is exotic about option spreads, they just combine basic option positions into a unique payoff structure. The butterfly spread is an exotic spread that can be approached in a couple of ways. It can be approached as a combination of bull and bear spreads which were covered in Chapters 7 and 8 or as a modified straddle which was discussed in Chapter 5. A version of the butterfly spread, the iron butterfly, was introduced in Chapter 6. These may be called exotic spreads, but if the strategies in the earlier chapters came across as the types of trades that can be mastered and implemented, there is no reason the same cannot be said for butterfly spreads by the end of this chapter.

INTRODUCTION TO BUTTERFLY SPREADS

A butterfly spread consists of positions in three or four options. The options have the same underlying and expiration. It is actually possible for a butterfly spread to consist of a combination of put and call options, or the spread may be created with all call or put options. Basically, there are a handful of methods to create the payoff structure of a butterfly spread. In this chapter, butterfly spreads created in all three of these methods as well as a couple of comparisons to strategies with similar payouts are covered.

To start, a basic butterfly using the same type of options will be introduced. When using all the same type of options, whether all calls or all puts, the butterfly spread will consist of three different options. In the case of a butterfly spread created with a combination of puts and calls, the spread will utilize four different options. This will be demonstrated further when the butterfly that mixes option types is introduced.

LONG CALL BUTTERFLY

A long call butterfly consists of three call options trading on the same underlying and having the same expiration. Each of the call options has different strikes and the strikes are usually equal distances from each other. For instance, a long call butterfly may involve a position in the 35, 40, and 45 strike calls. In some cases there may be an unequal distribution of options in a long call butterfly. As the combinations that may be created could be endless, the direct butterfly structure will be stuck with in this chapter.

To construct a long call butterfly, an equal number of the lowest and highest strike calls are purchased. The middle strike call option is sold, with twice as many of the middle strike options being sold as were purchased in either of the other strikes. The result is an equal number of long and short call options. Since this spread involves no naked short option positions, this spread is appropriate for many traders. In addition to having a high amount of potential risk associated with them, naked short option positions are often prohibited by brokerage firms for a variety of accounts.

The motivation behind a long call butterfly or any version of the other butterfly spreads that are referred to as long is actually a very specific stock outlook. This outlook or forecast consists of a stock reaching or settling at a specific level. A long call butterfly spread inherits this name due to

TABLE 9.1 Inputs and Output Used to Create an XYZ Jun 50/55/60 Long Call Butterfly

Inputs	
Days	45
Volatility	25%
Interest Rate	1.00%
XYZ Price	55.00
Output	
XYZ Jun 50 Call	5.35
XYZ Jun 55 Call	2.00
XYZ Jun 60 Call	0.45
XYZ Jun 50/55/60 Long Call Butterfly	1.80

the wings of the spread being long positions. The outside strike prices are purchased while the inside strike price is sold. The maximum payout of this spread occurs if the stock closes right at the middle strike price at expiration. In this case the only option that has value at expiration is the long call option with the lower strike price. Due to the payout structure, the long call butterfly is not really a position with a long bias, it is a trade that attempts to benefit from a stock landing at an exact price, or close to it, at expiration.

An example of spreads usually clears things up tremendously. This is especially true in this case, with different amounts of various options being bought and sold to create a payoff. Table 9.1 shows the option prices determined using an option calculator to create a sample long call butterfly spread.

In this case, XYZ is trading at 55.00 and there is a neutral stock outlook between now and June option expiration which is 45 days away. With an implied volatility of 25 percent, the XYZ Jun 50 Call is priced at 5.35 and the Jun 60 Call is priced at 0.45. These two options are purchased for a cost of 5.80, but then a short position is also taken in two of the XYZ Jun 55 Calls and a credit of 4.00 is realized for selling two of these options. With these transactions, the cost of the XYZ Jun 50/55/60 Long Call Butterfly is 1.80. Also as there are two long and two short call options in this spread, there are no naked option positions.

Before addressing the key levels for this trade, note something about the construction of the trade. Taking each of the long options and pairing it with one of the short XYZ Jun 55 Calls results in a combination of a bull call spread and a bear call spread. The bull call spread would consist of the long 50 Call and one of the short 55 Call positions. The bearish vertical spread in this case consists of the short position in the other 55 Call along with the long 60 Call.

TABLE 9.2 Key Levels for the XYZ Jun 50/55/60 Long Call Butterfly Spread

	Level	Explanation
Up Break-even Price	58.20	High Strike minus Cost of Spread
Down Break-even Price	51.80	Low Strike plus Cost of Spread
Maximum Dollar Gain	3.20	Maximum Spread Value minus Cost of Spread
Maximum Gain Price	55.00	Short Options Both Worthless
Maximum Dollar Loss	1.80	Cost of spread
Maximum Loss Prices	50.00 and Under	Low Strike of Spread
	60.00 and Over	High Strike of Spread

Using the assumption that the intention is to hold this trade to expiration, then the key levels may be calculated using expiration prices for the options. Table 9.2 covers the key levels for this butterfly spread.

The maximum potential gain for a long butterfly spread is always at a single point. In this case, if XYZ settles at 55.00 at expiration a maximum profit of 3.20 from this trade would be realized. In the case of the stock at 55.00 at expiration all of the options that make up the spread except for the 50 Call expire with no value. The 50 Call has 5.00 of value at expiration and the spread cost 1.80 to get into, so the profit at this level is 3.20.

As the stock price moves away from the center strike of 55, the spread begins to lose value. The break-even levels for this trade are at 51.80 to the downside and 58.20 to the upside. These two levels are determined by taking the cost of the spread and adding it to the lower strike price or subtracting it from the higher strike price.

Mechanically, if the stock is at 51.80 at expiration, once again the only option that has any value is the 50 Call. At this price point the value of the 50 Call is 1.80 and the cost of the spread was 1.80, which results in a break-even scenario. With the stock at 58.20 at expiration, the 50 Call and both 55 Call options are in the money. The 50 Call is worth 8.20 while the 55 Call is worth 3.20. As the position is long the 50 Call and short two of the 55 Calls, the math works out to 8.20 in the trader's favor and 6.40 against the trader for a net position of 1.80. Once again, the spread cost 1.80 and is worth 1.80, a break-even scenario.

Finally, the maximum potential loss of the spread is the premium paid to enter the spread of 1.80. With the stock at or below 50 at expiration all options expire out of the money or with no value. In this instance the cost was 1.80 and there is no value in the spread. At 60.00 or higher at expiration the value of the spread is also 0. For instance, if XYZ is at 70.00 at expiration the long 50 Call is worth 20.00 and the long 60 Call is worth 10.00 for a value of 30.00 for the long option positions. The 55 Call is worth 15.00, which due

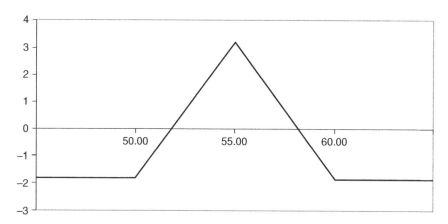

FIGURE 9.1 Payoff Diagram for the XYZ Jun 50/55/60 Long Call Butterfly Spread

to being short has a negative impact on an account. Since the spread is short 2 of the 55 Calls the impact is –30.00 (2 x –15.00). The 30.00 of long value minus 30.00 of value in the short options results in a spread with no value.

Figure 9.1 is a payoff diagram that is developed through the long call butterfly position. Upon glancing at the diagram it may be obvious where the term butterfly came from. That is, with some imagination the form of a butterfly may be seen. Note the peak of the payoff is right at 55.00 and then the payout drops when the stock moves in both directions. Between 50.00 and 60.00 the payout is similar to the payout for a short straddle. However, due to the long option positions in this spread that offset the short options, the potential maximum loss is limited unlike a short straddle.

Although in this case the long butterfly was initiated to benefit from very little price move, it is possible to trade a long butterfly with the anticipation that a stock is going to reach a certain level either higher or lower at expiration. In the previous case, if XYZ were trading at 50.00 and there was an expectation the stock was going to trade very close to 55.00 at expiration this may also be a viable trade.

LONG PUT BUTTERFLY

A long butterfly payoff may also be created using all put options. When considering a long butterfly spread, it is a worthwhile exercise to see if using put options or call options results in a slightly better entry price. Although the arbitrageurs keep option prices in line, there are times when

TABLE 9.3 Inputs and Output Used to Create an XYZ Nov
                30/35/40 Long Put Butterfly

Inputs	
Days	30
Volatility	30%
Interest Rate	1.00%
XYZ Price	35.00
Output	
XYZ Nov 30 Put	0.20
XYZ Nov 35 Put	1.70
XYZ Nov 40 Put	5.25
XYZ Nov 30/35/40 Long Put Butterfly	2.05

small price differences between the two similar payoffs occur that are too
slight or too small to be taken advantage of by the professional traders.

Not only is the payoff the same for the long put and call butterfly, but
the method to construct the positions is the same for both. A long put butterfly is initiated though a long position in equal numbers in two options
and a short position of twice as many options. The short options have a
strike price exactly halfway between the two long strikes. For instance,
if the trade motivation was to use the 20, 25, and 30 strike put options to
create a long butterfly payout, equal numbers of the 20 and 30 strike puts
would be purchased and twice as many of the 25 strike put options would
be shorted.

An example of a long put butterfly was developed using the options
in Table 9.3. The expectation is that XYZ will settle at 35.00, or very close
to this level, at expiration. This is the price the stock is also trading at
when the spread was entered. The anticipation is that this level will be
maintained over the next 30 days with November expiration 30 days off. To
benefit from this outlook one of the Nov 30 and Nov 40 puts are purchased
for a total of 5.45—0.20 for the XYZ Nov 30 Put and 5.25 for the XYZ Nov
40 Put. The spread is completed with two of the XYZ Nov 35 Put options
being shorted for 1.70 each or a total of 3.40. The cost of the spread comes
to 2.05, or the debit of 5.45 minus the credit received of 3.40.

As the trade was entered with the expectation of the stock being at
35.00 at November expiration, the key levels for this trade are based on
the stock at expiration. The levels are also determined in a similar fashion
to the long call butterfly discussed in the previous section. First, the maximum profit of the trade occurs if the stock settles at 35.00 at expiration. At
35.00 the only option that has value is the 40 Put. In the call example the
only option with any value was the lowest strike call. In this case the highest strike put is the only option that has value. The XYZ Nov 40 Put is worth

TABLE 9.4 Key Levels for the XYZ Nov 30/35/40 Long Put Butterfly Spread

	Level	Explanation
Up Break-even Price	32.05	High Strike plus Cost of Spread
Down Break-even Price	37.95	Low Strike plus Cost of Spread
Maximum Dollar Gain	2.95	Maximum Spread Value minus Cost of Spread
Maximum Gain Price	35.00	Short Options Both Worthless
Maximum Dollar Loss	2.05	Cost of spread
Maximum Loss Prices	30.00 and Under 40.00 and Over	Low Strike and High Strike of Spread

5.00, while the cost of the spread was 2.05. This results in a maximum profit of 2.95.

The break-even levels for this trade are determined exactly as they are for the long call butterfly spread. The lower breakeven is determined by adding the cost of the spread to the lower strike price and the higher break-even level is determined by subtracting the cost of the spread from the higher strike. However, the result at each level, or the way the spread works out to have the same value as the cost of the spread, is a bit different than with the call spread.

A summary of the key levels for this trade appear in Table 9.4. At the higher breakeven of 37.95, only the XYZ Nov 40 Put has any value. The 35 and 30 strike put options are out of the money and expire with no value. Therefore the XYZ Nov 40 Put is worth 2.05 which is the price paid for the spread. On the other end of the payoff diagram, at 32.05 both the 35 and 40 strike puts have value. The XYZ Nov 40 Put is worth 7.95 and the XYZ Nov 35 Put would be worth 2.95. Since the spread is short two of the Nov 35 Puts this would have a negative impact on the spread of 5.90. The long Nov 40 Put is worth 7.95, so subtracting the deficit associated with the 35 Put at 5.90 would result in a value of 2.05, or the cost of entering the spread.

The payout diagram for this spread is identical in shape to the payout that resulted from the long call butterfly position. Note in Figure 9.2 at 35.00 the maximum gain would be realized and at each of the other strike prices involved in the spread—30 and 40—there would maximum loss of 2.05 on the spread at expiration. Again, the long butterfly payout may be created with either all put or all call options.

Also similar to the long call butterfly, the long put butterfly may be broken down into a combination of two vertical spreads. Specifically a bull put and bear put spread. Using the XYZ Nov 30/35/40 Long Put Butterfly, the bull put spread would be a combination of the Nov 30 Put and one of the Nov 35 Puts. By taking a short position in the Nov 35 Put and purchasing

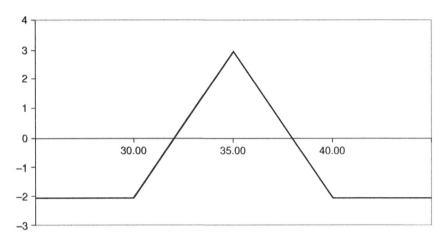

FIGURE 9.2 Payoff Diagram for the XYZ Nov 30/35/40 Long Put Butterfly Spread

the Nov 30 Put a bull spread is created. With a short position in the other Nov 35 Put and purchasing the Nov 40 Put a bear spread has been entered into. Putting these two positions together results in a long butterfly payout structure.

IRON BUTTERFLY

Not only may the long butterfly payout structure be created with all call or all put options, it also may be initiated with a combination of call and put options. This type of spread is called the iron butterfly. An iron butterfly has the same payout at expiration as either the long call butterfly or the long put butterfly. The method to create this spread is slightly different than the all call or all put butterfly spreads and is actually the preferred method of many traders.

An iron butterfly uses options with three different strike prices, the same as the previous two butterfly spreads. However, four different options are actually used when trading an iron butterfly. A put option with the lowest strike price is purchased and a put option at the middle strike price is sold. To complete the iron butterfly, a call option would be purchased at the highest strike price and a call option would be sold at the middle strike. Both the short put and call option would share a strike.

For example, an iron butterfly would be a combination of a long 25 Put, short 30 Put, short 30 Call, and long 35 Call. Another way to describe this spread is as a combination of a bull put spread and a bear call spread.

TABLE 9.5 Inputs and Output Used to Create an XYZ Dec
55/60/65 Iron Butterfly

Inputs	
Days	60
Volatility	20%
Interest Rate	1.00%
XYZ Price	60.00
Output	
XYZ Dec 55 Put	0.60
XYZ Dec 60 Put	2.40
XYZ Dec 60 Call	2.45
XYZ Dec 65 Call	0.80
XYZ Dec 55/60/65 Iron Butterfly	3.45

Both of these spreads are credit spreads, or a spread that takes in income when created so when an iron butterfly is initiated it is also done at a credit. This is a contrast to the long call and put butterfly spreads. Both of those spreads involved a cost to initiate the position.

As an example of an iron butterfly, XYZ is trading at 60.00 with December expiration 60 days off and an implied volatility of 20 percent. Using those pricing inputs, the Iron Butterfly option values appear in Table 9.5. Notice there are now four options in this table as opposed to the three options in the previous examples.

This iron butterfly would be initiated at a credit of 3.45 as both the 60 strike options would be sold while the XYZ Dec 55 Put and XYZ Dec 65 Call would be purchased. In both cases the more expensive option with regard to each type of option is sold so a credit is taken in from the combinations· of put options and the combinations of call options in the trade. Although a credit is taken in from putting on the XYZ 55/60/65 Iron Butterfly, the goal of the trade is the same as the long call butterfly and long put butterfly. Specifically for this trade, the goal is for the stock to settle at the middle strike price of the spread at expiration. At this price, the maximum profit of the spread would be realized.

Table 9.6 is a summary of the key levels for this Iron Butterfly. The payout levels are similar to the long butterfly spreads from the two previous sections, but the method of determining these payouts varies slightly. The maximum dollar gain is achieved if the stock settles at the middle strike, or 60.00, at expiration. However, this occurs in this case due to all options expiring with no value. With no value at expiration, the credit received from the trade is kept.

The break-even levels are mathematically determined by adding and subtracting the credit received when the trade was entered from the center

TABLE 9.6   Key Levels for the XYZ Dec 55/60/65 Iron Butterfly Spread

	Level	Explanation
Up Break-even Price	63.45	Middle Strike plus Credit from Spread
Down Break-even Price	56.55	Middle Strike minus Credit from Spread
Maximum Dollar Gain	3.45	Credit Received
Maximum Gain Price	60.00	Options All Worthless
Maximum Dollar Loss	1.55	Maximum Spread Value minus Credit
Maximum Loss Prices	55.00 and Under	Low Strike and High Strike of Spread
	65.00 and Over	

strike price. For this trade those two levels are 63.45 (60.00 + 3.45) and 56.55 (60.00 − 3.45). Finally, the maximum loss on this trade occurs and then is locked in outside the two outer strike prices. For each of these levels, the spread has a value of 5.00 and the credit received for this trade is subtracted from 5.00, resulting in the maximum loss. At 65.00 and any price level higher than 65.00, the two call options have value, with the short position in the 60 Call having 5.00 more value than the long position in the 65 Call. Since the trader is short the more valuable option, this is a negative result for him. This is the same as having a bear call spread end up at the maximum loss level. At the lower strike price of 55, the call options in this spread have no value, but the put options are both in the money. The short 60 put has 5.00 more value than the long 55 put so the spread is once again worth 5.00, but a negative 5.00 to the trader that is short the more valuable option. The payout here is very similar to the worst case scenario with a bull put spread.

The payout diagram for an iron butterfly is also a replication of the payout for either the long call or long put butterfly spreads. Figure 9.3 is a payout diagram displaying the profit or loss at expiration for the XYZ Dec 55/60/65 Iron Butterfly.

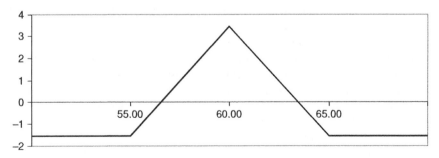

FIGURE 9.3   Payoff Diagram for the XYZ Dec 55/60/65 Iron Butterfly

TABLE 9.7 Iron Butterfly versus Long Call or Put Butterfly

Action	Iron Butterfly	Long Butterfly
Entry	Credit or Income	Debit or Cost
Max Profit Exit	No Action	Option Trade/Exercise Process
Max Loss Exit	Exercise Process	Possibly No Action
Options in Spread	2 Puts and 2 Calls	3 of same Type

The payout for this spread has the same levels as either of the other spreads although how those levels are determined occurs a bit differently. For instance with an expiration day settlement right at 60.00, all options in this spread would expire with no value and no action would need to be taken. If this butterfly were constructed using all call options, the call option with the 55 strike price would be 5 points in the money and the spread would have a long position in this option. Held through expiration this call option would be exercised and a long position in XYZ would appear in a trader's account on the following Monday morning. For this reason many traders prefer using an iron butterfly as opposed to a long butterfly with all options of the same type. Table 9.7 compares a long call or put butterfly with an iron butterfly.

Another factor that is different between the long butterfly with options that are all the same type and iron butterfly occurs upon entry into the position. The iron butterfly results in a credit for an account, while a trader would incur a debit or pay to enter one of the other long butterfly spreads. Additionally, while the same number of option contracts is used with both spreads, there is an extra individual option utilized with an iron butterfly. This is the result of both a put and call being sold at the middle strike price of the spread.

Finally, the maximum loss on a long butterfly may occur when all options are out of the money. In this case, there would be no trade that would occur to avoid going through the exercise process. It is possible for a long butterfly to have a maximum loss with all options in the money, but the assignment and exercise process would result in the buying and selling of shares netting out. With the iron butterfly, at either maximum loss level, stock would be bought and sold in the trader's account and be netted out.

When a long butterfly payout is considered, the factors of taking in income to initiate the trade through an iron butterfly structure should be weighed with the potential payout on an alternative construction through a long call butterfly or long put butterfly. The chance to improve on the potential profit and loss could outweigh incurring a cost upon initiating the trade.

In addition to approaching the iron butterfly as a combination of a bull put and bear call spread it is possible to consider the iron butterfly as a deviation of a short straddle. The short straddle involves selling a call and put option with the same strike and same expiration. The center of an iron butterfly is just that, a short position in a call and put option with the same strike prices.

If a trader begins with a short straddle, such as being short an XYZ Mar 25 Call and XYZ Mar 25 Put, they may create an iron butterfly by purchasing a call option with a higher strike and purchasing a put option with a lower strike, equal in distance from the center as the higher strike. This may also be referred to as buying the wings. To take the XYZ Mar 25 Short Straddle and turn it into an iron butterfly, the XYZ Mar 20 Put and XYZ Mar 30 Call could be bought. Now the short straddle has morphed into the XYZ Mar 20/25/30 Iron Butterfly.

SHORT STRADDLE COMPARISON

To begin with, a short straddle and iron butterfly both have the same goal, for a stock to land exactly at a certain price at expiration. In the case of the iron butterfly it would be the strike price in the middle of the spread. For the short straddle, the targeted price is the shared strike price of the short put and call options. Also, both trades are initiated with a credit to a trader's account.

The biggest contrast between the two spreads is the unlimited potential loss that the short straddle has exposure to as opposed to the limited downside risk that is incurred from an iron condor. A short straddle will consist of two short option positions that are naked or uncovered positions. Uncovered short call options have theoretically unlimited risk while naked short put options have a substantial potential loss that would occur if a stock were to go to 0.00. In the case of the iron condor, each of the short put and call options are covered by a long put and call option. For comparison, the options in Table 9.8 are used to create both an iron butterfly and short straddle.

The XYZ Feb 70 Short Straddle consists of a short position in both the XYZ Feb 70 Put and XYZ Feb 70 Call for a total credit of 5.85. The credit received for initiating the XYZ Feb 65/70/75 Iron Butterfly is lower than the credit of the straddle, or 3.70, which results from buying the wings. Buying the wings would be the purchases of the XYZ Feb 65 Put and XYZ Feb 75 Call for a total cost of 2.15. There is much less income for the iron butterfly, but also lower risk from the spread relative to the short straddle.

TABLE 9.8 Inputs and Output Used to Create an XYZ Feb 65/70/75 Iron Butterfly and XYZ Feb 70 Short Straddle

Inputs	
Days	30
Volatility	30%
Interest Rate	1.00%
XYZ Price	70.00
Output	
XYZ Feb 65 Put	1.05
XYZ Feb 70 Put	2.90
XYZ Feb 70 Call	2.95
XYZ Feb 75 Call	1.10
XYZ Feb 65/70/75 Iron Butterfly	3.70
XYZ Feb 70 Short Straddle	5.85

A comparison of the key levels for each of the two spreads appears in Table 9.9. The short straddle and iron butterfly both realize a maximum profit if XYZ settles right at 70.00 at expiration. At that level, all options in both spreads would expire with no value, with some being right at the money. Both spreads would keep the credit received for initiating their respective positions. Since the iron butterfly took in less than the short straddle, the short straddle has a higher profit when XYZ is at 70.00 at expiration.

Comparing the break-even levels, the short straddle has a wider range of levels where the spread would realize some sort of profit. At any price between 64.15 and 75.85 there would be some sort of partial profit for the trader from the XYZ Feb 70 Short Straddle position. In the case of the iron butterfly, the range where a partial profit may be realized is not quite as

TABLE 9.9 Key Level Comparison for the Feb XYZ 65/70/75 Iron Butterfly and Feb XYZ 70 Short Straddle

	XYZ 65/70/75 Iron Butterfly	XYZ 70 Short Straddle
Up Break-even Price	73.70	75.85
Down Break-even Price	66.30	64.15
Maximum Dollar Gain	3.70	5.85
Maximum Gain Price	70.00	70.00
Maximum Dollar Loss	1.30	Substantial/Unlimited
Maximum Loss Prices	65.00 and Under 75.00 and Over	0.00 and Unlimited

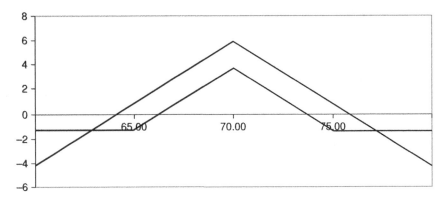

FIGURE 9.4 Payoff Diagram Comparison for the XYZ Feb 65/70/75 Iron Butterfly and XYZ Feb 70 Short Straddle

wide as the short straddle. Between 66.30 and 73.70 some sort of partial profit would be realized. Once again, this difference is a direct result of the lower amount of income taken in when the iron butterfly is initiated relative to the short straddle.

Finally, the maximum potential loss for the short straddle is theoretically unlimited. In the case that the stock takes off on a huge bullish move, the short straddle may possibly take on unlimited losses. Due to the purchase of the out-of-the-money XYZ 65 Put and XYZ 75 Call options, the maximum loss for the iron butterfly is limited to 1.30. A major tradeoff with this position is sacrificing some profit for protection against a very large potential loss.

The payoff diagram in Figure 9.4 displays the payoff at expiration for the XYZ Feb 65/70/75 Iron Condor and the XYZ Feb 70 Short Straddle. Both diagrams come to a head on the upside at the 70.00 level and then start to move away from a maximum gain level based on a stock move higher or lower. The difference between the break-even levels, where the payoff lines cross the 0 profit line, shows the superior payoff range of the short straddle. Finally the maximum potential loss, where the iron butterfly would be the better choice as the maximum loss is limited at both the outside strike prices is also displayed.

As noted in Chapter 5 many traders, for risk management purposes, will choose to purchase out of the money options as protection from a large move. This action turns a short straddle into an iron butterfly. Other traders may not have the ability to initiate naked short option positions so when they consider a short straddle they may be forced to buy the wings to adhere to the trading requirements dictated by their broker.

SHORT CALL BUTTERFLY

Like just about all option spreads, a long butterfly or iron butterfly may be reversed to create the opposite payout structure. The butterfly spreads created through the use of all the same type of options would be considered a short call or short put butterfly. In these cases the trade would basically be the opposite transaction of their long counterparts.

Before moving forward, a note about the naming of the long or short butterfly may be in order. The names come from the transaction that occurs with the wings of the spread. However, when looking at the payout structure or payout diagram, the payout of a long (call or put) butterfly is very similar to the payout of the short straddle, at least in the center of the butterfly spread. Conversely, the payout for the center of a short butterfly will look very similar to the payout diagram that is created when a long straddle is initiated. For a little more clarity on this, see Figure 9.5.

The first short butterfly to investigate is the short call butterfly. A short call butterfly is a combination of the same three options that would constitute an opposite long call butterfly. Once again, the middle options are traded in twice as many contracts as were traded on the outside strike prices. However, this time the middle contracts are purchased and the outside strike options, or wings, are sold. For instance a short call butterfly may consist of buying two 30 strike call options while selling a 25 strike call and a 35 strike call. The construction of the spread is exactly opposite

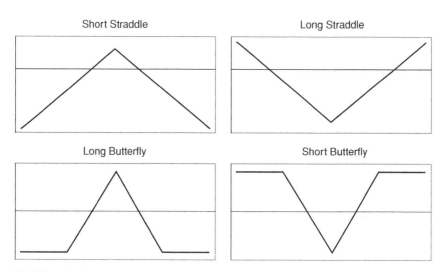

FIGURE 9.5 Comparison of Straddle and Butterfly Payouts

TABLE 9.10 Inputs and Output Used to Create an XYZ Apr 40/45/50 Short Call Butterfly

Inputs	
Days	50
Volatility	35%
Interest Rate	1.00%
XYZ Price	45
Output	
XYZ Apr 40 Call	5.60
XYZ Apr 45 Call	2.35
XYZ Apr 50 Call	0.75
XYZ Apr 40/45/50 Short Call Butterfly	1.65

of the long counterpart. The payout structure is exactly the opposite also, with the maximum gain being realized at the outside strikes and the maximum loss being realized with a settlement price at expiration equal to the middle strike price.

For an example of a short call butterfly, the option prices from Table 9.10 were taken from an option calculator. The assumption for this spread involves 50 days to April expiration, implied volatility on all options involved at 35 percent, and an underlying stock price of 45.00.

The output results in a short call butterfly being initiated for a credit of 1.65. The XYZ Apr 40 and XYZ Apr 50 Call options are sold for a total income of 6.35 (5.60 + 0.75), while two of the XYZ Apr 45 Call options are purchased for a total cost of 4.70 (2.35 each). The result is a credit of 1.65 to a trader's account. Another significant difference between the long counterparts to this trade is that the short call butterfly actually results in a credit to a trader's account. Also, this is a contributor to the naming of this spread. When options are sold, there is a credit, therefore as this trade brings in a credit it may be considered short.

The maximum loss for a short call butterfly occurs if the stock settles right at the middle strike price of the spread. In the case of the XYZ Apr 40/45/50 short call butterfly this would be with XYZ at 45.00 at expiration. If this were to occur, both the two 45 Calls and the 50 Call would expire with no value. The XYZ Apr 40 Call would be worth 5.00, but the spread is short this option, so the spread would be 5.00 against the trader. Subtracting the credit received for this trade, 1.65, results in a maximum loss of 3.35 with XYZ at 45.00 at expiration. The key levels are all summarized in Table 9.11.

There are two breakeven and areas of maximum gain for this spread. The break-even levels for this trade would involve a bearish move to 41.65 or a bullish move to 48.35. These levels are determined by combining the outside strike prices and the credit received from initiating the trade. For

TABLE 9.11 Key Levels for the XYZ Apr 40/45/50 Short Call Butterfly Spread

	Level	Explanation
Up Break-even Price	48.35	High Strike minus Credit Received
Down Break-even Price	41.65	Low Strike plus Credit Received
Maximum Dollar Gain	1.65	Credit Received
Maximum Gain Prices	40.00 and Under 50.00 and Higher	Spread Has No Value
Maximum Dollar Loss	3.35	Maximum Spread Value minus Credit
Maximum Loss Price	45.00	Middle Strike Price

the lower break-even level the credit is added to the strike (40.00 + 1.65) and for the higher break-even level the credit is subtracted from the higher strike price (50.00 − 1.65).

Finally the maximum gain for this spread occurs if the stock settles at or below the lower strike price or at or above the higher strike price. The math behind these two levels varies slightly, but the result is the same in both cases. Using the example trade, at 40.00 or below, all options in the spread expire out of the money and have no value. At 50.00 or any level higher than 50.00 all options are in the money. However, even though all options are in the money, the spread as a whole will be worth 0.00. To demonstrate this, consider XYZ at 60.00 at expiration. Table 9.12 shows the value of each component of the spread and the result.

At any level above 50.00 the option values of the long and short options actually cancel each other out. Using a settlement price of 60.00 the short options have a total value of 30.00, which works against the trader who is short these options. To offset these two short options, the long position in the two XYZ Apr 45 Calls is also worth 30.00. Being long, this is a benefit to the trader and the net result is a spread with no value at expiration.

Finally, in Figure 9.6, these key levels are displayed in a payoff diagram. The maximum loss level of 45.00 at the center strike price of the spread is the lowest point for the payout. Moving in either direction, the spread

TABLE 9.12 XYZ Apr 40/45/50 Long Call Butterfly Spread Value with XYZ at 60.00 at Expiration

	Profit / Loss
Short 1 XYZ Apr 40 Call	−20.00
Long 2 XYZ Apr 45 Calls	30.00
Short 1 XYZ Apr 50 Call	−10.00
XYZ Apr 40/45/50 Short Call Butterfly	0.00

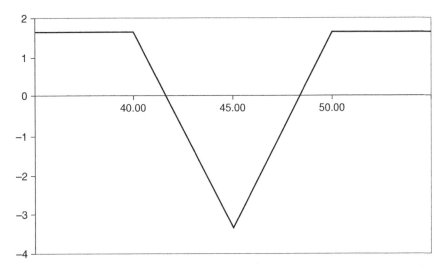

FIGURE 9.6   Payoff Diagram for the XYZ Jun 40/45/50 Short Call Butterfly Spread

begins to make money and approach the respective break-even levels. At the higher and lower strike prices, the payout tops out at the maximum level, which in this case is equal to the credit received for the spread.

SHORT PUT BUTTERFLY

The short put butterfly is very similar to a short call butterfly. Both positions will be initiated with a credit to an account and each of these spreads has a very similar payout structure. Also, each spread is constructed by purchasing twice as many of the middle strike options as are sold on each of the wings. The main difference between the two comes when determining the payout at certain levels.

As an example of a short put butterfly, the prices and options displayed in Table 9.13 were used. November options with 50 days to expiration with an implied volatility of 35 percent are priced out using a calculator. The underlying stock is trading at 70.00 which is also the strike of the middle option in the spread.

To enter into the XYZ Nov 65/70/75 Short Put Butterfly the 65 and 75 Put options would be sold for a net credit of 6.00 (0.50 + 5.50) while two of the XYZ Nov 70 Puts would be purchased for a cost of 4.40 (2.20 each). The net credit for this spread would be 1.60 (6.00 − 4.40), which also is the maximum potential profit of this trade.

TABLE 9.13 Inputs and Output Used to Create an XYZ Nov 65/70/75 Short Put Butterfly

Inputs	
Days	50
Volatility	35%
Interest Rate	1.00%
XYZ Price	45
Output	
XYZ Nov 65 Put	0.50
XYZ Nov 70 Put	2.20
XYZ Nov 75 Put	5.50
XYZ Nov 65/70/75 Short Put Butterfly	1.60

Table 9.14 displays the key levels of this trade at expiration. As mentioned before, 1.60 is the maximum potential profit of this trade and this occurs at any price above 75.00 or below 65.00 at expiration. In both of these cases, the spread has no value, like the Short Call Butterfly. However, the level where there is no value due to all options being out of the money is higher than the upper strike price in this spread. Below the lower strike price, all options are in the money, but the value of the short options is equal to the value of the long options.

The maximum loss for this trade is 3.40, which occurs if the stock settles directly on the middle strike price of 70.00 at expiration. Once again the math is slightly different when determining the value of this spread at that price. The 65 and 70 put options expire with no value if XYZ is at 70.00 at expiration. The only option that is in the money is the higher strike XYZ Nov 75 Put. In the case of the short call spread, the lower strike option would be the only option that is in the money. The XYZ Nov 75 Put would have 5.00 of value. As the spread is short this option that would be a debit

TABLE 9.14 Key Levels for the XYZ Nov 65/70/75 Short Put Butterfly Spread

	Level	Explanation
Up Break-even Price	73.40	High Strike minus Credit Received
Down Break-even Price	66.60	Low Strike plus Credit Received
Maximum Dollar Gain	1.60	Credit Received
Maximum Gain Prices	65.00 and Under 75.00 and Higher	Spread Has No Value
Maximum Dollar Loss	3.40	Maximum Spread Value minus Credit
Maximum Loss Price	70.00	Middle Strike Price

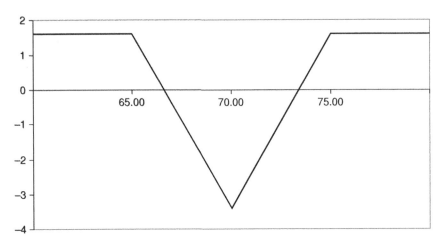

FIGURE 9.7   Payoff Diagram for the XYZ Nov 65/70/75 Short Put Butterfly Spread

of 5.00 to a trader, which is offset by the credit of 1.60 received to enter the spread.

The payout diagram in Figure 9.7 is a typical short butterfly payout with the maximum loss occurring right in the center of the spread and the profit being capped at each of the wing strike prices where options were sold.

REVERSE IRON BUTTERFLY

The iron counterpart to the long call and put butterfly spreads was the iron butterfly. The reverse iron butterfly is the opposite of an iron butterfly and is the iron counterpart to the short butterfly spreads. A reverse iron butterfly combines both call and put options to create a payout that is identical to the short butterfly diagrams in the previous two sections.

An approach to dissecting the iron butterfly was to consider the put and call options at the center strike to be a short straddle. The protection from the unlimited downside that comes from a short straddle was purchased through out-of-the-money options. The reverse iron butterfly starts out with a long straddle and then the wings—out-of-the-money options—are sold. The result is a payout that replicates a long straddle until either of the outside strike prices is reached. At this level the profit has matched the maximum potential payout.

The XYZ Dec 45/50/55 reverse iron butterfly, unlike the short butterfly spreads created with all similar options, is actually initiated with a debit or cost instead of a credit. Using the sample options from Table 9.15, the reverse iron butterfly would come at a cost of 3.35. The Dec 50 Put and Call

TABLE 9.15 Inputs and Output Used to Create an XYZ Dec 45/50/55 Reverse Iron Butterfly

Inputs	
Days	30
Volatility	40%
Interest Rate	1.00%
XYZ Price	50.00
Output	
XYZ Dec 45 Put	0.50
XYZ Dec 50 Put	2.25
XYZ Dec 50 Call	2.30
XYZ Dec 55 Call	0.70
XYZ Dec 65/70/75 Reverse Iron Butterfly	3.35

would be purchased for a total cost of 4.55 (2.25 + 2.30) and the Dec 45 Put and Dec 55 Call would be sold for a credit of 1.20 (0.50 + 0.70).

The key levels for this reverse iron butterfly are similar to the short butterfly spreads, but the math to determine these levels is a little different. Table 9.16 contains the key levels for the XYZ Dec 45/50/55 Reverse Iron Butterfly.

The maximum potential loss with this spread is limited to the capital outlay to enter the spread, or 3.35. At any level from 45.00 down or 55.00 and higher the spread has a value of 5.00, but the cost of the spread was 3.35 so the net profit is limited to 1.65. Above 55.00, only the Long 50 Call and Short 55 Call options are in the money. The 50 Call will have 5.00 more in value than the 55 Call. On the other end of the spectrum, with XYZ below 45.00 at expiration, the Long 50 Put and Short 45 Put options will have value with the 50 Strike Put having 5.00 more value than the 45 Put.

The break-even levels for this spread are determined by adding and subtracting the cost of the spread from the center strike price. To the upside, the spread is a profit anywhere over 53.35. On the downside it has

TABLE 9.16 Key Levels for the XYZ Dec 45/50/55 Reverse Iron Butterfly

	Level	Explanation
Up Break-even Price	53.35	Middle Strike plus Cost
Down Break-even Price	46.65	Middle Strike minus Cost
Maximum Dollar Gain	1.65	Max Spread Value minus Cost
Maximum Gain Prices	45.00 and Under 55.00 and Higher	Spread Has No Value
Maximum Dollar Loss	3.35	Cost of Spread
Maximum Loss Price	50.00	Middle Strike Price

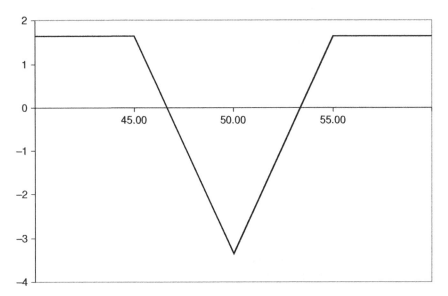

FIGURE 9.8   Payoff Diagram for the XYZ Dec 45/50/55 Reverse Iron Butterfly

value once 46.65 has been crossed. The payout diagram for this final butterfly example appears in Figure 9.8.

REVERSE IRON BUTTERFLY VERSUS STRADDLE

As the reverse iron butterfly involves a debit and has limited upside, the question may arise as to why not just stick with the long straddle and not worry about selling the wings. Selling the wings does bring some income and lowers the cost of the spread. In cases where options are expensive relative to the expected price move, taking in some income to offset this cost may make sense.

Also, there are levels where a reverse iron butterfly will have a better return relative to a long straddle. If the price projection is in line with one of these levels, the reverse iron butterfly is the preferred trade.

Using the options from the previous example that appear in Table 9.15, an XYZ Dec 50 Long Straddle would cost 4.55. This straddle is created through buying the XYZ Dec 50 Call at 2.30 and the XYZ Dec 50 Put at 2.25. Using this spread and the reverse iron butterfly from the previous section, the key levels were determined and appear in Table 9.17.

TABLE 9.17 Key Level Comparison for the Dec XYZ 45/50/55 Reverse Iron Butterfly and Dec XYZ 50 Long Straddle

	Reverse Iron Butterfly	Long Straddle
Up Break-even Price	53.35	75.85
Down Break-even Price	46.65	64.15
Maximum Dollar Gain	1.65	Unlimited
Maximum Gain Prices	45.00 55.00	Unlimited
Maximum Dollar Loss	3.35	4.55
Maximum Loss Price	50.00	50.00

Due to the lower cost of the spread, the reverse iron butterfly has a lower potential loss than the long straddle. Also, as the butterfly is a little less expensive, the break-even levels for this spread are a bit closer to the center strike price than the break-even levels for the straddle. The most significant difference between the two spreads comes when comparing the potential maximum gain. Due to there being no short options in the long straddle the theoretical potential profit for this spread is unlimited. With the reverse iron butterfly the maximum profit is capped at 1.65.

Figure 9.9 is a depiction of the payoff of the XYZ Dec 45/50/55 Reverse Iron Butterfly and XYX Dec 50 Long Straddle. The lower potential loss and

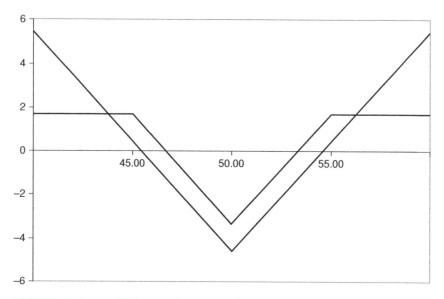

FIGURE 9.9 Payoff Diagram Comparison for the XYZ Dec 45/50/55 Reverse Iron Butterfly and XYZ Dec 50 Long Straddle

TABLE 9.18 Payoff Comparison of XYZ 45/50/55 Reverse Iron Butterfly and XYZ 50 Long Straddle

XYZ	Reverse Iron Butterfly		Long Straddle	
	Profit/Loss	% P/L	Profit/Loss	% P/L
40.00	1.65	49%	5.45	120%
45.00	1.65	49%	0.45	10%
50.00	−3.35	−100%	−4.55	−100%
55.00	1.65	49%	0.45	10%
60.00	1.65	49%	5.45	120%

closer break-even levels for the butterfly relative to the straddle are pretty apparent on this diagram. Also, the unlimited potential gain of the straddle also stands out.

At certain levels there is a preference for having put on the butterfly or reverse butterfly spread. Table 9.18 compares the profit and percent profit based on cost to enter the spread at a variety of levels. Between 40.00 and 45.00 on the downside and 55.00 and 60.00 to the upside, the long straddle becomes the preferred trade. In fact the levels where the straddle becomes the preferred trade is 43.20 on the downside and 56.80 on the upside. The spread would be worth 6.80 at either of these points, which is a profit of 2.25. This is very close to a 49 percent return on the trade.

In summary, there are a variety of ways to approach a butterfly, either through taking in a credit or paying a debit, regardless of what price outcome is expected when the trade is initiated. Also in situations where a long or short straddle is being considered, using a comparable butterfly spread may be a viable alternative.

CHAPTER 10

Condor Spreads

T here are two types of the spreads that are normally referred to as the winged spreads: the butterfly and the condor. The butterfly was introduced in Chapter 9 and the condor will be discussed in this chapter.

There are many similarities between butterfly and condor spreads. For instance there are versions of condors that utilize all the same type of options and then there is the iron version that uses a combination of both calls and puts. They both may be entered for a debit or a credit and share the naming of long or short based on the position taken with the outer strikes. Each has a comparable spread that will have a similar, yet more risky payout structure. Finally, they both may be approached as a combination of vertical bull and bear spreads.

INTRODUCTION TO CONDOR SPREADS

As mentioned there are many similarities between butterfly spreads and condors. The major difference is the construction of a condor. With a butterfly spread, the combination of options will consist of three or four unique options based on whether the options are all the same type for a butterfly. In a case where the options are all calls or puts, there are only three different contracts involved. The iron versions of butterfly spreads use a combination of two call and two put options, with a single strike price being shared by a call and put. In the case of a condor, there will always be four different options used, regardless of whether they are all the same type or not.

A condor constructed with all call or put options may involve four successive strike prices. For instance, a long or short call or put condor may use the 40, 45, 50, and 55 call options when it is being constructed. The two lower and two higher strike prices would need to have the same distance between them. The distance between the two middle strike prices may vary however; most of the examples in this chapter will keep an equal distance for simplicity.

When the spread is constructed with all the same type of options, the long version will be created through the purchase of the two outside options and selling the two inside strike options. This is similar to the long butterfly where the wings are purchased and the middle strike option is actually sold. The short version of a condor is created through selling the wings and buying the inside options. For examples, the long versions will be covered first and then the short condor spread will be discussed in the second half of the chapter. Iron condors and some comparable positions will also be discussed.

LONG CALL CONDOR

A long call condor takes four call options into account and creates a payoff that reaches the maximum potential profit if the underlying reaches a certain range at expiration. In the case of long butterfly spreads, a single point or price at expiration was the goal for initiating the trade. When using a long condor there is a little bit more room for error as the spread's maximum benefit is from a range of prices.

To construct a long call condor, the outside strike prices would be purchased. For example, using the strike prices in the examples at the beginning of this chapter (40, 45, 50, and 55) a long call condor would own the 40 and 55 strike calls and short the 45 and 50 strike calls.

To create an example of the long call condor, the levels from Table 10.1 were used. The goal of this spread is for XYZ, which is trading at 47.50 presently, to settle between 45.00 and 50.00 at January expiration, which is 60 days away. The option values are based on an implied volatility of 30 percent.

To create a long call condor with these options, the XYZ Jan 40 Call will be purchased for 7.75 and 0.35 will be paid for a long position in the XYZ Jan 55 Call. These two option purchases result in a cost of 8.10. The two inner strike options are sold, selling the XYZ Jan 45 Call for 3.75 and XYZ Jan 50 Call for 1.35. These two sales result in a credit to a trader's account of 5.10. The debit of 8.10 and credit of 5.10 are netted out to result in a cost of 3.00 to enter the XYZ Jan 40/45/50/55 Long Call Condor. In addition to

TABLE 10.1 Inputs and Output Used to Create an XYZ Jan 40/45/50/55 Long Call Condor

Inputs	
Days	60
Volatility	30%
Interest Rate	1.00%
XYZ Price	47.50
Output	
XYZ Jan 40 Call	7.75
XYZ Jan 45 Call	3.75
XYZ Jan 50 Call	1.35
XYZ Jan 55 Call	0.35
XYZ Jan 40/45/50/55 Long Call Condor	3.00

buying the wings, the fact that a long call condor will result in a cost to an account contributes to the name long.

Key levels for the long condor vary a bit from the long butterfly with the major difference being a wider maximum payout range. Also, due to an extra strike price being included in the spread, the range of break-even levels may be wider and the maximum loss level often is farther from the center of the spread. It is not a rule that the stock should be in the profit range when the trade is initiated, but it is common for long condors to be initiated in this manner. The key levels for the XYZ Jan 40/45/50/55 Long Call Condor appear in Table 10.2.

The maximum potential gain for this spread is 2.00, which is determined through the maximum potential value of this spread at expiration of 5.00 minus the cost of initiating the spread of 3.00. Between 45.00 and 50.00 the only two options in this spread that have value or are in the money are

TABLE 10.2 Key Levels for the XYZ Jan 40/45/50/55 Long Call Condor Spread

	Level	Explanation
Up Break-even Price	52.00	High Strike minus Cost
Down Break-even Price	43.00	Low Strike plus Cost
Maximum Dollar Gain	2.00	Maximum Spread Value minus Cost
Maximum Gain Prices	Between 45.00 and 50.00	Spread Worth Maximum Value
Maximum Dollar Loss	3.00	Cost of Spread
Maximum Loss Prices	40.00 and Under 55.00 and Over	Spread Has No Value

the XYZ Jan 40 Call and XYZ Jan 45 Call. At any value between 45.00 and 50.00, the 40 strike call will have 5.00 more value than the 45 strike call. Due to this difference and the spread being long the lower strike call, the spread will settle with a value of 5.00 which is a profit of 2.00 to the trader.

The break-even levels for a long call condor may be determined by adding the cost of the spread to the lowest strike price or subtracting the cost of the spread from the highest strike price. For this trade, in either case the spread would have 3.00 of value which is also the cost of the spread. At the lower break even price of 43.00 the math is fairly simple. The only option to have any value would be the XYZ Jan 40 Call, which would be worth 3.00. The spread is worth 3.00 and 3.00 was paid to enter the spread at 43.00.

The math behind the 52.00 break-even level is a little more involved. At 52.00 all options except the XYZ Jan 55 Call have value. The XYZ Jan 40 Call is worth 12.00, the XYZ Jan 45 Call is worth 7.00, and the XYZ Jan 50 Call is worth 2.00. As the 45 and 50 strike call options are short positions in this spread they offset the value of the XYZ 40 Call with the result being 3.00 of positive value (12.00 – 7.00 – 2.00). Once again the spread that cost 3.00 is worth 3.00 at expiration or a break-even trade.

The last of these key levels, the maximum loss for this trade, occurs anywhere above the high strike of 55.00 or below the low strike of 40.00. Below 40.00 all options expire with no value and the spread goes out worthless. The maximum loss of 3.00 or the price paid for the spread would be realized. At 55.00 the spread is also worth 0.00, but this is due to the value of the long options being equal to and offsetting the value of the short options and resulting in a net value of 0.00 for the spread. As an example of this scenario the option values in Table 10.3 were created, which assumes XYZ is at 60.00 at expiration.

Finally, a payoff diagram appears in Figure 10.1 that depicts the payout of the XYZ Jan 40/45/50/55 Long Call Condor. The condor inherits the name from the shape of this payout, and with a little imagination the image of a bird is there.

TABLE 10.3 XYZ Jan 40/45/50/55 Long Call Condor Value with XYZ at 60.00 at Expiration

	Profit/Loss
Long 1 XYZ Jan 40 Call	20.00
Short 1 XYZ Jan 45 Call	−15.00
Short 1 XYZ Jan 50 Call	−10.00
Long 1 XYZ Jan 55 Call	5.00
XYZ Jan 40/45/50/55 Long Call Condor	0.00

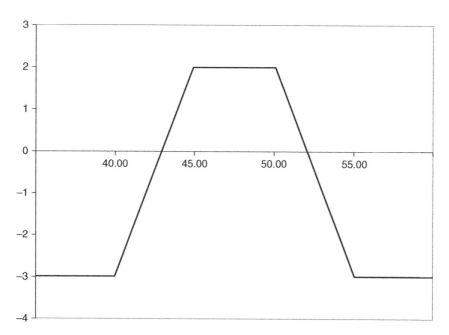

FIGURE 10.1 Payoff Diagram for the XYZ Jan 40/45/50/55 Long Call Condor Spread

Figure 10.1 shows that under the lower 40 strike and above the higher 55 strike, the maximum loss of this trade is limited. Between the 45 and 50 strike prices the spread will realize a maximum gain of 2.00. The other two ranges, which contain the angled lines, are areas of partial profit or loss. Finally, the profit and loss line crosses the 0 line twice, at 43.00 and at 52.00, showing where the spread turns into a winner from a loser.

LONG PUT CONDOR

A long put condor shares many common characteristics with a long call condor. They are both entered at a cost or debit, have the same payoff structures, and are created with the same type of options spaced out by strike in a similar manner. The long put condor payout is determined in a similar fashion to the payout structure of a long call condor, with some slight differences. When considering a long condor payout, exploring both for any potential price advantage is a worthwhile exercise.

The example used to demonstrate a long put payout was developed with the input and outputs displayed in Table 10.4. This long put condor

TABLE 10.4 Inputs and Output Used to Create an XYZ May 60/65/70/75 Long Put Condor

Inputs	
Days	45
Volatility	25%
Interest Rate	1.00%
XYZ Price	67.50
Output	
XYZ May 60 Put	0.25
XYZ May 65 Put	2.05
XYZ May 70 Put	4.65
XYZ May 75 Put	8.35
XYZ May 60/65/70/75 Long Put Condor	1.90

was initiated using May options that have 45 days to expiration. The implied volatility of these options is 25 percent and XYZ is trading at 67.50. The goal of this trade is to have XYZ settle between 65.00 and 70.00 at expiration.

The XYZ May 60/65/70/75 Long Put Condor is created through buying the XYZ May 60 Put and XYZ May 75 Put options for a total cost of 8.60 (8.35 + 0.25) and selling the XYZ May 65 Put and XYZ May 70 Put options for a total income of 6.70 (2.05 + 4.65). The net result is a cost of 1.90 for the spread.

Key levels for this trade are displayed in Table 10.5. Like the call version of the long condor, the maximum potential profit for this trade occurs between the two middle strike prices. At this level the spread has a maximum value of 5.00, based on two of the four options being in the money. With the long put condor the two options with value are the higher strike

TABLE 10.5 Key Levels for the XYZ May 60/65/70/75 Long Put Condor Spread

	Level	Explanation
Up Break-even Price	73.10	High Strike minus Cost
Down Break-even Price	61.90	Low Strike plus Cost
Maximum Dollar Gain	3.10	Maximum Spread Value minus Cost
Maximum Gain Prices	Between 65.00 and 70.00	Spread Worth Maximum Value
Maximum Dollar Loss	1.90	Cost of Spread
Maximum Loss Prices	60.00 and Under 75.00 and Over	Spread Has No Value

options. For this trade, the long position in the XYZ May 75 Put will be worth 5.00 more than the short position in the XYZ May 70 Put. The other two strike options are out of the money with XYZ between 65.00 and 70.00 at expiration and have no impact on the profit or loss for this spread. The spread is worth 5.00, but 1.90 was paid to enter the spread, so the net profit is 3.10.

The break-even levels are determined in the same method as the long call condor. Adding the cost of the spread to the lowest strike option or subtracting it from the highest strike option results in the break-even levels. At the higher break even of 73.10, only the XYZ May 75 Put has value and this value is equal to the cost of the spread, 1.90. The lower strike takes three of the four options into account as there is value in the 65, 70, and 75 strike options. The 75 strike option has 1.90 more in value than the combination of the short 70 and 65 strike options. At 61.90, the 75 Put is worth 13.10, the 70 Put is worth 8.10, and the 65 Put is worth 3.10. The short put values come to 11.20 (8.10 + 3.10) and the long put is worth 13.10. Once again, the spread is worth the cost of 1.90 (13.10 − 11.20).

Note the maximum loss matches the cost of the spread and this will occur at price levels below 60.00 and over 75.00. This maximum loss comes about as the spread has no value in either of these ranges. Above 75.00 this is a simple concept, all options expire with no value and the spread is worth 0.00. Below 60.00 the spread is worth 0.00, but getting to this point is a bit of a different exercise.

Below 60.00 all four options from the spread are in the money. Using a settlement price of 50.00 at expiration, the spread value is displayed in Table 10.6.

Note in the table there is 35.00 of long option value and 35.00 of short option value with the stock at 50.00 at expiration. The long and short option values in this spread will offset each other at any level below the lowest strike of 60.00, with the result being 0.00 and the loss limited to the cost of the spread.

TABLE 10.6 XYZ May 60/65/70/75 Long Put Condor Value with XYZ at 50.00 at Expiration

	Profit/Loss
Long 1 XYZ May 60 Put	10.00
Short 1 XYZ May 65 Put	−15.00
Short 1 XYZ May 70 Put	−20.00
Long 1 XYZ May 75 Put	25.00
XYZ May 60/65/70/75 Long Put Condor	0.00

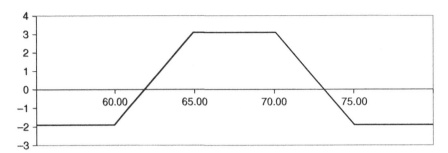

FIGURE 10.2 Payoff Diagram for the XYZ Jan 60/65/70/75 Long Put Condor Spread

Finally, the payout diagram in Figure 10.2 shows the payout for the XYZ 60/65/70/75 Long Put Condor at all of these levels. The range of maximum profitability is a range between 65.00 and 70.00. This graphical depiction is nice to see and can always be transposed to a stock price chart as support and resistance levels to be held until expiration. A similar exercise may be done with the breakeven and maximum loss levels to get another visual on how the trade may play out at expiration.

Both the long call and long put condors share many features. They have a similar potential payout structure and impose debits to a trader's account when the trade is initiated. The goal is the same, for a stock to land in a range at expiration.

As with the butterfly, there is an iron version of the long condor. An iron condor will take a combination of put and call options with the same strike makeup as the long versions, with all the same type of options and creates the same type of payout structure.

IRON CONDOR

An iron condor is one of the most popular strategies amongst intermediate-level traders. In fact there are many option strategists and educators who spend a big portion (if not all) of their time discussing and recommending trades in this strategy. The reasons for this are twofold.

First, the payoff at expiration of an iron condor is the same as the payoff for a long condor, which was covered in the previous two sections. The combination of a wide area of profitability and known risk and reward going into a trade is very attractive to traders. Also, in contrast to the previous two examples, an iron condor will be initiated with a credit as opposed to a debit to a trader's account. Many individuals like the idea of putting on a trade they find attractive and being paid to do so.

An iron condor, like the iron butterfly, is a spread that involves a combination of two put options and two call options. The first two strikes would be put options with the lowest strike being purchased and the higher strike being sold. The two call options would be higher strike options, in the same fashion as the long condor, consisting of the same type of options. The highest strike call would be purchased with the lower strike being sold.

There are two ways to approach and break down the iron condor. One would be as a combination of a bull put spread and a bear call spread. Each of these vertical spreads is always initiated as a credit, just as the iron condor always results in a credit. Another way to approach the iron condor is as a short strangle. The put and call options that are sold would result in a short strangle if it were not for the options that are purchased to complete the iron condor. The put and call that are purchased are less expensive than the sold options and offer protection from potential unlimited loss that comes with putting on a short strangle.

To create the sample iron condor, the options in Table 10.7 were used. For this position, XYZ is trading at 32.50 and August expiration is being targeted on a time basis. These options have 70 days until expiration and are trading based an implied volatility of 35 percent.

Using the options from this table, the XYZ Aug 25/30/35/40 Iron Condor is put on at a credit of 1.65. This credit is received due to the more expensive call and put options being sold and the less expensive of each type of option being purchased. On the put side of the trade, the XYZ Aug 25 Put is purchased for .10 and the XYZ Aug 30 Put is sold for .90, resulting in a credit of .80 from the puts. On the call side, the XYZ Aug 35 Call

TABLE 10.7 Inputs and Output Used to Create an XYZ Aug 25/30/35/40 Iron Condor

Inputs	
Days	70
Volatility	35%
Interest Rate	1.00%
XYZ Price	32.50
Output	
XYZ Aug 25 Put	0.10
XYZ Aug 30 Put	0.90
XYZ Aug 35 Call	1.05
XYZ Aug 40 Call	0.20
XYZ Aug 25/30/35/40 Iron Condor	1.65

TABLE 10.8   Key Levels for the XYZ Aug 25/30/35/40 Iron Condor Spread

	Level	Explanation
Up Break-even Price	36.65	Middle Call Strike plus Credit
Down Break-even Price	28.35	Middle Put Strike minus Credit
Maximum Dollar Gain	1.65	Spread Has No Value
Maximum Gain Prices	Between 30.00 and 35.00	All Options Expire Out Of The Money
Maximum Dollar Loss	3.35	Maximum Spread Value minus Credit
Maximum Loss Prices	25.00 and Under 40.00 and Over	Spread Has No Value

is sold for 1.05 and the XYZ Aug 40 Call is purchased for .20 resulting in income of .85. Both credits added together, 0.80 plus 0.85, result in income of 1.65.

In Table 10.8, the key levels for an iron condor are similar to the key levels for the long versions of this trade that use the same type of options. However, the method to determine these levels is a bit different. The maximum potential gain for this iron condor is the credit received for putting the trade on. Between the two inside strike prices of 35.00 and 40.00, all options in the spread expire with no value. When this occurs, the credit of 1.65 received is kept by the trader.

Break-even levels for this spread are determined by taking the middle strike prices of the spread and adding the credit to the higher of the middle strikes and subtracting the credit from the lower of the strikes. As the call options are the options with lower strikes, the credit would be subtracted from the strike of the XYZ Aug 30 Call to determine a downside breakeven of 28.35 (30.00 − 1.65). Put options are the highest two strike options in this spread. The lower of these two put options is the XYZ Aug 35 Put, and adding the credit of 1.65 to 35.00 determines the upside break-even level of 36.65.

Finally the maximum potential loss for this trade results with a close at expiration outside either of the highest or lowest strike prices in the spread. Much like the calculation of the maximum potential gain, the levels are the same as the long call and put condors, but the method of determining these varies a bit.

On the downside, any XYZ close below 25.00 would result in a maximum loss of 3.35 on this trade. At 25.00 the value of the spread is 5.00. This value comes from only two of the options in the spread. In a case of a close lower than 30.00, the call options are out of the money and have no value. Under 30.00, both of the put options in the spread have value, with the short option being worth 5.00 more than the long option. For example,

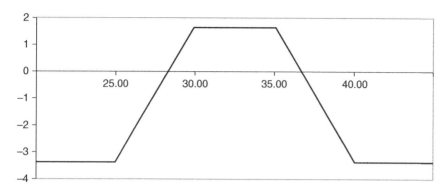

FIGURE 10.3 Payoff Diagram for the XYZ Aug 25/30/35/40 Iron Condor Spread

if XYZ were at 20.00 at expiration, the short XYZ Aug 30 Put would be worth 10.00 while the long XYZ Aug 25 Put would be worth 5.00. This results in a spread value of 5.00 against the position holder. The credit received of 1.65 may be added back to the 5.00 deficit to result in a loss of 3.35.

On the upside, the math is the same, but relates only to the call options in the spread. Over the highest spread strike price of 40.00, the put options in the spread expire with no value, but the two call options are both in the money. The short call option in the spread is 5.00 more in the money than the long call option, which results in a negative spread value of 5.00 to the trader. As an example, if XYZ is at 45.00 at expiration, the short XYZ Aug 35.00 Call would be worth 10.00 and the long XYZ Aug 40 Call would have 5.00 of value. As the spread is 5.00 against the trader, but a credit of 1.65 was received for initiating the spread, the trade ends up a 3.35 loser.

Figure 10.3 is a payoff diagram for the XYZ Aug 25/30/35/40 Iron Condor. The payout is a replication of the long call and put condor payouts from the previous two sections in this chapter. As mentioned before, many options traders consistently implement iron condor spreads in their accounts. With a wide payout range, limited risk, and the ability to implement this trade by taking in a credit, it makes sense that traders would see this as a preferable spread. Although a credit seems attractive, checking the comparable long call and put condors for a slightly better risk reward scenario should be done.

Note that the center of the iron condor payout diagram appears the same as a short strangle. Until the stock price reaches either of the outside strike prices with the condor, the payout is exactly the same. This raises the question as to why would a trader give up some potential profitability of this spread through buying the wings. The simple answer is risk management, as the short strangle results in potential unlimited loss. Buying the wings is a bit of insurance against maximum loss.

IRON CONDOR VERSUS SHORT STRANGLE

The short strangle was covered in Chapter 6, but a quick review is in order. A short strangle involves selling two options, a lower strike put option and a higher strike call option. Due to the spread having two naked short option positions, there is a high amount of risk if a trader's forecast is incorrect.

The motivations behind trading a short strangle or an iron condor are basically the same, the expectation that a stock is going to be in a certain range at expiration. If a trader's forecast is correct, the payout on a short strangle will be superior to the payout on an iron condor with the same forecast. This difference is due to no options being purchased to create a short strangle. With no options purchased for protection, more income would be realized when the short strangle was executed as opposed to the comparable iron condor.

For an example comparing the short strangle and iron condor, the same inputs and options that were used for the previous example will be used. The XYZ Aug 25/30/35/40 Iron Condor would be created in the same method as before and result in a credit of 1.65. A short strangle with the same profit range would be created by selling the XYZ Aug 30 Put for 0.90 and the XYZ Aug 35 Call for 1.05. The result is an XYZ Aug 30/35 Short Strangle at a credit of 1.95. These inputs are shown in Table 10.9.

A key level comparison of the two spreads is shown in Table 10.10. The differences are not terribly significant in this example. This is not

TABLE 10.9	Inputs and Output Used to Create an XYZ Aug 25/30/35/40 Iron Condor and XYZ Aug 30/35 Short Strangle	
Inputs		
Days		70
Volatility		35%
Interest Rate		1.00%
XYZ Price		32.50
Output		
XYZ Aug 25 Put		0.10
XYZ Aug 30 Put		0.90
XYZ Aug 35 Call		1.05
XYZ Aug 40 Call		0.20
XYZ Aug 25/30/35/40 Iron Condor		1.65
XYZ Aug 30/35 Short Strangle		1.95

TABLE 10.10 Key Level Comparison for the Aug XYZ 25/30/35/40 Iron Condor and Aug XYZ 30/35 Short Strangle

	XYZ Aug 25/30/35/ 40 Iron Condor	XYZ Aug 30/35 Short Strangle
Up Break-even Price	36.65	36.95
Down Break-even Price	28.35	28.05
Maximum Dollar Gain	1.65	1.95
Maximum Gain Prices	30.00 to 35.00	30.00 to 35.00
Maximum Dollar Loss	3.35	Substantial/Unlimited
Maximum Loss Prices	25.00 and Under 40.00 and Over	0.00 and Unlimited

always the situation; sometimes a good portion of the upside in a trade may be given up when some of the income from selling options is sacrificed in order to have some protection for a substantial or unlimited loss. As with every trade, options, or other instrument, there is always a tradeoff to consider with risk and reward.

As far as specific levels go, the potential profit of the strangle is 1.95 and 1.65 for the iron condor. So for paying 0.30 a trader has given up a small potential profit, but now has protection from potentially an unlimited or substantial loss. The iron condor holder would realize a maximum loss of 3.35 at any level over 25.00 or under 40.00, while the short strangle position theoretically has unlimited loss. Finally, the break-even levels are pretty close in this comparison; with the short strangle breaking even a little farther away from the middle strikes than the iron condor. Once again this difference is only 0.30. A trader considering this position would need to weigh whether paying out the 0.30 and giving up some small differences would be worthwhile on a risk reward basis.

Figure 10.4 displays the payoff differences between the two spreads. Due to the small difference in credits received on these two spreads, the payout lines almost overlap until the strike prices of 25.00 and 40.00 are reached. Outside of those two points a trader that puts on the iron condor is happy they chose to buy the wings to limit risk.

Due to the out-of-the-money nature of the outside strike prices on an Iron Condor the premiums for the options that would be purchased are usually pretty low. Even traders that have the ability or proper permission to put on naked short option positions often choose to buy the wings as cheap protection. When considering a short strangle, checking out how much upside may be given up by buying this protection is always worth a look.

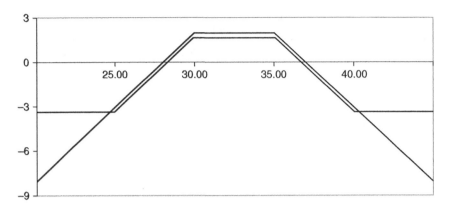

FIGURE 10.4 Payoff Diagram Comparing the XYZ Aug 25/30/35/40 Iron Condor and Aug 30/35 Short Strangle

SHORT CONDOR SPREADS

A short condor using all of the same type of options may be constructed with the result being a short call condor or short put condor. Like the short butterfly spreads with all of the same type of options, the short spread gets the name due to the wings being sold in the spread. Also, the fact that these spreads are done at a debit, or cost, contributes to this short naming.

There is also an iron version of the short condor, appropriately named the reverse iron condor as it is a reverse position of the iron condor. Each of these spreads will be covered in this section.

Short Call Condor

A short call condor is a spread that would be initiated with the expectation of a large move in one direction or another, with uncertainty as to which direction this move might be. The closest comparable to the payout of a short call condor may be the long strangle that was discussed in Chapter 6. There are often situations in the market where an announcement or event on the horizon that will have a dramatic impact on the price of a stock. The key unknown is whether this will be a positive or negative impact on the price of the stock. Initially, traders consider a long straddle or strangle to benefit from these events. However, as option prices usually anticipate events, to trade one of these events may be prohibitively expensive. In a situation like that, a short condor may be a viable alternative to a long strangle.

To create a short call condor, there are four different call options involved. All have the same underlying and expiration, but each is a different strike price. The distance between the first two strikes and the last two strikes should be equal, but this is not a requirement for the distance between the middle strike prices. In the past, this was not too much of an issue due to the limited number of strike prices, but there continue to be more option series offered in strike increments of a dollar. With more strike prices available, the possibility of creating even more customized payouts increases.

An example of a short call condor is going to assume XYZ has dollar strike prices available. With XYZ trading at 46.00, a trader believes the stock will either make a move to the upside or downside of around 15 percent in the next 40 days. November expiration is 40 days out and the implied volatility for those options is 32.50 percent. Table 10.11 summarizes the inputs and option outputs to determine the credit behind the short call condor.

To initiate this short call condor, the XYZ Nov 40 Call would be sold for a credit of 6.25 and the XYZ Nov 52 Call would also be sold for a credit of .30. These two option sales would bring in a total credit of 6.55. The call options trading at the inside strike prices would be purchased for a debit of 4.70, specifically buying the XYZ Nov 43 Call at 3.80 and the XYZ Nov 49 Call at 0.90. The result would be a credit of 1.85 (6.55 − 4.70) for putting on the XYZ Nov 40/43/49/52 Short Call Condor.

The key levels for this trade appear in Table 10.12. Due to the strike prices in this spread not being equidistant from each other, the calculation of the payouts are a little different than the previous condor and butterfly spreads.

TABLE 10.11 Inputs and Output Used to Create an XYZ Nov 40/43/49/52 Short Call Condor

Inputs	
Days	40
Volatility	32.5%
Interest Rate	1.00%
XYZ Price	46.00
Output	
XYZ Nov 40 Call	6.25
XYZ Nov 43 Call	3.80
XYZ Nov 49 Call	0.90
XYZ Nov 52 Call	0.30
XYZ Nov 40/43/49/52 Short Call Condor	1.85

TABLE 10.12   Key Levels for the XYZ Nov 40/43/49/52 Short Call Condor
Spread

	Level	Explanation
Up Break-even Price	50.15	Highest Strike minus Credit
Down Break-even Price	41.85	Lowest Strike plus Credit
Maximum Dollar Gain	1.85	Credit Received
Maximum Gain Prices	40.00 and Under	Spread has No Value
	52.00 and Over	
Maximum Dollar Loss	1.15	Maximum Spread Value minus Credit
Maximum Loss Prices	Between 43.00 and 49.00	Spread at Maximum Value

The maximum potential gain of this spread is the credit received of 1.85 that was taken to initiate the trade. This gain is realized if the underlying undergoes a pretty large move to the upside or downside. If XYZ is under 40.00 at expiration, all call options expire with no value and the credit taken in is kept. To the upside, if the stock is over 52.00 at expiration, the value of the spread is 0.00. The value of the two long options is offset by the value of the two short options in the spread. Once again the credit received is realized as the profit for this trade.

In a case of a maximum loss being realized, only the two lower strike options will come into play. The maximum loss in this particular trade occurs if XYZ is between 43.00 and 49.00 at expiration. Only the XYZ 40 and 43 strike call options have value in this case. As the XYZ Nov 40 Call would have 3.00 more value than the XYZ Nov 43 Call, the result would be a value of 3.00 against the trader. This 3.00 deficit is the result of being long the option that is worth 3.00 less than the short option. Since 1.85 was taken in to put this trade on, the result is a loss of 1.15 (3.00 − 1.15).

The payoff diagram for this short call condor appears in Figure 10.5. All short call and put condors have a payoff that flattens out between the middle strike prices and then start to benefit from stock price moves outside those strike prices. Above the highest or below the lowest strike price the profitability of the spread is capped. This cap is the result of the spread having no value at either of these levels.

Short Put Condor

A short put condor is a basic repeat of the previous spread. The payout calculations are slightly different for the maximum loss, but like the long counterpart, the motivation and construction of the trade is basically the same.

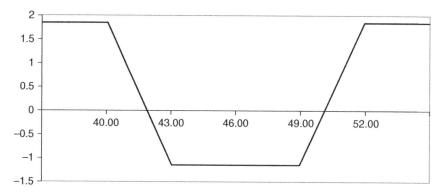

FIGURE 10.5 Payoff Diagram for the XYZ Nov 40/43/49/52 Short Call Condor

An example of a short put condor starts out with the options in Table 10.13. A trade is considered as there is an expectation of a 20 percent move either higher or lower out of XYZ in the next 55 days. To capitalize on this opinion, with XYZ at 33.00, the XYZ Jul 27/31/35/39 Short Put Condor is put on. A 20 percent move from XYZ would land the stock just past 27.00 on the downside or above 39 on the upside at expiration.

By selling the XYZ Jul 27 Put for 0.15 and the XYZ Jul 39 Put for 6.15, a credit is received of 6.30. Offsetting this is an outflow of 4.05 to pay for the XYZ Jul 31 Put and XYZ Jul 35 Put. The net result is a credit of 2.25 for initiating the XYZ Nov 27/31/35/39 Short Put Condor.

Like the short call condor, the maximum potential profit on this trade is the credit received of 2.25. If the stock is outside the higher or lower strike prices of the spread, the value of the spread will be 0.00. In the case

TABLE 10.13 Inputs and Output Used to Create an XYZ Jul 27/31/35/39 Short Put Condor

Inputs	
Days	55
Volatility	37.5%
Interest Rate	1.00%
XYZ Price	33.00
Output	
XYZ Jul 27 Put	0.15
XYZ Jul 31 Put	1.00
XYZ Jul 35 Put	3.05
XYZ Jul 39 Put	6.15
XYZ Jul 27/31/35/39 Short Put Condor	2.25

TABLE 10.14 Key Levels for the XYZ Jul 27/31/35/39 Short Put Condor Spread

	Level	Explanation
Up Break-even Price	36.75	Highest Strike minus Credit
Down Break-even Price	29.25	Lowest Strike plus Credit
Maximum Dollar Gain	2.25	Credit Received
Maximum Gain Prices	27.00 and Under 39.00 and Over	Spread has No Value
Maximum Dollar Loss	1.75	Maximum Spread Value minus Credit
Maximum Loss Prices	Between 31.00 and 35.00	Spread at Maximum Value

of the stock being over 39.00, this is an easy calculation as all options have no value. Under 27.00, all options would be in the money, but the value of the short options would be equal to the long options, netting out to a value of 0.00. In either case the credit received of 2.25 would be kept.

The maximum potential loss on this trade occurs if the spread reaches a value of 4.00. This is the most the spread can be worth at expiration and this would be the case with the stock between 31.00 and 35.00 at expiration. In this range, only the XYZ Jul 35 and XYZ Jul 39 Put options would be in the money. As the short position in the XYZ Jul 39 Put would have 4.00 more value than the long position in the XYZ Jul 35 Put, the spread would be worth 4.00. However, this would be a debit of 4.00 to the trader. Netted against the 2.25 taken in to initiate the trade results in a loss of 1.75.

Finally, the break-even levels for this trade are determined in the same way as for the call counterpart. On the downside the credit received is added to the lowest strike price and to the upside the credit is subtracted from the highest strike price. For this trade the result is a break even trade at 29.25 and 36.75. All key levels for this trade are covered in Table 10.14.

The payoff diagram for this trade appears in Figure 10.6. This payout has the same appearance as the short call condor in the previous example. These two trades are interchangeable as they both take in a credit and that credit is the maximum potential gain for the trade. The break-even levels are similar, just the math behind determining those levels is slightly different.

REVERSE IRON CONDOR

The final type of condor to be covered in this chapter is the reverse iron condor. This spread, like the iron condor, combines put and call options,

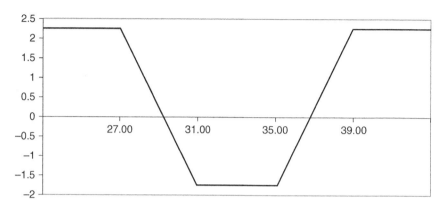

FIGURE 10.6 Payoff Diagram for the XYZ Jul 27/31/35/39 Short Put Condor

but unlike the iron condor the payoff on a reverse iron condor replicates a short condor. Although the reverse iron condor replicates a short call or put condor payout, the reverse iron condor will be initiated at a debit instead of a credit. As many traders prefer taking in a credit for this payoff, the reverse iron condor is usually considered as an afterthought to a long call or long put condor.

The options that will be used in this example appear in Table 10.15. December options have 60 days to expiration and an implied volatility of 35 percent. The underlying stock is trading at 42.50 and the price projection is for a move of 7.50 up or down over the next two months. To trade this, a trader decides to initiate the XYZ Dec 35/40/45/50 Reverse Iron Condor.

TABLE 10.15 Inputs and Output Used to Create an XYZ Dec 35/40/45/50 Reverse Iron Condor

Inputs	
Days	60
Volatility	35%
Interest Rate	1.00%
XYZ Price	42.50
Output	
XYZ Dec 35 Put	0.20
XYZ Dec 40 Put	1.25
XYZ Dec 45 Call	1.45
XYZ Dec 50 Call	0.40
XYZ Dec 35/40/45/50 Reverse Iron Condor	2.10

TABLE 10.16 Key Levels for the XYZ Dec 35/40/45/50 Reverse Iron Condor

	Level	Explanation
Up Break-even Price	47.10	High Middle Strike plus Cost
Down Break-even Price	37.90	Low Middle Strike minus Cost
Maximum Dollar Gain	2.90	Maximum Spread Value minus Cost
Maximum Gain Prices	35.00 and Under 50.00 and Over	Spread has Maximum Value
Maximum Dollar Loss	2.10	Cost of Spread
Maximum Loss Prices	Between 40.00 and 45.00	Spread has No Value

The reverse iron condor involves selling the wings and purchasing the inside options. In this trade, the XYZ Dec 35 Put and XYZ Dec 50 Call options are sold for a credit of 0.60 (0.20 + 0.40). The two options that are purchased, the XYZ Dec 40 Put and XYZ Dec 45 Call, cost a total of 2.70. The result is a debit of 2.10 to initiate this trade.

The key levels for this trade appear in Table 10.16 and are very similar to the key levels that might have resulted from using all call or all put options to trade a short condor. Once again, the method of calculating these levels is a bit different.

The maximum gain for the spread would be 2.90. This would be realized if the spread has a value of 5.00, which would occur below 35.00 or above 50.00 at expiration. If the stock is below 35.00, both the 35 and 40 strike put options are in the money and the call options are out of the money. At any value below 35.00, the long XYZ Dec 40 Put would be worth 5.00 more than the short XYZ Dec 35 Put. The spread would be worth 5.00, but 2.10 was paid to enter the trade with the result being a profit of 2.90.

If the stock rallies over 50.00 at expiration, the call options have value with the put options expiring out of the money. In this case the long call with a 45 strike would be worth 5.00 more than the short 50 call. Once again the result is a profit of 2.90 when the cost of 2.10 is subtracted from the spread value.

The two break-even levels would be determined by subtracting the cost of the spread from the lower of the middle strike prices and adding the cost to the higher of the middle strikes. In either of these cases, a long option would be worth 2.10 and neither of the short options would have any value. The spread would be worth 2.10 with a cost of 2.10 a break-even result.

Finally, a payout diagram for this trade appears in Figure 10.7. It has a very similar appearance to the short call and put condors, once again on the only difference between the all call and all put spreads is a credit for either of those versus a debit to put on the reverse iron condor.

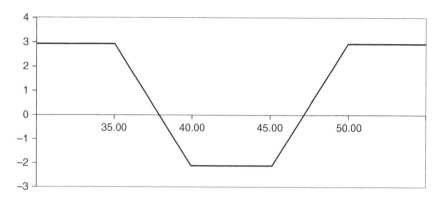

FIGURE 10.7 Payoff Diagram for the XYZ Dec 35/40/45/50 Reverse Iron Condor

REVERSE IRON CONDOR VERSUS LONG STRANGLE

The question arises, why purchase a reverse iron condor and limit potential gains when the income from the wings is not terribly significant. Or put another way, "Why not just purchase the long strangle?" A specific reason relates to the implied volatility of options and how the implied volatility of options reacts to known events. When a company or stock-specific event such as a quarterly earnings announcement is on the horizon, the implied volatility of options tends to rise. After the known event or announcement, the implied volatility will usually return to more normal or lower levels.

For example, if XYZ is going to announce a potential stock-moving event, the implied volatility of call and put options may rise to 40 percent versus a historical norm of 25 percent. Post the event, the implied volatility should return to the 25 percent level. With XYZ trading at 35.00, call and put options with 20 days to expiration and an implied volatility of 40 percent would be trading around 1.30. One day later, with the stock at 35.00 and the implied volatility at 25 percent, both options would have lost about 0.50 of value and be trading at 0.80. The possibility of an announcement having no price impact on XYZ is pretty remote, but this example shows what impact the drop in implied volatility will have on option values.

Both a long strangle and a reverse iron condor are strategies to use when trying to benefit from a big stock move. However, when attempting to benefit from a short-term move, consideration should be given to implied volatility returning to a more normal level after an announcement.

For example, XYZ is trading at 62.50 and earnings are going to be announced after the market close. The belief is that the stock should move

TABLE 10.17   Inputs and Output Used to Create an XYZ July 60/65 Long Strangle and XYZ July 55/60/65/70 Reverse Iron Condor

Inputs	
Days	15
Volatility	45%
Interest Rate	1.00%
XYZ Price	62.50
Output	
XYZ Jul 55 Put	0.30
XYZ Jul 60 Put	1.20
XYZ Jul 65 Call	1.30
XYZ Jul 70 Call	0.20
XYZ Jul 60/65 Long Strangle	2.50
XYZ Jul 55/60/65/70 Reverse Iron Condor	2.00

about 5.00 higher or lower based on past history. The idea behind the trade is to initiate the spread very near the close and then exit the following day.

In this case, the best options for the XYZ trade are the July expiration options. The July expiration is the next option expiration and there is very little time value left in these options. However, due to the anticipation of earnings, the implied volatility of XYZ July options has increased to 45 percent from a normal level of 25 percent. There are 15 days left until July expiration, post earnings there will be 14 days left. The options that will be used in this example appear in Table 10.17.

Note that both the long strangle and reverse iron condor are priced in Table 10.17. These are two of the best alternatives to consider for this short-term trade. The XYZ Jul 60/65 Long Strangle would cost 2.50, as 1.20 is paid for the XYZ Jul 60 Put and 1.30 in premium is paid for the XYZ Jul 65 Call. To put on the XYZ Jul 55/60/65/70 Reverse Iron Condor, both of these options are purchased, but the cost if offset by income taken in from selling the XYZ Jul 55 Put and XYZ Jul 70 Call. Selling these two options brings in 0.50 and reduces the cost of the trade to 2.00. In exchange, the upside to this trade is limited relative to the long strangle, but with the anticipated move of 5.00 higher or lower this may be a better alternative. Especially with the belief that implied volatility will move lower and reduce the value of all options.

The option values in Table 10.18 display the value of all four options assuming a day has passed and the implied volatility has dropped from 45 percent to a historically more normal level of 25 percent. The anticipation of this trade was for the stock to rally or drop 5.00 on earnings. This would result in a stock price of 57.50 or 67.50 the following day. Both the

TABLE 10.18   Long Strangle and Reverse Iron Condor Values with Implied Volatility of 25 Percent and 14 Days to Expiration

XYZ	55 Put	60 Put	65 Call	70 Call	Long Strangle	Reverse Iron Condor
55.00	1.10	5.05	0.00	0.00	5.05	3.95
57.50	0.30	2.80	0.00	0.00	2.80	2.50
60.00	0.05	1.15	0.10	0.00	1.25	1.20
62.50	0.00	0.35	0.40	0.00	0.75	0.75
65.00	0.00	0.05	1.30	0.10	1.35	1.25
67.50	0.00	0.00	2.85	0.35	2.85	2.50
70.00	0.00	0.00	5.10	1.35	5.10	3.75

long strangle and reverse iron condor trades make money, but the reverse iron condor makes 0.50 while the long strangle is up 0.30 or 0.35 depending on the direction of the stock move. The profit is a little bit lower on the long strangle and also on a larger investment in the trade of 2.50 versus 2.00 for the reverse iron condor.

To the upside, if the stock rallies well beyond anticipation, the long strangle would benefit, while the reverse iron condor would be limited in profitability due to the short option positions. In case the stock does not move as anticipated, both spreads would lose money. However, the reverse iron condor loses less as the out-of-the-money short options quickly lose their value with a drop in implied volatility.

The tradeoff here is limiting upside, but a cheaper method to trade the anticipated move from the underlying stock. Also, the benefit of a smaller loss in the case of the anticipated stock reaction not occurring exists due to the income realized from selling the options in the reverse iron condor.

Due to the known risk and reward associated with condors, especially iron condors, these spreads are some of the more popular exotic spreads for individual traders. Intermediate to advanced traders tend to turn to an iron condor when they believe a stock or index may be in a range for a period of time that coincides with the expiration date of the option contracts. Finally, even professional traders who have the ability to put on naked short option positions often turn to an iron condor for the protection offered by buying the wings.

Ratio Spreads

This chapter and Chapter 12 on backspreads are very closely related topics. Both a ratio spread and a backspread are the result of combining the same type of options in a spread, with one strike being long and the other strike being short. However, both these types of spreads consist of an unbalanced number of short and long options. The result is a unique payoff and risk structure. The idea behind splitting the strategies into two separate chapters is that the ratio spreads created with both calls and puts have a higher risk profile than the backspread. Also, ratio spreads are considered more neutral, while backspreads are considered more directional in nature.

A ratio spread, also called a vertical ratio spread or a front spread, consists of more short options than long options. Generally they are illustrated as two short options to one long option, but the number of options on each side or proportion of options relative to each other is unlimited. The key behind a spread being considered a ratio spread is that there are more short options than long options. To keep the examples simple in this chapter, a two-to-one ratio spread will be used in the example.

What is unusual about a ratio spread is that it shares some common traits with a long butterfly and with a short straddle. The payout of a ratio spread is maximized at a certain strike price, much like it would be for both a long butterfly and a short straddle. On the risk side, one direction is protected by a long option so there is limited risk, much like the long butterfly. The other direction does not have the long option protection in place, so there is substantial or unlimited risk in another direction, much like the short straddle.

There are two types of ratio spreads, call ratio spreads and put ratio spreads. Both are basically neutral in that the maximum profit from either results from a closing price right at a certain strike price. Also both of these ratio spreads have a price direction where there is substantial or unlimited risk. The interesting aspect of this is that the ratio spread created with call options has unlimited risk to the upside, while ratio spreads created with put options have unlimited risk to the downside.

CALL RATIO SPREAD

There are two types of ratio spreads, call ratio spreads and put ratio spreads. Both are basically neutral, in that the maximum profit from either results from a closing price right at a certain strike price. Also both of these ratio spreads have a price direction where there is substantial or unlimited risk. The interesting aspect of this is that the ratio spread created with call options has unlimited risk to the upside, while ratio spreads created with put options have unlimited risk to the downside.

A call ratio spread would be initiated through selling two call options at a high strike price and buying a single call option at a lower strike price. Once again, this two-to-one ratio is for simplicity, the ratio can differ as long as there are a higher number of short call options than long call options.

For example, a ratio call spread might be constructed by buying a 30 call and selling two 35 calls. Usually, these spreads may be initiated at a small credit or debit, depending on the time to expiration and where the underlying stock is trading at the time. Normally, the lower strike option will be in the money and the higher strike options will be out of the money, with the goal of the trade that the stock lands very close to the higher strike at expiration. If the trade is put on at a credit, then a small profit may also be made at any price below the higher strike. However, the risk to this trade is a very bullish move in the underlying stock. With one of the higher strike short call options uncovered, the potential for unlimited losses exists with this trade.

The options in Table 11.1 were used to develop an example of a ratio call spread. With XYZ trading at 34.00, the May options have 90 days to expiration and an implied volatility of 50 percent. The XYZ May 30 Call is trading at 5.60 and the XYZ May 35 Call is trading at 2.95. To create the XYZ May 30/35 Ratio Call Spread, two of the May 35 Calls are sold for a total of 5.90 (2.95 each) and one of the XYZ May 30 Calls is purchased for 5.60. The result is a net credit of 0.30 for initiating this spread.

TABLE 11.1 Inputs and Output Used to Create an
XYZ May 30/35 Call Ratio Spread

Inputs

Days	90
Volatility	50%
Interest Rate	1.00%
XYZ Price	34.00

Output

XYZ May 30 Call	5.60
XYZ May 35 Call	2.95
XYZ May 30/35 Call Ratio Spread	0.30

Table 11.2 shows the key levels for this call ratio spread. These figures are a unique combination of levels and prices. Each will be covered closely due to their complex nature relative to most of the other spreads discussed thus far in this book.

The first key levels to focus on are the maximum dollar gain and maximum gain price. The maximum potential gain from this trade is 5.30. This is determined through two factors. First, the 0.30 credit received from initiating the trade and then the profit at 35.00 that would be realized from the option positions. At 35.00 at expiration, the two short May 35 Call options would have no value. However, the single long May 30 Call would have 5.00 in value. With 5.00 from the long call position and 0.30 from initiating the trade, a maximum profit of 5.30 at 35.00 is determined.

Since the option spread has two short call option positions and one long call option position, the spread has a naked short call position. Due to this short call, the risk profile for this spread results in a theoretically unlimited loss scenario. This is more academic than reality, but the

TABLE 11.2 Key Levels for the XYZ May 30/35 Call Ratio Spread

	Level	Explanation
Break-even Price	40.30	Difference Between Strikes plus High Strike plus Credit
Maximum Dollar Gain	5.30	Credit plus High Strike minus Low Strike
Maximum Gain Price	35.00	Spread Worth Maximum Value
Maximum Dollar Loss	Unlimited	Stock Rallies
Maximum Loss Price	Unlimited	Second Short Call Value Unlimited

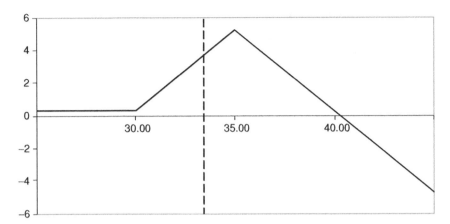

FIGURE 11.1 Payoff Diagram for the XYZ May 30/35 Call Ratio Spread

fact exists that there is a short call option that will incur losses as the stock rises.

Finally, the break-even level is determined through a number of factors. At 40.00 the options would net out to a value of 0.00. The long 30 Call would be worth 10.00 and the two short 35 strike call options would have a value that is a negative 10.00 to the trader. Of course this does not take the credit for initiating the spread into consideration. So at 40.00, there is still a credit of 0.30 that was kept by the trader for initiating the trade. The result is a breakeven comes at 40.30, where the naked short option has moved 0.30 higher to offset that credit received.

Figure 11.1 is a payoff diagram for the XYZ May 30/35 Call Ratio Spread. Note the left side of the diagram looks very similar to a long butterfly spread while the right side of the diagram is like the short straddle. At any price level below 40.30, there is some sort of profit realized from this spread. As the pricing of XYZ moves lower from 40.30 and approaches the higher strike price of 35.00, the profit of this strategy increases. This increase is due to the value of the two short options decreasing at a faster rate than the value of the single long option.

Below 35.00 the value of the short call options is 0.00, but there is still value in the long 30 strike call, as long as the stock closes above 30.00 at expiration. Below 30.00 there is no value in any of the options that comprise the ratio spread, but the small premium of 0.30 that was received when the spread was initiated is kept by the trader.

Note there is a vertical dashed line on the chart depicting the price of the underlying stock when the trade was initiated. XYZ was at 34.00, which is comfortably in the range of profitability at expiration. Although it

TABLE 11.3 Inputs and Output Used to Create an XYZ Mar 30/32 Call Ratio Call Spread

Inputs	
Days	60
Volatility	35%
Interest Rate	1.00%
XYZ Price	29.00
Output	
XYZ Mar 30 Call	1.45
XYZ Mar 32 Call	0.80
XYZ Mar 30/32 Call Ratio Spread	0.15

is common for a trader to initiate a ratio spread when the stock is in this area, it is not a rule. The next example is a ratio spread that was initiated with a stock at a level that is outside this range.

There is also the possibility of using a ratio spread as a more directional trading vehicle. For instance, if XYZ is trading at 29.00 and a trader believes the stock is going to trade up to 32.00 in 60 days, there may be a ratio spread that matches this price projection. After searching option chains, the option values in Table 11.3 are used to develop an example of a directionally based ratio spread.

With XYZ trading at 29.00, combining the Mar 30 and 32 Call options to create a call ratio spread looks attractive on a pricing basis using an implied volatility of 35 percent. The XYZ Mar 30 Call is trading at 1.45, while the XYZ Mar 32 Call is pricing at 0.80. If two of the 32 strike call options are sold and a single 30 call is purchased the result is a credit of 0.15.

The key levels for this trade appear in Table 11.4. If the stock settles right at the targeted price of 32.00 at expiration, the trade results in a profit of 2.15. This profit breaks down as 2.00 coming from the value of the long

TABLE 11.4 Key Levels for the XYZ May 30/32 Call Ratio Spread

	Level	Explanation
Break-even Price	34.15	Difference Between Strikes plus High Strike plus Credit
Maximum Dollar Gain	2.15	Credit plus High Strike minus Low Strike
Maximum Gain Price	32.00	Spread Worth Maximum Value
Maximum Dollar Loss	Unlimited	Stock Rallies
Maximum Loss Price	Unlimited	Second Short Call Value Unlimited

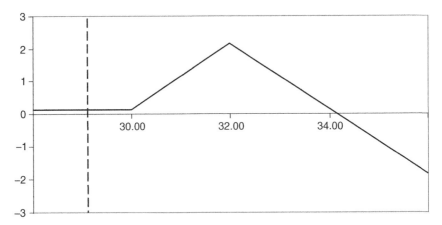

FIGURE 11.2   Payoff Diagram for the XYZ Mar 30/32 Call Ratio Spread

30 Call and 0.15 from the income taken in through initiating the trade. At 32.00 the two short 32 strike call options expire with no value.

Over 32.00, the spread begins to lose value and then breaks even at 34.15. As the stock moves higher the spread begins to lose value. This loss in value comes from the extra short call option that is not covered by either another long call option or a long stock position.

The payoff diagram, Figure 11.2, is similar to the first ratio spread example, except the price level that the stock is trading upon initiation of the spread is highlighted by a vertical dashed line, which in this case is not in the proximity of the maximum profit level as in the previous example. The purpose behind highlighting this level is to demonstrate that if the price prediction of XYZ is wrong in two directions—that is if the stock does not move at all or moves in a bearish direction—the trade will still end up being a small profit.

A call ratio spread would be a strategy that is employed when a trader believe a stock is going to possibly land very close to a certain strike price at expiration. Usually a butterfly spread also comes to mind in this situation, but the butterfly spread does not allow room for error in either direction. In the case of a ratio spread, if the trader is wrong, but wrong where the stock sells off, a small profit would still be made if the stock dropped. This is not true in the case of a long butterfly.

On the risk side, since there is a naked option involved, the ratio spread has tremendous risk on the upside relative to the price of the stock. This also differs from a butterfly, but is very similar to the exposure that is taken on when a short strangle is traded.

TABLE 11.5   Inputs and Output Used to Create an XYZ Mar 40/45 Put Ratio Spread

Inputs	
Days	120
Volatility	40%
Interest Rate	1.00%
XYZ Price	41.00
Output	
XYZ Mar 40 Put	3.15
XYZ Mar 45 Put	6.15
XYZ Mar 40/45 Put Ratio Spread	0.15

PUT RATIO SPREAD

A put ratio spread would be traded in a case where a trader is expecting a stock to settle close to a strike price and the trader is also willing to take on risk that the stock will not trade lower. With the call ratio spread the risk was for a stock that may trade much higher, but with the put ratio spread there will be a naked short put option, which exposes a trader to downside price risk and a substantial potential loss.

An example of a put ratio spread was developed with the options from Table 11.5. With March expiration 120 days out, an implied volatility of 40 percent and XYZ trading at 41.00, the XYZ Mar 40 Put is trading at 3.15 and the XYZ Mar 45 Put is trading at 6.15. To trade an XYZ Mar 40/45 Put Ratio Spread, two of the Mar 40 Put options would be sold and one of the Mar 45 Puts would be purchased. The result is a small credit of 0.15.

The maximum potential gain from a put ratio spread is the same as a call ratio spread, where a single price point is the maximum potential profit point. With respect to a call ratio spread, the maximum profit point is the

TABLE 11.6   Key Levels for the XYZ Mar 40/45 Put Ratio Spread

	Level	Explanation
Break-even Price	34.85	Lower Strike minus Strike Difference minus Credit
Maximum Dollar Gain	5.15	Credit plus High Strike minus Low Strike
Maximum Gain Price	40.00	Spread Worth Maximum Value
Maximum Dollar Loss	34.85	Stock Goes to Zero
Maximum Loss Price	0.00	Second Short Put Value at 0.00

higher strike price, using a put ratio spread results in the maximum profit point being the lower strike price.

For the XYZ Mar 40/45 Put Ratio spread, the maximum profit would be reached with a price for XYZ of 40.00 at expiration. The maximum profit would be 5.15 for this trade, which is determined by 5.00 in value for the long 45 put and the 0.15 taken in from initiating the trade.

Another factor that differentiates a ratio call and ratio put spread is the potential maximum loss from the two spreads. A ratio call spread has a potential maximum loss that is theoretically unlimited. The ratio put spread has risk to the downside, but the downside is limited to a stock going to 0.00. With this spread, if XYZ were to go to 0.00, the spread would incur a loss of 34.85. This is the loss associated with being naked short one XYZ Mar 40 Put, with the profit of the income from initiating the trade and 5.00 points profit from the positions created with the other two options in the spread.

The payoff diagram (see Figure 11.3) for a put ratio spread is opposite of that for a call ratio spread. The similarities of having one side look like a long butterfly and the other side replicating a short straddle do exist. However, the sides have switched. The left side of the payout has the extreme downside exposure like a short straddle and the right side of the spread has the limited exposure from the higher strike price like a long butterfly.

The dashed line represents the stock price when this trade was initiated, or 41.00. This spread does have some room for error as the trade does not become unprofitable until the stock trades under 34.85 at expiration. Also, if the stock takes an unforeseen bullish turn, the trade is a small profit from 45.00 and higher.

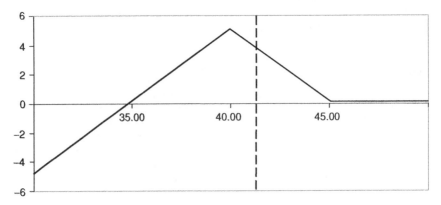

FIGURE 11.3 Payoff Diagram for the XYZ Mar 40/45 Put Ratio Spread

TABLE 11.7 Inputs and Output Used to Create an XYZ Aug 50/54 Put Ratio Spread

Inputs	
Days	60
Volatility	30%
Interest Rate	1.00%
XYZ Price	48.00
Output	
XYZ Aug 50 Put	3.45
XYZ Aug 54 Put	6.50
XYZ Mar 50/54 Put Ratio Spread	0.40

Like the call ratio spread, a stock does not necessarily need to be close to the maximum profit range to justify putting on a trade using a put ratio spread. It is possible that upon initiation of the trade the stock may even be at a price that would result in a loss at expiration. The thought behind one of these trades would be where the stock is expected to be on exit or, in this case, at expiration. The options used to create an example of this type of trade appear in Table 11.7.

XYZ is trading at 48.00 and a trader believes the stock should trade up to the 50.00 range in the next couple of months. It is possible the stock may take off from there, but the trader is at the very least moderately bullish on XYZ. The trader explores a variety of potential trades and then decides to initiate a put ratio spread using the XYZ Aug 50 and XYZ Aug 54 Put options. These options are valued at 3.45 for the XYZ Aug 50 Put and 6.50 for the XYZ Aug 54 Put. Through selling two of the lower strike put options for a credit of 6.90 and buying one of the higher strike options for 6.50, the trader takes in a credit of 0.40 to initiate the trade.

The key levels for this trade, shown in Table 11.8, demonstrate that even if this trade is erroneous and the stock trades lower, there is a buffer

TABLE 11.8 Key Levels for the XYZ Aug 50/54 Put Ratio Spread

	Level	Explanation
Break-even Price	45.60	Lower Strike minus Strike Difference minus Credit
Maximum Dollar Gain	4.60	Credit plus High Strike minus Low Strike
Maximum Gain Price	50.00	Spread Worth Maximum Value
Maximum Dollar Loss	45.60	Stock Goes to Zero
Maximum Loss Prices	0.00	Second Short Put Value at 0.00

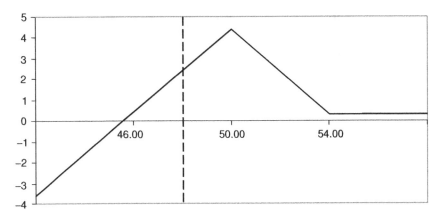

FIGURE 11.4 Payoff Diagram for the XYZ Mar 50/54 Put Ratio Spread

of 2.40 from the current stock price to the break-even point of 45.60. This level is determined by adding the spread difference to the credit received for the trade and then subtracting that sum from the lower strike price of the spread.

The maximum potential profit of this trade is 4.40 which would be realized if the stock settles at 50.00 at expiration. There would be 4.00 of value in the long XYZ Aug 54 Put, no value for the two short XYZ Aug 50 Put options, and 0.40 received from initiating the trade. With the stock over the higher strike price of 54.00, the stock would settle in a range that would result in all options expiring with no value and the profit from the trade resulting in the premium kept for putting the trade on.

Finally, the payoff diagram in Figure 11.4 shows the profit or loss of this trade at a variety of price points. Looking at the vertical dashed line, which represents the stock price upon initiation of the trade, the buffer that exists before the trade is not a profit is seen. Also, the upside to the right of this line peaks at 50.00 and drops off to the higher strike of 54.00, but never reaches the loss area.

RATIO SPREAD COMPARISONS

In this chapter ratio spreads have been compared to being a combination of a short straddle and a long butterfly. To illustrate this further, this section will take options with the same time to expiration and implied volatility and create a put ratio spread, long put butterfly, and a short straddle. All three of these spreads have a single price point at expiration where the

TABLE 11.9 Inputs and Output Used to Create a Put Ratio, Long Put Butterfly, and Short Straddle

Inputs	
Days	60
Volatility	45%
Interest Rate	1.00%
XYZ Price	43.00
Output	
XYZ Oct 40 Put	1.70
XYZ Oct 43 Put	3.10
XYZ Oct 43 Call	3.15
XYZ Oct 46 Put	4.90
XYZ Oct 40/43 Put Ratio Spread	1.30
XYZ Oct 40/43/46 Long Put Butterfly	(0.40)
XYZ Oct 43 Short Straddle	6.25

maximum profit would be realized. This point is what all three of these spreads will have in common.

Table 11.9 displays all the inputs and options needed to create the three spreads for this comparison. With XYZ trading at 43.00 a trader believes the stock will stay in a tight range over the next 60 days. This results in the actual price target of this trade being the same as the price where the stock was when the trade was initiated or 43.00.

October options expire in 60 days and have an implied volatility of 45 percent.

Using the available options in this table the XYZ 43/46 Put Ratio Spread could be initiated for a credit of 1.30. This would involve selling two of the XYZ Oct 43 Put options at 3.10 each for a credit of 6.20, and then paying 4.90 for a single XYZ Oct 46 Put. A long put butterfly is created by selling two of the XYZ Oct 43 Put options, once again for a credit of 6.20. The XYZ 40 Put would be purchased for 1.70 and the XYZ Oct 46 Put would be bought for 4.90 for a total cost of 6.60. The result is a debit of 0.40 to put on this butterfly spread. The final spread in this section is the XYZ Oct 43 Short Straddle which brings in 6.25 through selling one XYZ Oct 43 Put for 3.10 and an XYZ Oct 43 Call for 3.15.

The first comparison involves the put ratio spread and the long put butterfly. The primary difference between these two positions is the butterfly is put on at a cost or for a debit, while the put ratio spread brings in a credit. Getting paid to put on a position is always a positive, but should not be the only reason to choose one strategy over another. The key levels

TABLE 11.10   Key Levels for XYZ Oct 40/43 Put Ratio Spread and XYZ Oct 40/43/46 Long Put Butterfly

	XYZ Oct 40/43 Put Ratio Spread	XYZ Oct 40/43/46 Long Put Butterfly
Up Break-even Price	None	45.60
Down Break-even Price	38.70	40.40
Maximum Dollar Gain	4.30	2.60
Maximum Gain Price	43.00	43.00
Maximum Dollar Loss	38.70	0.40
Maximum Loss Prices	0.00	40.00 and Lower
		46.00 and Higher

in Table 11.10 should all be considered when choosing which strategy to implement.

Using the break-even levels as a starting point, note that the there is no break-even price related to the stock moving higher in the put ratio spread, while there is a break-even price associated with the long put butterfly. This is due to the put ratio spread turning out to be profitable at any level above the down break-even price. However, to the upside the long put butterfly does show a profit, but only as long as the stock closes under 45.60 at expiration. As a review, this level is determined by subtracting the cost of the spread (0.40) from the upper strike price of 46.00.

On the downside the break-even level for the long put butterfly is 40.40, which compares unfavorably to the much lower break-even level for the put ratio spread of 38.70. However, the trade off between these break-even levels can be seen in the other key levels.

The maximum potential loss that may be realized from the put ratio spread is substantial, or specifically 38.70, which would occur if the stock were to drop all the way to 0.00. For the butterfly spread, the potential loss is actually capped at the cost of the spread, or 0.40, which occurs if the stock is over 46.00 or under 40.00 at expiration. This low potential maximum loss definitely favors the put butterfly.

The maximum potential gain from the spreads occurs at the same price point of 43.00. However, the amount of these gains differs greatly. The potential maximum gain from the long put butterfly is 2.60, while the maximum potential gain from the put ratio spread is 4.30. This is a good example of how risk and reward works—there is more risk associated with the put ratio spread and there is a higher reward. Figure 11.5 is a payoff diagram that compares the payout for these two strategies at expiration.

The payout diagram comparing these two strategies is pretty dramatic. The risk to the downside is a cause of concern regarding the put ratio

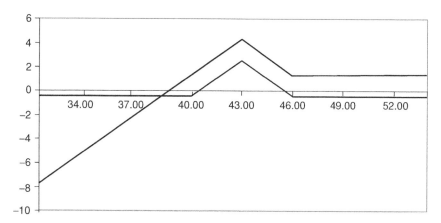

FIGURE 11.5 Payoff Diagram comparing the XYZ Oct 40/43 Put Ratio Spread and XYZ Oct 40/43/46 Long Put Butterfly

spread. On the upside, the put ratio spread does not become unprofitable with any move to the upside from the underlying stock. There is basically a tradeoff here that must be considered before deciding which strategy to pursue.

One final important note regarding comparing a put ratio spread and long put butterfly. Margin would be required for the ratio spread due to the uncovered option in the ratio spread, while the only outlay involved in the butterfly spread would be the initial cost to initiate the spread.

Table 11.11 has the key levels for the put ratio spread and initiating a short straddle with the same maximum payout level. As in the previous example, the most striking initial difference between the put ratio spread and the short straddle is the break-even price point to the upside. The short straddle will start to become a losing trade if the stock is above 49.25 at

TABLE 11.11 Key Levels for XYZ Oct 40/43 Put Ratio Spread and XYZ Oct 43 Short Straddle

	XYZ Oct 40/43 Put Ratio Spread	XYZ Oct 43 Short Straddle
Up Break-even Price	None	49.25
Down Break-even Price	38.70	36.75
Maximum Dollar Gain	4.30	6.25
Maximum Gain Price	43.00	43.00
Maximum Dollar Loss	38.70	36.75 Unlimited
Maximum Loss Prices	0.00	0.00 Unlimited

expiration. Admittedly this is a pretty big move before the trade goes from a profit to a loss, but at 49.25 the put ratio spread would still have a profit.

To the downside the break-even level is more favorable for the short straddle as the position becomes a losing trade at 36.75, while the ratio spread starts to lose money below 38.70. The maximum potential losses are somewhat similar between the two spreads. The risk in the put ratio spread is only to the downside, but there is basically no protection from a potentially substantial loss if the stock trades to 0.00. The short straddle does have substantial risk to the downside, but unlike the put ratio spread also has unlimited loss to the upside.

Finally, the maximum potential gain favors the short straddle with a profit of 6.25 versus 4.30 for the put ratio spread. Both realize this maximum gain if the stock settles at 43.00 at expiration. As in the previous comparison, this higher potential profit reflects the more risky of the trades. There is more potential risk associated with the short straddle than the put ratio spread. With a higher potential loss or risk level, the reward for putting the trade on is more lucrative.

Figure 11.6 is a graphical depiction of the potential payouts of the two strategies. Although with different price levels, the left side of the diagram has very similar characteristics. Both the short straddle and put ratio spread lose one for one with the stock to the downside. The right side, which shows what the payouts would be with a bullish move in the stock, is where the true difference exists between the two trades. The short straddle incurs a high level of risk, while the put ratio spread does not have a level where it becomes a losing trade.

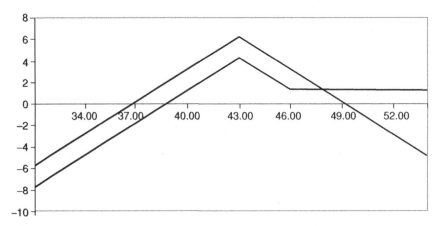

FIGURE 11.6 Payoff Diagram comparing the XYZ Oct 40/43 Put Ratio Spread and XYZ Oct 43 Short Straddle

A ratio spread—whether with a put or call option—is a trade that results in a naked option and exposure either to a strong bullish or bearish move in the underlying stock. Either the put ratio or call ratio spread should be approached with caution due to this high level of risk. However, there are times where a specific stock price is projected and either of these spreads may be the best alternative to trade this option.

When considering a neutral outlook for a stock, a long put butterfly, put ratio spread, and short straddle are all alternatives to investigate. Take into account the potential risk and reward of each strategy, along with exactly how each strategy will match up to a price projection.

CHAPTER 12

Backspreads

A ratio spread is a strategy that is used to target a certain price at option expiration. On the other end of the strategy spectrum, the backspread is a trade that is put on with the expectation of a large move in the underlying stock. Like a ratio spread, the backspread has the same features as a straddle and butterfly, however, the backspread is more like a combination of a long straddle and short butterfly. The payoff is capped in one direction, like a butterfly, but unlimited (or substantial) in the other price direction.

Finally, the backspread is initiated by purchasing more options than are sold. The purchased options are less expensive than the options that are sold, so the result is usually a very inexpensive trade or even a credit to the trader's account. As in the previous chapter, the ratio of options long to short can be of a wide variety, but for simplicity, the examples in this chapter are going to focus on two long options to one short option.

CALL BACKSPREAD

A call backspread would involve trading a disproportionate number of call options. The difference between a backspread and a ratio spread is more options would be purchased than sold. With a call backspread, the higher strike options would be purchased and the lower strike options would be sold. For example, selling a call option with a 30 strike and buying two call options with a 35 strike. Selling the more expensive lower strike option and

TABLE 12.1 Inputs and Output Used to Create an XYZ Mar 50/55 Call Backspread

Inputs	
Days	60
Volatility	30%
Interest Rate	1.00%
XYZ Price	52.50
Output	
XYZ May 50 Call	4.00
XYZ May 55 Call	1.60
XYZ Mar 50/55 Call Backspread	0.80

buying the cheaper higher strike option should result in a fairly inexpensive trade or even a trade initiated for a credit to an account.

An example of a call backspread is created using the options from Table 12.1. March expiration is 60 days out, the options are trading with an implied volatility of 30 percent, and XYZ is trading at 52.50. Using these levels, an XYZ Mar 50 Call is trading for 4.00 and an XYZ Mar 55 Call would be trading at 1.60. The trades involved are selling the XYZ Mar 50 Call for a credit of 4.00 and purchasing two of the XYZ Mar 55 Call options for 1.60 each, or a total cost of 3.20. The result from these trades is a net credit of 0.80 for initiating the XYZ Mar 50/55 Call Backspread.

The goal behind a backspread is to benefit from a large price move in a certain direction, although a move in the opposite direction may also result in a profit. With a call backspread, the direction is a bullish move from the underlying as being long more call options than short results in net long exposure to the underlying security. The key levels for the XYZ Mar 50/55 Call Backspread appear in Table 12.2.

TABLE 12.2 Key Levels for an XYZ Mar 50/55 Call Backspread

	Level	Explanation
High Break-even Price	59.20	High Strike plus Spread Difference minus Credit
Low Break-even Price	50.80	Low Strike Plus Credit
Maximum Dollar Gain	Unlimited	Stock Rallies
Maximum Gain Price	Unlimited	Long Option Profit
Maximum Dollar Loss	4.20	Short Option has Maximum Value Relative to Long Options
Maximum Loss Price	55.00	Higher Strike Price

The XYZ Mar 50/55 Call Backspread has a pretty wide range of prices where the trade would result in a loss at expiration. However, the expectation of a large move from the underlying is a key component to deciding to initiate a backspread. The upper break-even level is 59.20 and the lower break even is 50.80. The stock price upon initiation of the trade was 52.50, so the downside breakeven may be reached through a relatively small price move of 1.70. To the upside, the break-even level would be reached with a pretty significant stock move of 6.70.

The upside profit of this trade is unlimited based on the price of the stock rallying to lofty levels. As far as a maximum loss, this level occurs at 55.00 per share, which would result in a value of 5.00 for the 50 strike call and no value for the two 55 strike call options. As the spread is short a single 50 strike call, the spread would have a total value of −5.00, but some of this is offset by the premium received of 0.80 when the spread was implemented.

Figure 12.1 shows the payoff diagram for this trade. Note the vertical dotted line on the diagram which indicates the level where XYZ was trading upon initiation of this spread. From this chart, the distance to cover to reach an area where the strong upside may be realized is pretty apparent. The other direction, where a small profit consisting of the income taken in on the spread is realized does not involve quite as big a move.

The first example of a call backspread involves initiating a trade where the stock is in a range where a loss would be incurred at expiration if the stock price were to stay stagnant. The second example does just the opposite. With XYZ trading at 29.50, the belief is that in the next 45 days there may be a significant announcement that would push shares dramatically higher. However, the risk is the expected announcement may not come to

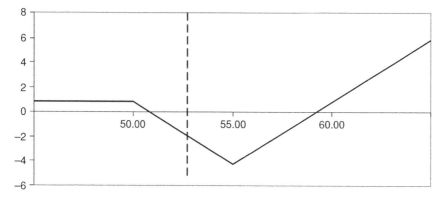

FIGURE 12.1 Payoff Diagram for the XYZ Mar 50/55 Call Backspread

TABLE 12.3 Inputs and Output Used to Create an XYZ Dec 30/33 Call Backspread

Inputs	
Days	45
Volatility	30%
Interest Rate	1.00%
XYZ Price	29.50
Output	
XYZ Dec 30 Call	1.05
XYZ Dec 33 Call	0.25
XYZ Dec 30/33 Call Backspread	0.55

fruition in the next 45 days. In that case, a very stagnant stock price would be anticipated.

Using the options from Table 12.3, an XYZ Dec 30/33 Call Backspread with 45 days to expiration and an implied volatility of 30 percent is created. The lower strike 30 call is sold for 1.05 and two of the higher strike 33 calls are purchased for 0.25 each, or a total cost of 0.50. The result is a credit of 0.55 for putting on this spread.

The key levels displayed in Table 12.4 show that this spread matches up well with the goals intended when the trade was placed. Both break-even levels are above the current stock price of 29.50. The lower break-even price of 30.55 is 1.05 higher than the initial price, and the second break-even price is at 35.45 or a move of to the upside of 6.05. This price would involve more than a 20 percent move from the current XYZ price of 29.50, which was one of the potential outcomes anticipated when initiating this trade.

At the higher strike price of 33.00, the 30 strike call option has 3.00 of value, but as the spread is short this option that is a negative 3.00 to the

TABLE 12.4 Key Levels for an XYZ Dec 30/33 Call Backspread

	Level	Explanation
High Break-even Price	35.45	High Strike plus Spread Difference minus Credit
Low Break-even Price	30.55	Low Strike plus Credit
Maximum Dollar Gain	Unlimited	Stock Rallies
Maximum Gain Price	Unlimited	Long Option Profit
Maximum Dollar Loss	2.45	Short Option has Maximum Value Relative to Long Options
Maximum Loss Price	33.00	Higher Strike Price

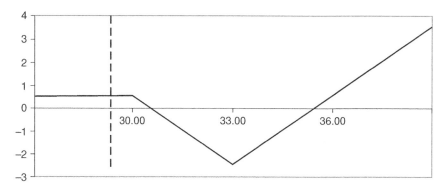

FIGURE 12.2 Payout Diagram for the XYZ Mar 30/33 Call Backspread

trader. The resulting loss is 2.45, as some of this negative value is offset by the 0.55 credit taken in when the trade was put on.

Figure 12.2 shows the payout for this spread, along with the stock price for XYZ when the trade was initiated highlighted on the diagram. This is a good depiction of just how far the stock needs to go to start moving into that potentially unlimited profit range. A stagnant or bearish move in the stock works well for this spread also.

PUT BACKSPREAD

The put backspread is similar to the call backspread as it may benefit from both a bullish or bearish move from the underlying. The big difference between the two is that the put backspread will benefit more if the stock has a big bearish move or loses value. This differs in that the call backspread is set up to have maximum benefit from a bullish move.

A put backspread also differs somewhat in the construction of the position. As a call backspread was created by selling lower strike calls and buying more of the higher strike call options, a put backspread is created by selling higher strike puts and buying more of the lower strike put options. A put option with a lower strike price should have a lower value than a put option with a higher strike price, as the put with the lower strike is the right to sell something at a lower price than the higher strike. This pricing difference in the options stems from the logic that the right to sell anything at a higher price should have move value than the right to sell something at a lower price.

The options that were used to develop the first example of a put backspread appear in Table 12.5. With XYZ trading at 42.00, a trader believes

TABLE 12.5   Inputs and Output Used to Create an XYZ Mar
                  41/44 Put Backspread

Inputs	
Days	45
Volatility	30%
Interest Rate	1.00%
XYZ Price	42.00
Output	
XYZ Mar 41 Put	1.25
XYZ Mar 44 Put	2.95
XYZ Mar 40/45 Put Backspread	0.45

a stock is going to experience a large move higher or lower with a bias toward a downward stock move. After weighing different potential strategies, the trader decides to create an XYZ Mar 41/44 Put Backspread by selling one XYZ Mar 44 Put and purchasing two XYZ Mar 41 Put options.

The specific transactions are buying two XYZ Mar 41 Puts at 1.25 each for a total cost of 2.50, and selling one XYZ Mar 44 Put, taking in a credit of 2.95. The net result is a credit of 0.45 to put the spread on. Although a credit is received when the trade is initiated, if XYZ settles at the current price of 42.00 at expiration, it actually would turn out to be a losing trade. This is shown along with the other key levels of this trade in Table 12.6.

This trade is entered into when the stock is trading at 42.00, which is a little bit higher than the maximum loss level of 41.00. If XYZ were to drift down by 1.00 and settle at 41.00 at expiration, the short 44 strike put would be worth 3.00 and the two long 41 put strike options would have no value. With the spread worth −3.00, adding back the credit of 0.45 that was realized when the trade was put on results in a loss of 2.55.

TABLE 12.6   Key Levels for an XYZ Dec 41/44 Put Backspread

	Level	Explanation
Lower Break-even Price	38.45	Low Strike minus Strike Spread plus Credit
Higher Break-even Price	43.55	High Strike minus Credit
Maximum Dollar Gain	38.45	Stock Goes to Zero
Maximum Gain Price	0.00	Long Put Profit
Maximum Dollar Loss	2.55	Short Option has Maximum Value Relative to Long Options
Maximum Loss Price	41.00	Lower Strike Price

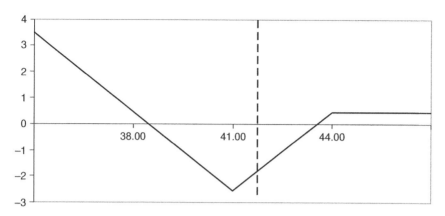

FIGURE 12.3 Payout Diagram for the XYZ Mar 41/44 Put Backspread

To the downside the stock would need to drop from 42.00 to the lower break-even point of 38.45 before profits start to kick in. Under 38.45, the spread starts to profit on a one-for-one basis with the stock moving lower. The higher break-even price is 43.55, where the spread also starts to become profitable. However, in this direction the profit is capped at 0.45 at any price level from 44.00 up. At any price above and including 44.00, all of these put options expire out of the money with no value.

Figure 12.3 is a payout diagram for the XYZ Mar 41/44 Put Backspread. Note the level where the stock was trading when the trade was initiated is once again highlighted by a dashed vertical line.

With the stock not moving at all and XYZ closing at 42.00 at expiration, the trade would end up being a loser. However, to get to the downside levels where the stock starts to reach prices where the spread begins to see strong profits, the stock must go through the level of maximum loss. In the other direction, just a couple of points stand between where the stock is upon putting the trade on and the maximum potential profit on the upside. In the next example, the stock is at a level where things are a bit different when the trade is initiated.

Another example of a put backspread was created from the options priced in Table 12.7. This trade was actually initiated at a level where the stock is equal the maximum loss pricing level of the spread.

With this trade the options only have 15 days left to expiration. This would be a trade where a quick move is expected in the near term, such as a move associated with an earnings announcement or some other stock-moving event. Usually a long straddle comes to mind when putting on a trade to benefit from a large anticipated move from a stock, however, if there is a directional bias a backspread may also be appropriate. In

TABLE 12.7 Inputs and Output Used to Create an XYZ Jul 36/38 Put Backspread

Inputs	
Days	15
Volatility	30%
Interest Rate	1.00%
XYZ Price	36.00
Output	
XYZ Jul 36 Put	0.90
XYZ Jul 38 Put	2.20
XYZ Jul 36/38 Put Ratio Spread	0.40

this case there is a bearish bias regarding the potential reaction from the stock.

The trade is placed by selling the XYZ Jul 38 Put for a credit of 2.20 and purchasing two of the XYZ Jul 36 Puts for a cost of 1.80 (.90 each). The XYZ Jul 36/38 Put Ratio spread takes in a credit of 0.40.

Key levels for this trade appear in Table 12.8. Note, again, unlike the previous example, the maximum loss level is equal to where the stock is trading when the spread was initiated. If the stock settles at 36.00 at expiration the spread loses 1.60. This is determined by the short 38 strike option having a value of 2.00 while the long 36 strike options expire with no value. This 2.00 of negative value is offset a little by the credit received when the trade was initiated.

There is a narrow range that needs to be covered to reach the two break-even levels, but also there are only 15 days to option expiration. This gives the trade very little time for the stock to make a move that would result in a profit. In both directions the stock needs to move 1.60 for this spread to break even. Only when the stock reaches the higher strike price

TABLE 12.8 Key Levels for an XYZ Jul 36/38 Put Backspread

	Level	Explanation
Lower Break-even Price	34.40	Low Strike minus Strike Spread plus Credit
Higher Break-even Price	37.60	High Strike minus Credit
Maximum Dollar Gain	34.40	Stock Goes to Zero
Maximum Gain Price	0.00	Long Put Profit
Maximum Dollar Loss	1.60	Short Option has Maximum Value Relative to Long Options
Maximum Loss Price	36.00	Lower Strike Price

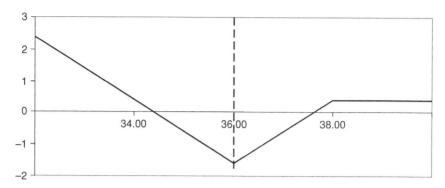

FIGURE 12.4 Payout Diagram for the XYZ Jul 36/38 Put Backspread

of 38.00 does the spread realizes a profit of 0.40, which is set at any price higher than this level. On the downside, the break-even level is 34.40, and as the stock continues under that level the spread profits along with the stock's move to the downside.

The payout diagram in Figure 12.4 depicts the profit and loss of this trade at expiration. With the stock at the maximum loss point when the trade was initiated the line that represents this price is in the middle of the diagram. It is also equidistant from both break-even levels.

At any price under 38.00, this put backspread has a payout structure that is very similar to a long straddle. From 38.00 on up, that structure changes a bit and the spread replicates a short butterfly. Both those strategies would be utilized when the expectation is for some sort of quick move expected from a stock. All three strategies benefit from a large move if the underlying is near the area where there would be a maximum loss incurred. The next section takes a look at comparing all three.

BACKSPREAD COMPARISONS

In the previous chapter a ratio spread is compared to a straddle and butterfly spread that have the same target or market outlook. This section will perform the same exercise using a put backspread, a long straddle, and a short put butterfly. The spreads used in this section are created using the inputs and resulting options in Table 12.9.

The motivation behind all of the trades in this section is the expectation of a large move from the underlying stock in a short period of time. Therefore, the options in this table have only 10 days to expiration and a

TABLE 12.9 Inputs and Output Used to Create a Put Backspread, Short Put Butterfly, and Long Straddle

Inputs	
Days	10
Volatility	35%
Interest Rate	1.00%
XYZ Price	44.00
Output	
XYZ Aug 41 Put	0.15
XYZ Aug 44 Put	1.05
XYZ Aug 44 Call	1.10
XYZ Aug 47 Put	3.15
XYZ Aug 44/47 Put Backspread	1.05
XYZ Aug 41/44/47 Short Put Butterfly	1.20
XYZ Aug 44 Long Straddle	(2.10)

big move is expected within this time period. The underlying stock is trading at 44.00 and the options have an implied volatility of 35 percent.

The first comparison is between the XYZ Aug 44/47 Put Backspread and the XYZ Aug 41/44/47 Short Put Butterfly. A credit would be received for entering both trades. In the case of the backspread, two of the 44 strike put options would be purchased for a cost of 2.10, while a credit of 3.15 would be received for selling the 47 put for a net result of a credit of 1.05. The butterfly spread would result in a credit of 1.20 as two of the 44 put options would be purchased for a cost of 2.10 and a credit of 3.30 would be taken for selling the 41 and 47 put options.

After determining the initial credit associated with each of the spreads, the key levels would need to be analyzed. Table 12.10 is a comparison of the

TABLE 12.10 Key Levels for XYZ Aug 44/47 Put Backspread and XYZ Aug 41/44/47 Short Put Butterfly

	XYZ Aug 44/47 Put Backspread	XYZ Aug 41/44/47 Short Put Butterfly
Up Break-even Price	45.95	45.80
Down Break-even Price	42.05	42.20
Maximum Dollar Gain	42.05	1.20
Maximum Gain Prices	0.00	47.00 and Over
		41.00 and Under
Maximum Dollar Loss	1.95	1.80
Maximum Loss Price	44.00	44.00

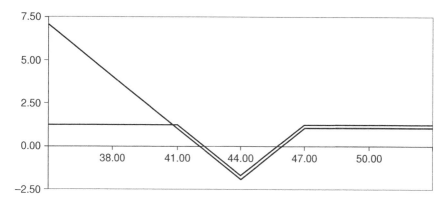

FIGURE 12.5 Payoff Diagram comparing the XYZ Aug 44/47 Put Backspread and XYZ Aug 41/44/47 Short Put Butterfly

key levels of the XYZ Aug 44/47 Put Backspread and the XYZ Aug 41/44/47 Short Put Butterfly.

The potential maximum loss for each spread occurs if at expiration the stock is trading at 44.00, the same level it is trading when the spread was initiated. These two spreads have very similar potential maximum loss levels at 1.95 for the backspread and 1.80 for the short butterfly. Also the break-even levels in both directions are both very similar, with the difference being only 0.15 more for the backspread in each direction.

The contrast between the two spreads shows up when considering the maximum potential gain of each spread. On the upside the maximum gain for the put backspread would be capped at 1.05 and the maximum profit for the butterfly spread would top out at 1.20. However, to the downside, there is the potential for the spread to make up to 42.05 if the stock trades to 0.00. At minimum, the spread continues to profit on a one-for-one basis as the stock moves lower, with the potential profit not being limited in this direction as it is for the butterfly spread.

Figure 12.5 is a payoff diagram comparing the payoffs at a variety of price points for both the XYZ Aug 44/47 Put Backspread and the XYZ Aug 41/44/47 Short Put Butterfly. Note the payoffs practically overlap at every price point under 41.00. At 41.00 the backspread starts to take off in value, while the butterfly does not continue to benefit from this price move.

Comparing these two spreads should result in a trader deciding that the backspread is the preferred trade. The downside risk and break-even levels for both of these trades are similar, while the reward differs greatly. If a trader was expecting a large move in either direction, the backspread has a very similar breakeven and potential profit to the up-side. If the stock trades dramatically lower, the backspread could end up

TABLE 12.11 Key Levels for XYZ Aug 44/47 Put Backspread and XYZ Aug 44 Long Straddle

	XYZ Aug 44/47 Put Backspread	XYZ Aug 44 Long Straddle
Up Break-even Price	45.95	46.15
Down Break-even Price	42.05	41.85
Maximum Dollar Gain	42.05	Unlimited
Maximum Gain Price	0.00	Unlimited
Maximum Dollar Loss	1.95	2.15
Maximum Loss Price	44.00	44.00

realizing a much more dramatic profit than if a short put butterfly had been traded.

Once again using the options in Table 12.9 the XYZ Aug 44/47 Put Backspread is put on for a credit of 1.05. To purchase the long straddle actually results in a debit. An XYZ Aug 44 Long Straddle is created through purchasing both the XYZ Aug 44 Call for 1.10 and the XYZ Aug 44 Put for 1.05 with the result being a cost of 2.15.

The other comparison considers the put backspread and a long straddle. Each shares 44.00 as a common price point for a maximum loss from the position. As the stock is at 44.00 upon initiation of the trade, the motivation behind either spread is for the stock to move away from this price point as dramatically and quickly as possible.

Using the levels from Table 12.11 to analyze which is the better trade yields a trading decision that varies from the previous example. The maximum potential loss for each spread occurs at the same price for 44.00 and is very similar for each spread at 1.95 for the backspread and 2.15 for the long straddle. This difference is pretty small at only 0.20 between the two spreads. Break-even levels for both spreads are also very similar, with XYZ needing to move just 0.20 more in either direction for the long straddle to break even compared to the backspread.

The contrast between these two spreads shows up when considering the maximum potential gain from either trade. With a downside move in XYZ stock both spreads benefit on a one-for-one basis with the stock under the break-even levels. However, the profitability of the backspread is capped to the upside, while it is theoretically unlimited for the long straddle.

Figure 12.6 is a good graphical depiction of the difference between these two spreads. Any price above 47.00 is where there is a discernable difference between the two trades. This difference where the straddle continues to add to profits as the stock moves higher is why the long straddle is actually a preferred trade to the backspread in this case.

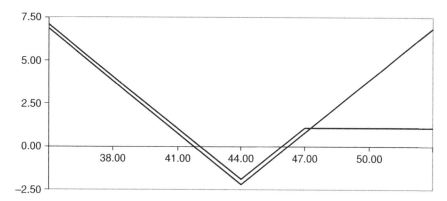

FIGURE 12.6 Payoff Diagram comparing the XYZ Aug 44/47 Put Backspread and XYZ 44 Long Straddle

This final example is a good depiction of why comparing a variety of strategies can be a worthwhile endeavor. The risk associated with both spreads is very similar, while the potential reward, at least to the upside, is superior when considering the long straddle.

A backspread is a unique trade that may work in a variety of situations. Although initiated with a credit in the examples, it is always possible to place one of these trades through paying a debit. If a stock is being analyzed and a large move is expected, considering a backspread is always in order and much more so if there is a bias in the expectation of a potential move.

CHAPTER 13

The Stock
Repair Strategy

T he stock repair strategy is not exactly a spread trade, but is an interesting use of options against a current stock position. In a situation where a loss has occurred in a stock and a trader is hoping for a better exit price, a stock repair spread is a good method to benefit from a rebound in the stock. This benefit may allow the trader to recoup losses from the stock, possibly break even on a trade, and not increase their downside risk exposure to the stock. As with all trading prospects that sound too good to be true there is a tradeoff. The tradeoff here is giving up future profits on the stock if the stock rebounds above a certain point.

Unfortunately the first step in this trade is to have a losing stock. No one starts out buying a stock with the expectation that it will go lower, but this does happen. When it does, a natural reaction is to buy more to improve the break-even price and hopefully get out at less of a loss or possibly at a profit when the stock moves higher. However, along with this ability to break even at a lower price comes more risk. With a stock repair trade there is actually the ability to recoup losses and possibly break even, but without taking on the additional risk of doubling down.

This chapter does not jump right into the stock repair, but first expolores what is involved in doubling down on a stock when there has been a loss and then explores the stock repair trade as an alternative. The stock repair trade involves buying a call option to benefit from a rebound in the stock. However a trader also sells two out-of-the-money call options on the underlying and uses those proceeds to pay for the long call. This may be done for a small credit, debit, or even as a costless transaction.

DOUBLING DOWN ON A POSITION

The first step in a stock repair trade involves being involved in a long stock position that has not worked out particularly well. In fact, the stock trade is usually a stock that has been purchased with the result being a quick loss of around 5 to 10 percent. After a quick loss like this, one method that may be used to try to get some of the losses back would be doubling down on shares. Doubling down is basically buying the same number of shares that are already owned in order to have a lower break-even level.

For instance, if 100 shares of XYZ are purchased at 60.00 and the stock quickly trades down to 50.00, 100 more shares may be bought at 50.00. The result of this activity is a long position of 200 shares with an average cost of 55.00. If the stock rebounds to 55.00, the trader may sell 100 shares and now have a new break-even level of 55.00 on the remaining 100 shares, or may choose to sell all 200 shares, break even on the trade, and look for a new opportunity. The trader may also just keep the 200 shares and continue to profit from more price appreciation.

The downside to doubling down at 50.00 on XYZ is the added risk taken on by now being long 200 shares. Now, instead of being long just 100 shares if the stock goes lower, for each point drop in the stock there is a loss of 2.00 on the position. This additional risk should definitely be taken into consideration before doubling down on a position. Table 13.1 shows the results of doubling down and not doubling down on shares of XYZ at a variety of price points.

Another potential strategy to attempt to regain some losses from a rebound in the stock could be doubling down through the purchase of a call option. There is limited downside to owning a call option, but there is also a time value component to owning a call that works against a trader. The finite life of a call option works against a trader as the rebound would need to occur before the option expires.

Again consider a trader having purchased XYZ at 60.00 and the stock suddenly drops to 50.00. With XYZ trading at 50.00 and a call option with

TABLE 13.1 Comparison of Not Doubling Exposure and Doubling Exposure to XYZ

XYZ	100 Shares at 60.00	200 Shares at 55.00
40	(20.00)	(30.00)
45	(15.00)	(20.00)
50	(10.00)	(10.00)
55	(5.00)	Break Even
60	Break Even	10.00
65	5.00	20.00

TABLE 13.2 Comparison of Buying a Call, Not Doubling Exposure, and Doubling Exposure to XYZ

XYZ	100 Shares at 60.00 1 XYZ 50 Call at 2.50	100 Shares at 60.00	200 Shares at 55.00
40	(22.50)	(20.00)	(30.00)
45	(17.50)	(15.00)	(20.00)
50	(12.50)	(10.00)	(10.00)
55	(2.50)	(5.00)	0.00
60	7.50	0.00	10.00
65	17.50	5.00	20.00

60 days until expiration trading for 2.50, then a call may be purchased to attempt to benefit from a rebound in shares of XYZ. However, the break-even level is now a bit higher than the midpoint between where shares were originally purchased and where they are now trading. If the stock only rebounds to 55.00 in 60 days, the profit on the option is 2.50 and the stock loss is at 5.00. Still an improvement over just holding 100 shares, but not quite as good a break-even point as doubling down. Table 13.2 shows the profit and loss of doubling down with this call option at a variety of prices relative to the two other strategies.

The actual break-even level for this trade is now at 56.25. At this price point, there is a 3.75 loss in the stock, but the XYZ 50 Call would have a profit of 3.75 for a break-even trade. Also note that if the stock does not move and closes at 50.00 at option expiration then the loss on the whole trade is now 12.50, or 2.50 worse than the 10.00 loss for either of the other strategies.

Finally, the other alternative if a rebound is hoped for would be to just hold the original 100 shares with a cost of 60.00. A full move of 10 points would be needed to break even, but there would be no extra downside risk exposure or cost associated with doing nothing and waiting.

All three of these decisions—doing nothing, doubling down, and doubling down with options—have pros and cons as far as added risk or a change in the profit profile. The stock repair strategy has an added dimension where there is no additional risk, but there is a sacrifice of potential upside on the trade.

THE STOCK REPAIR TRADE

An alternative to the do nothing or doubling down strategies is the stock repair trade. In a stock repair trade a call option in purchased to benefit from the potential increase of the stock. This is much like the strategy where a

TABLE 13.3   Comparison of Stock Repair, Buying a Call, Not Doubling Exposure, and Doubling Exposure to XYZ

XYZ	Stock Repair	100 Shares at 60.00 1 XYZ 50 Call at 2.50	100 Shares at 60.00	200 Shares at 55.00
40	(20.00)	(22.50)	(20.00)	(30.00)
45	(15.00)	(17.50)	(15.00)	(20.00)
50	(10.00)	(12.50)	(10.00)	(10.00)
55	0.00	(2.50)	(5.00)	0.00
60	0.00	2.50	0.00	10.00
65	0.00	7.50	5.00	20.00

call was purchased to improve the upside of the stock. However, the added component to the stock repair trade is the selling of two call options in order to pay for the long call. Covering the cost of the long call with the sale of two higher strike call options contributes to there being no increase in the downside risk exposure to XYZ.

Returning to the previous example, with XYZ having gone from 60.00 to 50.00, a 60-Day call option with a 50.00 strike could be purchased for 2.50. To offset this cost, and negate any additional downside risk, two of the 55 Calls may be sold for 1.25 each, or a total of 2.50. The result is a transaction with no cost that results in a break-even level of 55.00 for the trade.

Table 13.3 shows the profit and loss for the stock repair strategy relative to the other three alternatives regarding what to do with XYZ after the 10-point drop in the stock. The downside risk is not increased over the alternative of doubling down with either a call option or 100 more shares. The downside to this strategy is sacrificing all potential profitability from XYZ through the stock repair strategy. The strategy should be used in cases where the true hope is just to get a return to break even while taking on no additional risk.

Figure 13.1 is a payoff diagram comparison between the stock repair strategy and doing nothing with respect to XYZ and not improving the break-even point. In all three of the next diagrams, the payout of the stock repair will be depicted by the solid line, while the dashed line will represent the payout of the strategy that the stock repair strategy is being compared to.

For the comparison to just holding the stock or doing nothing, the benefit from the stock repair strategy exists at the price points between 50.00 and 60.00. In this price range, the stock repair trade has a superior return relative to the alternative of just holding the stock and waiting for a rebound to exit shares. On the downside, as the stock moves lower, the loss

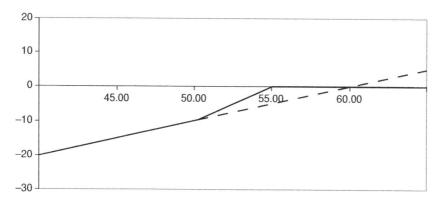

FIGURE 13.1 Payoff Diagram of Stock Repair versus Holding Stock

incurred by the stock repair is the same as the loss that would be realized by holding stock. Finally, above 60.00 holding the stock would be the preferred trade as being long stock from 60.00 starts to become a profitable transaction.

Doubling down with a call versus the stock repair is displayed in Figure 13.2. When doubling down with a call, there is the benefit of making money on the upside that does not exist with the stock repair. Above the break-even price of 56.25 for the trade and adding a call option to the long stock position, the stock repair trade would not have been a superior choice. Below this point, the cost associated with purchasing the call comes into play and the stock repair strategy outperforms doubling down with a call.

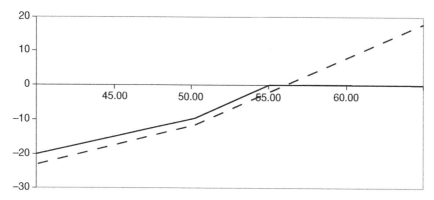

FIGURE 13.2 Payoff Diagram of Stock Repair versus Doubling Down with a Call

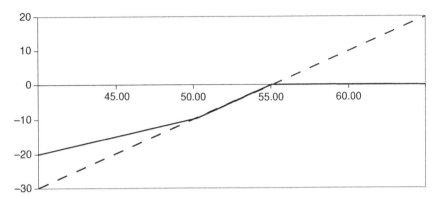

FIGURE 13.3 Payoff Diagram of Stock Repair versus Doubling Down with Shares

Finally, Figure 13.3 compares the stock repair trade to doubling down through the purchase of more shares of XYZ. The potential upside for doubling down is much higher than that of the stock repair strategy. Also, the break-even levels are equal for the two strategies. Where the stock repair strategy is a better choice than doubling down is if the stock continues to go lower. Through doubling down, the risk is doubled compared to the stock repair strategy.

Every stock that is purchased and goes lower may not be a candidate for any of these strategies. Sometimes it is best to just sell a loser and walk away. When there is an expectation that a stock is going to rebound some and the hope is to exit at break even, the stock repair strategy may be a good alternative to consider. If doubling down on shares is being considered to exit at break even, the stock repair trade is a superior choice. It is superior since a trader is not doubling down and taking on added downside risk.

Finally, the stock repair strategy is an interesting use of options that gives traders and investors a chance to get out of a trade at break even without increasing their risk. Also, the stock repair strategy may be used by most traders as there are no naked short option positions in the trade. Two call options are sold, but one is covered by the call that is purchased and the other is covered by the long stock position. Even though upside is sacrificed, the major goal of the stock repair trade is trying to get losses back through the use of options and breaking even on the trade.

CHAPTER 14

Calendar Spreads

T here are actually two general classifications of calendar spreads. First there is a traditional calendar spread, which is covered in this chapter. This would consist of two options of the same type and strike, but with different expiration dates. One option would be sold and the other purchased with the hope of benefiting from differing time value deterioration between the two. Specifically, the goal would be for the long option to lose less value based on the passage of time relative to the short option. The second is called a diagonal spread, which is discussed further in Chapter 15.

The traditional calendar spread is considered a neutral strategy that attempts to benefit from the difference in how time deterioration may occur over the life of an option. Considered a long calendar spread, a near-term option would be sold while a longer-dated option may be purchased. The strike price of the two options is usually very close to the level where the underlying is trading when the trade is initiated. This is due to options with a strike price close to where the underlying stock is trading losing their time value at a faster rate than options with more time to expiration. At-the-money options lose time value at an increasing magnitude as the expiration date approaches. A long calendar spread will take advantage of this difference.

Until now, the majority of trades in this book have focused on how an option spread profits or loses money based on where the stock and options are at expiration. This is different for a calendar spread. In the case of a calendar spread, there is a trading decision to be made when the near-dated option has expired. That decision may be to exit the option that is still held by the spread, possibly create a new calendar spread using the open option position, or just hold the open option position as a directional trade.

TIME VALUE EFFECT

Chapter 4 covered the common pricing factors that impact option values, known as the Greeks. The Greeks indicate how much an option value or another Greek changes related to a one-unit change in a pricing factor. When considering a calendar spread, the pricing factor that is a focus is the time to option expiration, specifically how the passage of time impacts the value of the options in the spread.

The Greek that relates to how the passage of time impacts an option's value is theta. The unique feature of theta is that for options that have strike prices very close to or at the same level as the underlying security, the passage of time does not decrease the option's value at a linear rate.

Theta for an at-the-money option increases as the time to expiration decreases. With 60 days to expiration, an option may lose .02 a day in value. When there is just 15 days left to expiration, this same option may be losing .10 or even .15 a day in value. All else being the same, if a trader were long an option losing .02 a day and short an option losing .15 a day, this would be a good trade on a day-to-day basis.

Figure 14.1 shows the value of a 50 Strike Call option based on a stock trading at 50.00 a share and implied volatility of 25 percent. The bottom of the chart depicts the number of days to expiration, counting down from 90 to 0 days.

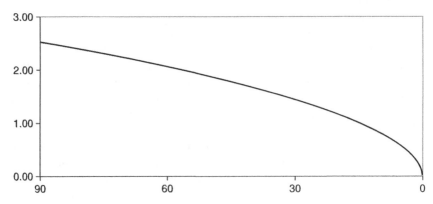

FIGURE 14.1   Effect of Time Passage on At-the-money Call Option Value

Note the value for this option loses value at a pretty consistent rate for the time period from 90 to 60 days left to expiration. During the second 30-day period, from 60 to 30 days remaining on the life of this option, the value begins to deteriorate at a more rapid rate. Finally, in the final 30 days, the value loss accelerates, with more than half the value of the option being lost to time deterioration in this last third of the chart.

Through putting on a long option position that has less exposure to time deterioration than a short-dated option, a trader can benefit from a range bound stock over the life of the shorter-dated short option. This strategy actually may work with either call or put options.

LONG CALL CALENDAR

A long call calendar spread consists of a long position in an option that has longer to expiration than a corresponding short option. Both call options have the same strike price and underlying, the only difference is the time to expiration. A sample transaction to create a long call calendar spread would be:

Buy 1 Aug 50 Call at 2.50—90 Days to Expiration
Sell 1 Jun 50 Call at 1.45—30 Days to Expiration

The net result of these two trades is a long call calendar spread with the short leg expiring in 30 days on June expiration. At June expiration the August call options will still have 60 days left until expiration. The underlying stock in this example was priced at 50.00 when the trade was initiated. Therefore with all pricing factors staying the same, this August 50 Call would have a value of about 2.05, while the June 50 Call would expire with no value. In this case there would be a profit of 1.45 from the short position in the Jun 50 Call and a loss of 0.45 in the long Aug 50 Call position. This imbalance in the loss of option value based on time to expiration is the motivation behind putting on a long call calendar spread.

For a full example of a long call calendar spread, the options created from the inputs in Table 14.1 were used. With XYZ trading at 40.00 the at-the-money Jul 40 Call is trading at 1.40 and the XYZ Oct 40 Call would be valued at 2.85. The assumptions behind these prices are a consistent implied volatility of 30 percent for both option series, along with 30 days until July expiration and 120 days until October expiration.

Using the options from this table, the cost of a long calendar spread would be 1.45. This is the result of paying 2.85 for the October call and receiving 1.40 for selling the near-dated call option that expires in July.

TABLE 14.1   Inputs and Output Used to Create a Long XYZ
Oct 40/ Short XYZ Jun 40 Call Calendar Spread

Inputs	
Days to July Expiration	30
Days to October Expiration	120
Volatility	30%
Interest Rate	1.00%
XYZ Price	40.00
Output	
XYZ Jul 40 Call	1.40
XYZ Oct 40 Call	2.85
XYZ Jul/Oct 40 Call Calendar Spread	1.45

The 1.45 outflow to initiate this trade is actually also the amount that is the potential maximum loss. All key levels for this trade that are determined when the trade is initiated appear in Table 14.2.

The maximum loss of 1.45 would be the balance of the trade if XYZ moves dramatically higher or lower. At these levels for the underlying stock, the spread would have a value that is equal to the premium paid for the position. The exact levels would be based on other market conditions, specifically the implied volatility component of the long option that has time remaining until expiration. Also, since this is still an open position, in the case of a reversal of the share price of XYZ, the possibility that the option may gain back some value does exist.

The maximum potential gain for this trade occurs if the stock settles at the strike price of 40 at June expiration. At this level, the October call would have maximum value relative to the June call. Using a pricing

TABLE 14.2   Key Levels for the Long XYZ Oct 40/ Short XYZ Jun 40 Call
Calendar Spread

	Level	Explanation
High Break-even Price	42.50	Long Option minus Short Option equals Premium Paid
Low Break-even Price	37.90	Long Option equals Premium Paid
Maximum Dollar Gain	1.40	Long Option at Maximum Value Relative to Short Option
Maximum Gain Price	40.00	Strike Price for Both Options
Maximum Dollar Loss	1.45	No Value in Either Option
Maximum Loss Price	26.50	Remaining Long Option has No Value

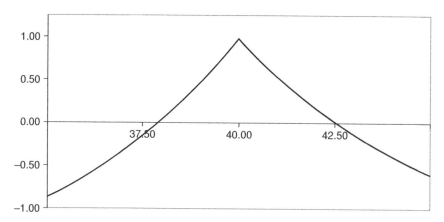

FIGURE 14.2 Payoff Diagram for Long XYZ Oct 40 / Short XYZ Jun 40 Call Calendar Spread

calculator again, and not changing assumptions other than days to expiration, the October option would be worth 2.45. Subtracting the 1.45 cost of this spread from 2.45 results in a trading profit of 1.00.

Finally, the break-even points for this trade are determined through assumptions regarding the pricing of the open option position when the short call option position expires. To the downside, the short option would have no value at expiration. Since there is no value in the short option, the long XYZ Oct 40 Call has a value of 1.45 if XYZ is trading at about 37.90. To the upside, at 42.50, the XYZ Jun 40 Call is in the money by 2.50. Using a stock price of 42.50 to get a value for the XYZ Oct 40 Call results in an option value of 3.95, which is 1.45 higher than the short option. With a premium paid of 1.45 at inception of the trade, and a spread value of 1.45 at expiration, this trade would be a break-even result. These key levels are highlighted in the payoff diagram in Figure 14.2.

Note the shape of this payoff diagram is not linear. This is a result of the non-linear nature of the effect of time on the value of option prices. At different pricing levels and times to expiration the nature of changes in time have a different impact on the value of an option. The curve of this line relates to the time value associate with the long call option that still has time left to expiration.

Also, always remember that upon expiration of the front or near-term month in a calendar spread, there will still be an open option position. This open position may be closed out, with the selling proceeds contributing to the profit of the trade or offsetting some of the loss incurred from the short option position.

LONG PUT CALENDAR

In addition to creating a calendar spread with call options, the same strategy may be employed using all put options. In fact this may be executed with the same forecast that exists with the all call option calendar spread. As with any strategy that may be executed with a choice of options, considering a put alternative when looking at a call calendar spread is worth spending a few extra minutes before pulling the trigger on the trade.

Also, although considered a neutral strategy, a calendar spread may have a bullish or bearish bias to it. This bias would stem from where the strike price is for the options used to create the spread relative to where the underlying stock is when the trade is initiated. For example, if XYZ is trading at 47.50 and a calendar spread is created using options with a 45 strike, the maximum profit of this spread at expiration of the near-term option would occur with the stock at 45.00. As 45.00 is less than the price of XYZ at initiation of the trade, there is a bearish bias to this calendar spread.

Table 14.3 contains options that were created to demonstrate a long put calendar spread. This spread also has a slight bearish bias to it, as the stock is trading at 34.00 and the spread is created using the February 33 and August 33 strike put options. The February options have 35 days to expiration, while the August options have 215 days to expiration. With an underlying stock price of 34.00 and an implied volatility of 30 percent the XYZ Feb 33 Put is priced at 0.80 and the XYZ Aug 33 Put is priced at 2.50. The result here is a cost of 1.70 for the XYZ Feb/Aug 33 Put Calendar Spread.

As with all long calendar spreads, the goal is to attain maximum value from the long option that will remain open at expiration relative to the

TABLE 14.3 Inputs and Output Used to Create a Long XYZ Aug 33 / Short XYZ Feb 33 Put Calendar Spread

Inputs	
Days to February Expiration	35
Days to August Expiration	215
Volatility	30%
Interest Rate	1.00%
XYZ Price	34.00
Output	
XYZ Feb 33 Put	0.80
XYZ Aug 33 Put	2.50
XYZ Feb/Aug Put Calendar Spread	1.70

shorter-dated option which will have expired. This value would be realized if the underlying stock is trading at the strike price of the two options. In the case of this trade, this level is 33.00 and using a pricing calculator to estimate the value of the long option at expiration results in a profit of 1.00 with the stock at 33.00 at expiration. With the stock at this level, the XYZ Aug 33 Put would be trading at 2.70. This assumes no change in the implied volatility input to the equation.

The maximum potential loss for this calendar spread is equal to the premium paid to initiate the trade. In a situation where neither option has any value at the near term expiration, the position would have a loss of 1.70. There would be a long position remaining in the XYZ Aug 33 Put that could remain open for the next 180 days. Over the course of 180 days it is possible the stock could move lower and some value could be realized from the long put position. Using the short-term option expiration date to determine the key levels results in a potential maximum loss of 1.70 upon expiration of the first option.

Finally, the break-even levels are also determined using a pricing calculator. As a stock moves farther away from the strike price of an option the result is a lower time value for that option. Since the profitability of a calendar spread is based on the time value differences between a long and a short option, when a large price move occurs the time value components may not work out in the spread's favor. With a move to the upside, the break-even level of 35.50 is based on there being intrinsic value in neither option, but the time value component of the open long put dropping enough to result in no profit from the trade. To the downside, both options have value, but the time value of the long option has been negatively impacted to the point of the trade becoming a losing proposition from 31.00 and lower. All of these key levels are covered in Table 14.4.

TABLE 14.4 Key Levels for the Long XYZ Aug 33 / Short XYZ Feb 33 Put Calendar Spread

	Level	Explanation
High Break-even Price	35.50	Long Option equals Premium Paid
Low Break-even Price	31.00	Long Option minus Short Option Equals Premium Paid
Maximum Dollar Gain	1.00	Stock at 33.00 at Expiration
Maximum Gain Price	33.00	Maximum Long Option Value Relative to Short Option Value
Maximum Dollar Loss	1.70	No Value in Either Option
Maximum Loss Price	50.00	Remaining Long Option has No Value

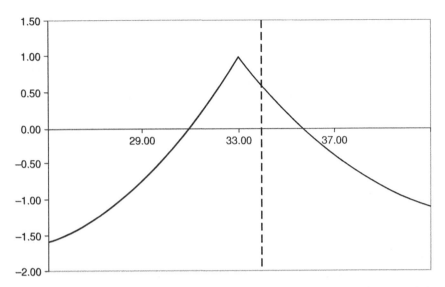

FIGURE 14.3 Payoff Diagram for Long XYZ Aug 33 / Short XYZ Feb 33 Put Calendar Spread

Figure 14.3 is a payoff diagram showing the profit or loss of this spread at expiration of the short-term option. It is very similar to Figure 14.2 which depicted the payout for a long call calendar spread. One difference is that the call example from this chapter had a neutral stock bias, while this trade has a bit of a bearish bias. To display this, a line was added to show where XYZ would have been upon initiation of the trade.

Although in the area of profitability, the stock is not at the exact point of maximum profitability when this trade was put on. A slight move to the downside is needed to settle at that perfect spot to realize a large profit from this trade. A final motivation behind putting this trade on in a manner where a slight bearish bias exists can be seen in this payoff diagram.

With a bearish bias toward XYZ, using a lower strike price results in a larger range of profitability for the trade based on a downside move from XYZ. The profit area to the left of the vertical line covers more price levels than the profit area to the right. To the downside, XYZ would need to lose 3.00 to 31.00 before the trade becomes a loss. On the bullish side, there is only 1.50 of price range available before the trade reaches the break-even point.

A calendar spread may be neutral, but also have a slight directional bias to it. In addition to having a bias, calendar spreads may be combined to create a wider range of potential profitability. The next section takes the trade from this section and adds another calendar spread to it to change the profile of the trade to some degree.

COMBINED CALENDAR SPREAD

Chapter 10 discussed condor spreads, with the iron condor being a combination of a bull and bear spread. A combined calendar spread may be thought of in the same light, as a combination of a couple of spreads—one bearish and one bullish that results in a market neutral outlook.

For example, if a stock is trading at 46.00 and a long calendar spread is initiated with put options that have a strike price for 45, this would represent a slightly bearish outlook for the stock. The strike price represents the maximum profit level at expiration for the short put and is lower than the stock price. If a more neutral outlook exists, another calendar spread might be initiated with a bullish bias.

A bullish bias calendar spread might involve selling a near-expiration 47 strike call and buying a longer-term expiration 47 strike call. By choosing the 47 strike, the result is a maximum profit for this spread at 47.00 on near-term expiration. This is a slightly bullish move from the current stock price from 46.00.

Table 14.5 is an expansion of the options created with Table 14.3 in the long calendar put spread example from the previous section. The

TABLE 14.5 Inputs and Output Used to Create Combined Calendar Spread

Inputs	
Days to February Expiration	35
Days to August Expiration	215
Volatility	30%
Interest Rate	1.00%
XYZ Price	34.00
Output	
XYZ Feb 33 Put	0.80
XYZ Aug 33 Put	2.50
XYZ Feb 35 Call	0.90
XYZ Aug 35 Call	2.75
XYZ Feb/Aug 33 Put Calendar Spread	1.70
XYZ Feb/Aug 35 Call Calendar Spread	1.85

TABLE 14.6 Key Levels for the Combined Calendar Spread

	Level	Explanation
High Break-even Price	37.00	Remaining Long Option Values equal To Premium
Low Break-even Price	31.75	Long Option equals Premium Paid
Maximum Dollar Gain Range	1.15–1.35	Short Options Expire with No Value
Maximum Gain Price Range	33.00–35.00	Stock Rallies
Maximum Dollar Loss	3.55	Both Premiums Lost
Maximum Loss Price	Extreme Move	High Strike minus Low Strike

inputs and put option pricing are the same. Pricing for 35 strike call options with the same expiration months as the put options have been added, along with the cost of initiating an XYZ Feb/Aug 35 Call Calendar Spread. The call spread would result in a debit of 1.85 and combined with the cost of the put spread results in a cost of 3.55 to initiate this combined calendar spread.

The key levels for this combination of calendar spreads appear in Table 14.6. Considering these levels relative to the put spread from the previous example is worthwhile. Both of these trades are based on the same stock and a similar outlook for that stock with the slight difference that there is a more bearish bias to the previous spread.

The break-even levels shift a bit, with the lower break-even level moving from 31.00 to 31.75 when comparing the put-only spread to the combined spread. This results in a little less room to the downside that would result in a profit. Considering a possible bullish move, the break-even level is around 37.00, which is 1.50 higher than the break even for the more bearish biased spread. The result is a different, but wider range of profitability by combining the two spreads.

The maximum potential gain for this spread would occur if the stock were to land at 35.00 at expiration. At this level, the remaining value of the two long options would be 4.90, or 1.35 greater than the 3.55 cost of the spread. At 33.00, the remaining long call and put options would be worth a combined value of 4.70, which would result in a profit of 1.15 at February expiration. The maximum profit for the put calendar spread was 1.00, so the difference between the two spreads favors the combined spread, but not by a significant amount.

The 3.55 cost of the spread also represents the maximum potential loss. This is a significant difference when compared to the previous spread. There is a higher potential profit and a wider range of potential profitability.

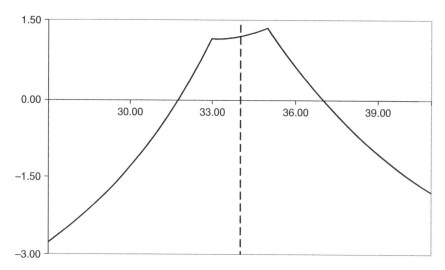

FIGURE 14.4 Payoff Diagram for Combined Calendar Spread

Expressed differently, there is more potential reward. To gain more potential reward, there is also more risk associated with the combined spread. This risk is represented by the higher cost and potential maximum loss of the combined spread.

The unusual looking payoff diagram in Figure 14.4 shows the payout at expiration of the February options. Like the previous diagram, the price where XYZ was trading upon initiation of the trade is highlighted with a vertical line. Note that it is right in the middle of the range where there would be a maximum payout at expiration. Also, note between the 33 and 35 strike prices on this diagram there is a slight upward slope adjustment to the payout. The unusual slope relates to the impact of interest rates on call prices relative to put prices.

This diagram somewhat resembles a short strangle, with curved lines as opposed to straight lines. This spread was covered in Chapter 6 where it was mentioned that due to a short strangle consisting of naked short option positions it may not be appropriate for all individual traders. Since there are no naked option positions with the combined calendar spread, this spread may be considered as an alternative to the short strangle or any other neutral spread.

As a quick review, calendar spreads involve two different option expiration dates, with a potential trading decision being part of the overall trading plan of the spread. All option trades are at minimum a two-step trading decision involving time and price projections. A calendar spread is at minimum a three-step trade, with a plan for what to do with the long option at expiration being part of the equation.

Finally, there are assumptions that come into play when projecting the long option's price at the outcome at expiration of the short option. The pricing inputs—specifically implied volatility—for an option usually vary greatly over the life of an option. Projecting this level is a key element when considering a calendar spread.

CHAPTER 15

Diagonal Spreads

A diagonal spread shares characteristics of both calendar spreads covered in the previous chapter, along with vertical spreads which were discussed in Chapters 7 and 8. The calendar portion stems from the spread consisting of options that have two different expiration dates. When compared to a calendar spread, the difference with a diagonal is that the strike prices are not the same for both options. As far as the similarity with a vertical spread, this relates to a diagonal spread consisting of two of the same type of options (put or call) and the options having different strike prices, with one option being long and the other being a short position.

Also, as calendar spreads may be created using long positions in LEAPS options, there are also some that consider a diagonal spread as a viable alternative to a covered call or buy write. Using a LEAPS call option in place of a stock for a covered call was covered in Chapter 2, but will be reviewed again in this chapter.

CALL DIAGONAL SPREAD

A basic diagonal spread using call options would be created through the purchase of a call option with longer time to expiration than a corresponding call option that is sold short. The shorted option would also have a higher strike price than the option that was purchased. With a shorter time to expiration combined with a higher strike price, the option being sold short should have a lower premium than the option that is purchased. For instance, if a call option with a strike price of 50 and 30 days left to

TABLE 15.1 Inputs and Output Used to Create a Long XYZ Jul
35 / Short XYZ May 45 Diagonal Call Spread

Inputs	
Days to May Expiration	30
Days to July Expiration	90
Volatility	35%
Interest Rate	1.00%
XYZ Price	44.25
Output	
XYZ May 45 Call	1.45
XYZ Jul 35 Call	9.60
XYZ May 45 / Jul 35 Diagonal Call Spread	8.15

expiration were sold, and a call option on the same underlying with a
strike price of 40 and 90 days to expiration were purchased, then a diagonal spread would have been established.

With this spread involving a near-term call with a 50 strike price and a
longer-term call option with a 40 strike price, the goal and maximum profit
would be reached with the stock trading right at 50.00 at expiration. The
spread will have a profit if the stock is over 50.00 at expiration, but this
profit would be cut a little due to the effect of time and price movement on
the remaining long option and placing this option farther in the money.

An example to help with more understanding of the call diagonal
spread was created using the options appearing in Table 15.1. Using an
implied volatility of 35 percent for both options and an underlying stock
price of 44.25, the May 45 Call with 30 days to expiration would be trading
for 1.45 while the longer-term July 35 Call that has 90 days to expiration
would be quoted at 9.60. Initiating a long position in the Jul 35 Call and a
short position in the May 45 Call would result in a net debit of 8.15.

Table 15.2 displays the key levels for this diagonal spread based on the
assumption that the implied volatility for the remaining Jul 35 Call will remain steady at 35 percent. Implied volatility does move around, sometimes
dramatically over the course of a single day, but an assumption needs to be
made to determine some sort of value for the remaining long call position
at May expiration. Assuming a steady implied volatility level is consistently
applied throughout this chapter.

The maximum potential loss for this call diagonal spread is 8.15, which
is also the cost of the spread. If the stock drops dramatically, to the point
where the remaining long call has no value, then the remaining long option
would theoretically have no value on expiration of the short option. The
result is a loss equal to the premium paid to initiate the spread. Using a

TABLE 15.2 Key Levels for Long XYZ Jul 35 / Short XYZ May 45 Diagonal Call Spread

	Level	Explanation
Break-even Level	42.80	Long Option Value equal to Debit Paid to Enter Trade
Maximum Dollar Gain	2.00	Maximum Long Option Value versus Short Option Value
Maximum Gain Price	45.00	Short Option Strike Price
Maximum Dollar Loss	8.15	Premium Paid for Trade
Maximum Loss Price	23.50	Long Option Has No Value

pricing calculator, this level is approximately 23.50, a pretty big drop from the current price of 44.25. This option does still have 60 days remaining until expiration, so the possibility of the stock rebounding and there being some sort of value in this Jul 35 Call over the next 60 days does exist.

The desired profit result at expiration of the short option on a diagonal spread occurs if the stock is at the strike price of the short option. At this level, the remaining long in-the-money call option will have maximum value relative to the expiring option. For the diagonal spread in this example, this level would be 45.00. At 45.00 the Jul 35 Call would have a value of 10.15, which is 2.00 more than the debit that was paid to initiate this spread.

Finally, the break-even level of this spread is estimated at around 42.80. At this level and again using an assumption that the implied volatility has remained steady at 35 percent, the long option would be valued at 8.15. The spread cost 8.15 to initiate and with 8.15 in value for the open long call position, the result is a break-even trade.

The payoff diagram for a diagonal spread created with call options generally will look like the diagram in Figure 15.1. Note the curved nature of the payout above and below the upper strike of 45. This is due to the impact of time to expiration and what this does to the value of the remaining open option position.

At the maximum profit level of 45.00, the line starts to move lower in both directions. However it starts to move dramatically lower when the stock price drops, while the drop is pretty miniscule as the stock price moves higher, as this represents the impact of how deep in the money options lose time value as the stock moves farther in the money.

Finally, note that the diagonal spread has a very similar appearance to a covered call payout. The difference is the line curves more as the stock price moves lower. Also, a very big difference is that the diagonal spread has a much lower maximum potential loss than a corresponding covered call. Creating a covered call instead of a diagonal spread results in a

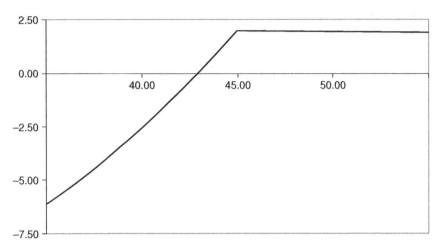

FIGURE 15.1 Payoff Diagram for Long XYZ Jul 35 / Short XYZ May 45 Diagonal Call Spread

maximum loss exposure that is almost equal to the full stock value, which is much higher than that of the long call option.

LEAPS CALL DIAGONAL SPREAD

A diagonal spread may also consist of a longer-term option that has more than a year to expiration as the long portion of the trade. These options are known as Long Term AnticiPation Securities, or LEAPS. Not all stocks with options trading on them have LEAPS available, but generally stocks that have active option markets also have LEAPS available.

Creating a diagonal spread using a LEAPS call as the long option in the position would result in a similar payout as the diagonal spread with a shorter time to expiration. However, there is an increase in similarity to a covered call when the long option is a LEAPS option. The time value component of a deep in-the-money LEAPS call will lose value at a very slow pace. Also, a deep in-the-money LEAPS call will have a delta very close to 1.00 where the option will gain and lose value on almost a dollar-for-dollar basis as the underlying stock gains and loses value. Since the LEAPS option will change value similarly to the underlying stock, it can be an excellent substitute for the underlying stock when considering a covered call position.

To demonstrate a diagonal call spread using a LEAPS option, the securities in Table 15.3 were used. Two January expiration dates represent

TABLE 15.3 Inputs and Output Used to Create a Long XYZ Jan 2012 30 / Short XYZ Jan 2011 50 Diagonal Call Spread

Inputs	
Days to Jan 2011 Expiration	45
Days to Jan 2012 Expiration	410
Volatility	30%
Interest Rate	1.00%
XYZ Price	48.75
Output	
XYZ Jan 2011 50 Call	1.55
XYZ Jan 2012 30 Call	19.40
XYZ Jan 2012 30/Jan 2011 50 Diagonal Call Spread	17.85

the options with January 2011 being 45 days out and January 2012 expiration occurring in 410 days. Using an implied volatility of 30 percent with an underlying stock price of 48.75, the two options are priced at 1.55 for the near-term call and 19.40 for the longer term January 2012 LEAPS call.

From these two options a diagonal spread would be initiated for a cost of 17.85. As far as option spreads go, this may be considered somewhat expensive. However, if the stock is purchased and the near-term Jan 2011 Call options were sold, the price would be almost three times the spread cost of 17.85. Using stock in this example, purchasing shares would cost 48.75 and the cost would be slightly offset by the income from selling the call and receiving 1.55. This would result in a cost of 47.20, which is a large difference than the debit of 17.85 to replicate the payout using a LEAPS instead of purchasing shares.

Table 15.4 covers the key levels for this diagonal spread using the Jan 2012 Call option as the long option in the spread. At 50.00, which is the strike price of the short call option, the spread would result in a dollar gain

TABLE 15.4 Key Levels for Long XYZ Jan 2012 30 / Short XYZ Jan 2011 50 Diagonal Call Spread

	Level	Explanation
Break-even Level	47.25	Long Option Value equal to Debit Paid to Enter Trade
Maximum Dollar Gain	2.65	Maximum Long Option Value versus Short Option Value
Maximum Gain Price	50.00	Short Option Strike Price
Maximum Dollar Loss	17.85	Premium Paid for Trade
Maximum Loss Price	12.50	Long Option Has No Value

of 2.65. This result uses assumptions due to there being an open option position in the LEAPS option when the key levels are determined. That assumption, as in the previous example, is that the implied volatility level of 30 percent is the same at the expiration of the near-term option as it was when the spread was initiated.

The maximum dollar loss for this spread is the amount paid to initiate the trade, or 17.85. Theoretically this occurs if the stock trades down to 12.50 at expiration of the short option. This would be, to say the least, a pretty dramatic move. A factor to keep in mind regarding the maximum potential loss is in comparison to a covered call. If the stock were purchased instead of the LEAPS call, the maximum loss is the amount paid for that trade, or 47.20. The dollar risk of the diagonal spread is lower than the dollar risk of the covered call.

Finally, the break-even level for this trade is 47.25. Using a pricing calculator to estimate the value of the option at 47.25, the LEAPS option would be worth 17.85. This is the same price paid to enter the trade.

The payoff diagram in Figure 15.2 appears very much like a covered call payout. If the diagram were expanded to include all prices down to 0.00, the difference between a covered call and a diagonal spread would be much more obvious. As the underlying stock price moves lower, the line that represents the payout at expiration of the short term option would start to lose the angle that moves lower and almost become flat, as the closer to 0.00 the stock price gets, the less value the remaining call option has until it is equal to 0.00 at 12.50.

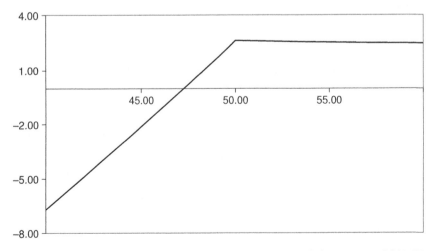

FIGURE 15.2 Payoff Diagram for Long XYZ Jan 2012 30 / Short XYZ Jan 2011 50 Diagonal Call Spread

PUT DIAGONAL SPREAD

When there is a bearish bias regarding the future direction of a stock, a diagonal spread may also be created using put options. A diagonal spread using puts is very similar to the call version, with one of the goals being benefitting from the time deterioration of an option with less time to expiration relative to an option that has more time left until expiration. The long option will have a higher strike price, which will result in even less loss of time value over the course of the trade.

For example, a put diagonal spread may consist of selling a put option with a 35 strike and 30 days to expiration and buying a put option with a 45 strike and 120 days to expiration. If the underlying stock is trading around 36.00, then the longer term option is deep in the money. The near term 35 strike put is slightly out of the money, but still very close to the underlying price of 36.00. With 30 days remaining, this option should lose value at a much quicker rate than the long option. The combination of being long a deep in-the-money option with a longer time to expiration and short a near-term put option that has less time to expiration would result in the short option losing more value than the long option over the following 30 days.

The options in Table 15.5 illustrate how the difference between expirations and strikes works in a diagonal spread created with put options. The options are priced to create the put diagonal spread by using an implied volatility of 30 percent along with options expiring in 40 and 100 days and an underlying stock price of 20.25. April expiration is 40 days out and the XYZ Apr 20 Put is trading at .70. The longer-term option is the June expiration option and an in-the-money XYZ Jun 25 Put would be quoted at 4.85.

TABLE 15.5 Inputs and Output Used to Create Long XYZ Jun 25 / Short XYZ Apr 20 Diagonal Put Spread

Inputs	
Days to April Expiration	40
Days to June Expiration	100
Volatility	30%
Interest Rate	1.00%
XYZ Price	20.25
Output	
XYZ April 20 Put	0.70
XYZ June 25 Put	4.85
XYZ Jun 25 / Apr 20 Diagonal Put Spread	4.15

TABLE 15.6 Key Levels for Long XYZ Jun 25 / Short XYZ Apr 20 Diagonal Put Spread

	Level	Explanation
Break-even Level	20.80	Long Option Value Equal to Debit Paid to Enter Trade
Maximum Dollar Gain	0.85	Maximum Long Option Value versus Short Option Value
Maximum Gain Price	20.00	Short Option Strike Price
Maximum Dollar Loss	4.15	Premium Paid for Trade
Maximum Loss Price	33.50	Long Option Has No Value

The result of selling the XYZ Apr 20 Put and receiving 0.70 and buying the XYZ Jun 25 Put and paying out 4.85 would be a debit of 4.15. This debit is also the maximum potential loss that could be realized at April expiration from this diagonal put spread. Using a pricing calculator to determine at what price to the upside there is no value remaining in the open long option position results in an estimated break-even price of 33.50.

Continuing with the key levels for this trade that are shown in Table 15.6, the maximum profit for this trade is 0.85. If the stock settles down just 0.25 from where the trade was initiated at 20.00 the short April put will expire with no value. The profit from this short position will be the 0.70 that was taken in when the trade was initiated. In addition, the long Jun 25 Put should be worth 0.15 more than it was when the trade was initiated The long option does lose some time value, but this is made up through the stock moving a bit lower. The combination of these two profits results in 0.85 for the overall trade.

Finally, the break-even level for this trade would occur if the stock were to trade up to 20.80 at expiration. The short option would once again expire with no value, but the long put would have lost value to the point of being priced at 4.15. At 20.80 with 60 days to expiration and an implied volatility level of 30 percent, the XYZ Jun 25 Put would be valued at 4.15 or the cost to initiate the trade.

Figure 15.3 depicts the payout of the put diagonal spread at April expiration. The peak of profitability comes at the 20.00 level and then tapers off a bit as the stock price moves lower. Below 20.00 the short option will be in the money and the time value component of the long option will diminish as the price moves lower. This results in the curved nature of this line. To the upside, the remaining long option continues to lose value, until at 33.50 there is no value left at April expiration.

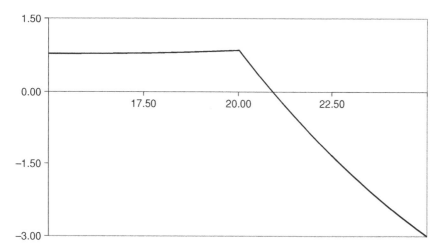

FIGURE 15.3 Payoff Diagram for Long XYZ Jun 25 / Short XYZ Apr 20 Diagonal Put Spread

LEAPS PUT DIAGONAL SPREAD

Just like the call version of the diagonal spread, a put version may be constructed using a LEAPS option as the underlying long option. In this case a deep in-the-money put option would be the underlying and in addition to representing the long leg of a spread may also be used to express a short opinion in the underlying stock. Selling a near-term put with a strike price close to the underlying stock will be the other part of the spread. As in the other diagonal spreads, this near-term option should lose time value more quickly than the long option.

The options in Table 15.7 were used to create the put diagonal spread to demonstrate the underlying being a longer-term option or a LEAPS put. With XYZ trading at 62.85, an XYZ Jun 60 Put with 50 days until expiration would be trading at 1.90, and a longer-term in-the-money XYZ Jan 75 Put would trade at 15.15. This January option expires 260 days in the future—the following year. These prices are based on an implied volatility of 35 percent for both options.

Using these prices, the Jan 2012 75 Put would be purchased for a debit of 15.15. This cost would be offset by the sale of the slightly out-of-the-money Jun 60 Put which would bring in 1.90. Combining these two transactions would result in a cost of 13.25 for this diagonal spread.

TABLE 15.7   Inputs and Output Used to Create Long XYZ Jan
2012 75 / Short XYZ Jun 60 Diagonal Put Spread

Inputs	
Days to Jun 2011 Expiration	50
Days to Jan 2012 Expiration	260
Volatility	35%
Interest Rate	1.00%
XYZ Price	62.85
Output	
XYZ Jun 2011 60 Put	1.90
XYZ Jan 2012 75 Put	15.15
XYZ Jan 2012 75 / May 60 Diagonal Put Spread	13.25

This 13.25 cost is also the first key level to discuss in Table 15.8. The cost of this trade is also the maximum potential loss based on both options having no value at expiration. This would involve a large rally in the underlying to a price of 160.00 according to a pricing calculator. This is a gain of almost 150 percent, so the possibility is pretty unlikely over the next 50 days.

Using the pricing calculator, the Jan 2012 75 Put would have a value of 16.75 if the stock were at 60.00 at expiration of the near-term option. With the other option expiring with no value, this would result in a profit of 3.35 for the spread and would represent the maximum profit for this trade at June expiration.

Finally, the break-even level for this trade would occur with the stock at 64.90 at June expiration. Using the pricing calculator with the assumption that the implied volatility for the Jan 2012 option stays steady at 35 percent would result in a value for the long put of 13.25. As this is also

TABLE 15.8   Key Levels for Long XYZ Jan 2012 75 / Short XYZ Jun 60 Diagonal
Put Spread

	Level	Explanation
Break-even Level	64.90	Long Option Value equal to Debit Paid to Enter Trade
Maximum Dollar Gain	3.35	Maximum Long Option Value versus Short Option Value
Maximum Gain Price	60.00	Short Option Strike Price
Maximum Dollar Loss	13.25	Premium Paid for Trade
Maximum Loss Price	160.00	Long Option Has No Value

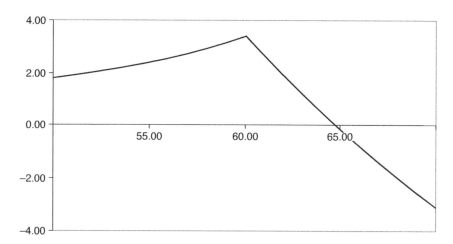

FIGURE 15.4 Payoff Diagram for Long XYZ Jan 2012 75 / Short XYZ Jun 60 Put Spread

the debit incurred when the trade was initiated the result is a break-even trade.

The payoff diagram for this trade appears in Figure 15.4. The lines are a bit more curved than the other LEAPS example, where the time difference between the two options is much closer. Because the longer-term long put option has much more time to expiration than the previous example, the lines are less linear than in the previous example.

DOUBLE DIAGONAL SPREAD

The final example in this chapter involves combining two diagonals to create a unique payout. A very similar approach would involve combining two vertical spreads to create an iron condor. This strategy was described in Chapter 10.

When two vertical spreads are combined to create an iron condor, both of the verticals spreads are done at a credit, with one being a bull spread and the other a bear spread. The result of a double diagonal is similar, with one being bullish and the other bearish. As a result of both sides of the spread being done at a debit, the double diagonal will be put on at a debit where an iron condor would bring in a credit.

As mentioned earlier in this chapter, a diagonal spread may have a slightly bullish or bearish bias to it. By combining two spreads that have different directional tilts to them, a market-neutral spread that benefits from

TABLE 15.9 Inputs and Output Used to Create Double
Diagonal Spread

Inputs	
Days to August Expiration	40
Days to November Expiration	100
Volatility	35%
Interest Rate	1.00%
XYZ Price	48.00
Output	
XYZ Aug 46 Put	1.30
XYZ Nov 50 Put	4.60
XYZ Nov 46 Call	4.60
XYZ Aug 50 Call	1.40
XYZ Aug 50 / Nov 46 Call Diagonal	3.20
XYZ Aug 46 / Nov 50 Put Diagonal	3.30
Double Diagonal	6.50

the difference in time deterioration between longer term and shorter-term options may be created.

The options from Table 15.9 will demonstrate how combining a bullish biased and bearish diagonal can result in a spread that will benefit from a stock that is expected to settle in a certain range at expiration of the short options in the spread. In addition to a price forecast resulting in a profit, the other piece of the trade that should work in the trader's favor is the time deterioration difference between the short and long option positions.

Using an implied volatility of 35 percent and a stock price of 48.00, put and call option prices with expirations in 40 and 100 days were determined. The expirations used are August for the near-term options and November for the 100-day options. Although this spread uses non-LEAPS oriented options, it is also possible to use options with much more time to expiration as the long in the spreads.

To keep this example simple, the two legs of the overall spread will be discussed separately, then they will be combined for the overall payout. The put diagonal will consist of buying an in-the-money XYZ Nov 50 Put for 4.60, and selling the out-of-the-money XYZ Aug 46 Put for a credit of 1.30 to create a put diagonal spread at a cost of 3.30.

The call spread involves selling the out-of-the-money and near-term XYZ Aug 50 Call for a credit of 1.40, and then purchasing the in-the-money XYZ Nov 46 Call, also for a cost of 4.60. The result is a cost of 3.20 for the call leg of the double diagonal spread.

TABLE 15.10 Key Levels for Double Diagonal Spread

	Level	Explanation
Upper Break-even Level	52.50	Call Spread Gain equals Put Spread Loss
Lower Break-even Level	44.25	Put Spread Gain equals Call Spread Loss
Maximum Dollar Gain Range	1.25–1.50	Maximum Long Option Value versus Short Option Value
Maximum Gain Price Range	46.00–50.00	Short Option Strike Prices
Maximum Dollar Loss	2.60	Premium Paid for More Expensive Leg
Maximum Loss Price	31.50	Loss on Call Leg offset by Put Leg Profit

By taking the cost of both the call and put legs of the double diagonal spread, the result is a cost of 6.50. Interestingly, the maximum potential loss on this spread is much less than the cost of the spread. In fact it basically is about half this amount. If the stock rallies, the put spread would have no value, but there would be some value in the call spread, specifically the remaining open position in the long call option. In a case where the stock falls dramatically, there would be no value in the call options, but the remaining long put option would have value. The result is a maximum potential loss of around 2.60 if the stock were to fall dramatically to the low 30 s at near term expiration.

Continuing with the break-even levels in Table 15.10, there is a range where a maximum profit exists. Between the two short strike prices of 46.00 and 50.00, the short options would expire with no value, but there would be value remaining in the open long option positions. This value would result in a profit in a range between 1.25 and 1.50.

Finally, break-even levels for this spread are determined using the same assumption that implied volatility is steady into expiration. To the downside, at 44.25 the spread would break even, and to the upside, the stock settling at 52.50 or higher would result in a loss for this spread.

Figure 15.5 demonstrates the payout at expiration of the August options for this double diagonal spread. The shape is similar to a long condor or iron condor, with the exception of the lines having a much more curved nature to them. Note even the area between the strike prices is not a straight line and dips slightly toward the 48.00 price level, which is also the price where the stock is when the trade is initiated.

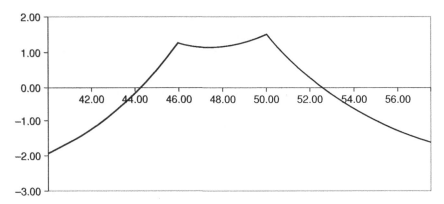

FIGURE 15.5 Payoff Diagram for Double Diagonal Spread

Although this chart is limited to prices from 40.00 to 58.00, as the stock moves farther out in either direction the line representing the profit or loss of the spread begins to flatten out and become basically linear.

The diagonal spread has multiple projections that should be made when considering the trade. A price level is projected to the expiration of a single option and then possibly a projection would be in place for a farther out expiration. Combining these two projections may be difficult enough, but there is also the question of implied volatility changing around between the time a trade is initiated and when the first option expires. The examples in this chapter assumed the implied volatility would be pretty steady over the life of the short option, but this is not always the case when actually trading a diagonal spread.

CHAPTER 16

Delta Neutral Trading

D elta neutral trading refers to a method of putting on positions where the main concern is not necessarily a move in the underlying stock price. If anything, a spread that is delta neutral is used to avoid risk to a move in the underlying stock. The goal might be to benefit from how the passage of time may impact the relative value of options. Another potential motivation behind a delta neutral trade may be based on the assumption that there might be a change in implied volatility that would positively impact the price of a spread. Once again this positive impact on the value of a spread would have nothing to do with a price forecast for the underlying stock.

Another aspect to delta-neutral positions relates primarily to market makers. An option market maker is continuously trying to buy options for less and sell for greater than what they believe the option is worth based on their model. When a market maker is able to trade an option at one of these favorable prices, they will lock in their profit and hedge their position through an offsetting trade in the underlying stock. The combination of these two trades results in a delta-neutral situation. When delta neutral, a relatively small price move will have little impact on the profit or loss related to the spread.

DELTA REVIEW

Although delta and all the Greeks were covered in Chapter 4, this section will quickly review the concept of delta and demonstrate what impact initiating a spread trade has on delta. The delta of an option is an indication of how much in value that option is expected to change based on a one-point change in the underlying security. If an XYZ 50 Call has a delta of 0.50, then the value of that option would be expected to gain 0.50 if XYZ goes up by a point. A call option is limited to a minimum delta of 0.00 and a maximum delta of 1.00. An option should not go up by more than a point based on price change if an underlying stock goes up by a point. Conversely, for an option with little or no value if a stock moves by a point, it is possible for the option to experience no price change based on delta. This case would be an option with a delta of 0.00.

Put options have negative deltas as a put is expected to lose value when a stock moves higher, and gain value when a stock moves lower. For example, if a put option has a delta of -0.50, a one-point drop in the underlying should result in a gain for the option of 0.50. This goes back to early math education, and the concept that a negative multiplied by a negative equals a positive.

DELTA-NEUTRAL POSITIONS

A delta-neutral position results from taking positions in instruments that have exposure to the same underlying security. These positions will have a combination of long and short delta exposure to the underlying. The result will be limited price exposure to the stock or market that is being traded. The exact exposure that is taken on through each individual stock or option contract is determined. They are then matched up to eliminate price exposure. For example, if one position has a delta exposure equivalent to long 500 shares of XYZ and another position is held that has a delta exposure of short 500 shares of XYZ then the combination results in a delta neutral position.

The first example of how a position may be considered delta neutral will use a spread that is similar to a covered call or buy write, as it would be called in this case. To obtain delta neutrality, the spread will involve an unequal amount of call options relative to the long position in the underlying stock. This is due to the underlying stock having a delta equal to 1.00, while the call options sold to obtain negative delta positions have a delta of less than 1.00.

The positions in Table 16.1 are combined to demonstrate how a delta-neutral position appears or is created. The trader holds a long position of 700 shares of XYZ stock. A stock always has a delta equal to 1.00, as a one-point move up or down in a stock results in a one-point gain or loss,

TABLE 16.1 Sample Delta-Neutral Position

Position	Security	Price	Delta	Position Delta
Long 700	XYZ Stock	37.50	1.00	700
Short 10	XYZ 35 Call	1.50	0.70	(700)

depending on the position held in that stock. Since the stock has a delta of 1.00, the result is a delta position of long 700.

The other position involves a short position in the XYZ 35 Call options of short 10 options. As an option contract represents 100 shares, this is equivalent to 1000 shares. Since the delta of the XYZ 35 Call is 0.70, 10 XYZ 35 Call options have a delta position equal to 700 shares. However, since these options are short, the result is a delta short position of 700 for the option position. After combining the two positions, the result is delta-neutral exposure to XYZ.

Delta-neutral positions should result in no gain or loss through the combined positions for a small price change in the underlying. Whenever prices undergo large changes, the delta of underlying options changes also. When there is a change in the delta, the neutral price exposure that the position had does not exist anymore. The Greek that relates to this concept is known as Gamma and will be covered in the next section. However, for now the focus will be directly on delta and some small price moves.

In the case of a small price move in XYZ, the profit or loss impact for the combined position should be a net break even. To demonstrate, the profit and loss impact of a rise of 0.50 and a drop of 0.50 in XYZ are displayed in Tables 16.2 and 16.3.

The first case involves a rise in XYZ of 0.50 and the price impact this has on the stock and the XYZ 35 Call. In the case of XYZ stock, the stock price would go from 37.50 to 38.00. A long position of 700 shares with a 0.50 gain per share results in a $350 gain on the long stock position.

The option price change and dollar loss is a little more complex. With a delta of 0.70 the price impact on a 0.50 gain in XYZ on the option would be a change of 0.35, or 0.70 times 0.50. As the account holder has a position of 10 contracts this would have an impact of $350 with the math behind this

TABLE 16.2 Impact of a 0.50 Price Gain in XYZ

Position	Security	Price	Delta	Position Delta	XYZ Change	Profit/ Loss
Long 700	XYZ Stock	37.50	1.00	700	+0.50	+$350
Short 10	XYZ 35 Call	1.50	0.70	(700)	+0.50	−$350

TABLE 16.3 Impact of a 0.50 Price Drop in XYZ

Position	Security	Price	Delta	Position Delta	XYZ Change	Profit/Loss
Long 700	XYZ Stock	37.50	1.00	700	−0.50	−$350
Short 10	XYZ 35 Call	1.50	0.70	(700)	−0.50	+$350

being 0.35 times 100 times 10. Each option contract represents 100 shares, and 10 is the number of contracts held by the account. Since this account is short 10 contracts, the final result is a loss of $350. Therefore, these two positions result in a net break even for the account.

If the stock were to drop by 0.50, the impact would be a loss of $350 from the long stock position of 700 shares. With the loss of 0.50 in the underlying stock, the XYZ 35 Call would see a loss of 0.35 (again 0.70 times 0.50) per contract. Using the same math as in the example where XYZ gained .50, the price impact is $350 on the option position, but in this case the $350 is a benefit to the account, as this was a short position. The net result with a drop of 0.50 in XYZ is a gain of $350 on the short option position and a net break even for the account.

Delta-neutral spreads may also be created using a combination of options and excluding any direct exposure to the underlying stock through a long or short stock position. One of the most common delta neutral spreads is the straddle. Whether long or short, if a straddle is initiated with options that have a strike price that is very close to where the underlying is trading at the time, it should probably be very close to a delta-neutral position.

For example, the two long option positions in Table 16.4 would be combined to create a trade with neutral delta exposure to XYZ. In this example, the underlying stock is trading at 40.00, equal to the strike price of the corresponding options.

The spread in Table 16.4 is a long straddle with the motivation behind this trade being an increase in volatility. The goal would be a large and hopefully quick price move, either higher or lower. However, initially this trade appears to gain no benefit from a price move. For example, in Tables 16.5 and 16.6, there are the results from a 0.50 move higher and 0.50 move lower in XYZ.

TABLE 16.4 Straddle Resulting in a Delta-Neutral Position

Position	Security	Price	Delta	Position Delta
Long 10	XYZ 40 Call	1.60	0.50	500
Long 10	XYZ 40 Put	1.60	−0.50	(500)

TABLE 16.5 Impact of a 0.50 Price Gain in XYZ

Position	Security	Price	Delta	Position Delta	XYZ Change	Profit/Loss
Long 10	XYZ 40 Call	1.60	0.50	500	+0.50	+$250
Long 10	XYZ 40 Put	1.60	−0.50	(500)	+0.50	−$250

    With XYZ moving up by 0.50, the expectation would be a positive price impact on the long call position and a negative impact on the long put option position. With a delta of 0.50 for the long call position, the result is a gain of $250. The math to determine this profit comes from there being a long position in 10 contracts, which represents 1000 shares. With a delta of 0.50 multiplied by 1000 shares, the result is a delta of 500. Taking the price change of 0.50 multiplied by the delta of 500 results in a profit of $250.

    For the long position in the XYZ 40 Put options, the result is a reciprocal loss of $250. This result comes from the combination of a positive price change in the underlying and the exposure to the underlying being a negative delta. This negative delta results from the long position in the options combined with the negative delta per put option. With a delta of −500 for the 10 XYZ 40 Puts, multiplied by the price change of a positive 0.50, results in a dollar loss of $250 on the put position.

    In a case where the stock moves lower, the opposite profit and loss effect would occur with the spread. The call position would lose an equal amount as the put position gained. The math is the same as when the stock moves higher, just with the XYZ 40 Put gaining $250 and the XYZ Call losing $250.

    If the expectation behind putting on a straddle involves the price movement of the underlying, then how does this trade begin to become profitable when the delta of the position in 0.00? The answer to this question is in time, as the stock moves farther in direction, the delta of one option becomes much greater than the offsetting delta of the other option. How the delta changes with larger price moves is covered in this next section.

TABLE 16.6 Impact of a 0.50 Price Drop in XYZ

Position	Security	Price	Delta	Position Delta	XYZ Change	Profit/Loss
Long 10	XYZ 40 Call	1.60	0.50	500	−0.50	−$250
Long 10	XYZ 40 Put	1.60	−0.50	(500)	−0.50	+$250

GAMMA

As mentioned in the previous section and in Chapter 4 where the Greeks were covered more in depth, the delta can constantly change based on the underlying price changes. The Greek that indicates the expected change in delta based on a change in the underlying security is known as gamma.

As a quick review, if the gamma of an option is .05, then the delta would be expected to rise by 0.05 with a 1 point increase in the price of the underlying and the delta would drop by 0.05 with a one-point decrease in the price of the underlying. Gamma has a varying impact on the value of options as the underlying stock moves higher or lower.

Using the trade from the previous example and a pricing calculator, the impact of price changes, both higher and lower, appear in Table 16.7. This table has a lot of information packed into a fairly small space, and gamma was excluded to keep things fairly simple. The price of the underlying stock was at 40.00 when the price of 1.60 for both the put and call options were determined for the straddle.

As the stock price moves higher or lower, with all else staying the same, the straddle does make money. This occurs as the option that is benefitting from the price move gains more than the corresponding option loses in value. Taking a look at a move from 40.00 to 38.00, the XYZ 40 Put gains 1.16 moving from 1.60 to 2.76. The XYZ 40 Call would lose value, but only 0.84. This results in a profit of 0.32 for the long straddle position. As the stock moves lower, the profit of the put option continues to more than offset the loss from the call option until a very big move down. Eventually,

TABLE 16.7 Option Prices and Deltas at a Variety of Price Levels

XYZ	40 Put Price	40 Put Delta	40 Call Price	40 Call Delta	Spread Price	Spread Delta	Spread P/L
30.00	10.00	−1.00	0.00	0.00	10.00	−1.00	6.80
32.00	8.02	−0.99	0.02	0.01	8.04	−0.98	4.84
34.00	6.08	−0.94	0.08	0.06	6.16	−0.88	2.96
36.00	4.29	−0.84	0.29	0.16	4.58	−0.68	1.38
38.00	2.76	−0.68	0.76	0.32	3.52	−0.36	0.32
40.00	1.60	−0.50	1.60	0.50	3.20	0.00	0.00
42.00	0.83	−0.30	2.83	0.70	3.66	0.40	0.46
44.00	0.39	−0.16	4.39	0.84	4.78	0.68	1.58
46.00	0.16	−0.07	6.16	0.93	6.32	0.86	3.12
48.00	0.06	−0.03	8.06	0.97	8.12	0.94	4.92
50.00	0.02	−0.01	10.02	0.99	10.04	0.98	6.84

the stock moves far enough away from the strike price of 40.00 that there is no value in the 40 Call at all and the 40 Put moves almost dollar for dollar with the stock.

In the other direction, as the stock moves higher, the call option gains value at a more rapid pace than the put option loses value. Once again eventually the put option has no more value to give up and the call continues to benefit from a higher price move. This deep in the money, the 40 Call will move at almost a dollar for dollar basis with XYZ.

MARKET MAKER TRADING

An option market maker is an individual or firm that posts prices where they are a willing buyer or seller of options. The prices they are willing to buy or sell are based on a fair value for the option that has been determined by one of a few option-pricing models. A market maker will take this price and post a buy price, or bid, below this fair value and a sell price, or ask, higher than this fair value. They have a two-part goal throughout the day, first buy below the fair value and sell above the fair value whenever a customer order is placed. Second have as little exposure to price moves in the underlying security as possible.

This first goal is achieved through the posting of accurate market prices while the second goal is achieved through trading the underlying security or other options on this security to maintain a neutral exposure. Delta neutrality is a piece of this goal, so a very basic example is used to demonstrate the transactions a market maker might use to keep their exposure to price movements in the underlying at a minimum.

If a market maker receives an order to sell call options on XYZ that is equal to the bid price he is posting for this option he would facilitate it by buying these call options. Immediately after purchasing these call options, he would have long exposure to the underlying stock. In order to reduce this exposure, he would execute an order to sell short shares of XYZ.

A market maker may also take on negative exposure to the underlying stock moving higher when executing public orders. For instance if a public order to sell put options on XYZ were facilitated by the market maker, he would take the other side of this transaction and purchase those puts. Through buying this XYZ put he now has risk that the stock would move higher. To mitigate this risk he would purchase a certain number of shares of XYZ.

As an example, the figures from Table 16.8 would represent the needed outputs for a market maker to initiate a delta-neutral trade. With XYZ

TABLE 16.8 Model Output for XYZ 40 Call

XYZ Price	40.00
XYZ 40 Call FV	2.00
XYZ Delta	0.50

trading at 40.00, a 40 strike call has a fair value of 2.00. Also, the market maker's software determines the Delta of this option is 0.50.

With a fair value of 2.00, a market maker wants to purchase this option at a price lower than 2.00 and sell this option at a level higher than the fair value of 2.00. In order to do this he will quote a bid price lower than the fair value and an offer price above the fair value. The quote for this option may be something like what appears in Table 16.9.

A market maker is willing to purchase 10 contracts of the XYZ 40 Call for 1.90 and sell 10 contracts of the XYZ 40 Call for 2.10. These are prices where a market order for 10 contracts, either buy or sell, should be executed immediately. If a market order to sell 10 XYZ 40 Calls is entered, it should be traded at 1.90 with the market maker being the purchaser of those contracts. A market order to buy 10 XYZ 40 Calls would be traded at 2.10, with the market maker being the seller at this price.

These two prices also represent a level where the market maker would do an offsetting trade in the underlying stock to remain hedged or delta neutral to small changes in the underlying stock. A specific example of this would be if a sell order comes in for 10 XYZ 40 Calls and the market maker fills this order through purchasing these options for 1.90 each.

Assuming the market maker had no position in XYZ options, the market maker's position is now Long 10 XYZ 40 Calls. This position exposes the market maker to price risk in XYZ stock, specifically if the stock goes lower, the call options would be expected to lose value. In order to offset this risk, the market maker would sell shares of XYZ. The specific number of shares sold would be based on the delta of the option.

The XYZ 40 Call has a delta of 0.50 and the market maker has purchased 10 of these contracts. As each contract represents 100 shares of stock the options represent 1000 shares of XYZ. However, the market maker thinks more in terms of delta than in terms of shares. With a delta of 0.50 and 1000 shares represented, the market maker has a long delta

TABLE 16.9 Market Maker Quote Based on Model Fair Value

	Bid Size	Bid	Ask	Ask Size
XYZ 40 Call	10	1.90	2.10	10

TABLE 16.10 Market Maker Positions after Executing 40 Call Trade

Buy/Sell	Contracts/ Shares	Instrument	Price	Delta	Delta Position
Buy	10	XYZ 40 Call	1.90	0.50	+500
Sell	500	XYZ	40.00	1.00	−500

position of 500. To get delta neutral he would need to sell 500 shares of XYZ. These transactions are shown in Table 16.10.

The market maker buys calls and sells shares with the result being neutral price exposure to XYZ. This neutral exposure exists only for small moves in the underlying price. Shortly after engaging in this transaction, XYZ drops 1.00 to 39.00. Table 16.11 shows the new levels that the market maker's pricing model gives that are relevant to this trade and his position. The delta drops some and so does the fair value of the XYZ 40 Call, which loses 0.50 from 2.00 to 1.50.

With a fair value of 1.50, the market maker is now displaying a bid–ask of 1.40 by 1.60 with a willingness to pay 1.40 for the XYZ 40 Call or sell them at 1.60. Before any other trades come in or the market maker changes his hedge, a public order comes in to purchase 10 XYZ 40 Calls at the market and the market maker executes this order by selling 10 XYZ 40 Calls at 1.60. With this he has now bought and sold 10 XYZ 40 Calls and would have a flat position in this contract. In addition to executing this trade, he would also buy back the 500 shares of XYZ that were sold short and do so at the market price of 39.00. A summary of all transactions appears in Table 16.12.

The market maker incurs a loss of $300 due to the transactions he executes to facilitate the public orders that have come into the marketplace. However, this loss is more than offset through transactions that were executed in XYZ stock to maintain a neutral position. The profit from the stock transactions came to $500 with a net result of $200 of profit to the market maker.

This example of a market maker's trading activity is extremely basic and truly more for illustrative purposes than an example of how individuals should approach delta-neutral trades. A market maker is responsible

TABLE 16.11 New Values after 1.00 Drop in XYZ

XYZ Price	39.00
XYZ 40 Call FV	1.50
XYZ Delta	0.45

TABLE 16.12 Trading Results Associated With Buy and Sell of 40 Call

Instrument	Buy	Buy Price	Sell	Sell Price	Profit/ Loss	$ Profit/ Loss
XYZ 40 Call	10	1.90	10	1.60	−0.30	−$300.00
XYZ	500	39.00	500	40.00	+1.00	+$500.00

for a variety of option strikes and expirations. They respond to order flow throughout the trading day and may hold a large number of option positions at any single moment. However, even with several positions their basic goal is to have as little exposure to price risk in the underlying security and buy and sell options at prices that allow them to be paid as liquidity providers.

CHAPTER 17

Executing a Spread Trade

T he majority of positions discussed in this book involve more than a single trading instrument. To initiate what should be considered a single position, although made up of more than a single security, more than one trade may need to be executed at the same time. As this may be a costly and short-term risky proposition, some consideration as to exactly how to go about getting into and out of a spread trade should be considered. Also, as all trades should have a plan for going into and coming out of the trade, the execution of the trade on both sides should be part of that plan.

Before jumping into executing a trade with two or more instruments at the same time (legs to the trade), single equity and option contract executions will be quickly covered. Then trades involving a stock and an underlying option will be discussed. The chapter progresses along to include trades that use a variety of legs. Finally, executing different components of a spread trade at different times will be covered, where a trader tries to take advantage of market swings to improve the profit and loss profile of a spread.

As a final note, many brokerage firms offer the ability to enter spread trades as a single transaction on their platforms. This functionality may take some of the risk out of making sure a spread trade is executed efficiently and correctly. If you are considering trading spreads, check with your broker on exactly the best method to execute a trade on their platform.

EXECUTING A STOCK OR OPTION TRADE

The true market for a stock or option is not always the last price. All actively traded securities have a price where the ability to quickly sell a certain number of shares or contracts and a price where shares or contracts may be purchased. The price where the ability to sell exists is known as the bid, or where the market is bidding to buy securities. The offer or ask, which is the price where the market is offering to sell, is also the price where a purchase may be made.

If a trader is long or owns a stock and they are considering selling this stock, the most important real time price for this stock is the bid price. The bid price is where shares may be sold quickly, at least at the current moment. In a case where a trader may have a short position he is considering covering or is thinking about purchasing shares of a stock to create a new long position, the most important price is the offer or ask.

In addition to a bid and ask there is a component to the quote known as the size. The size refers to the number of shares or contracts that are being offered for sale or bid by the marketplace. An example of a market quote for a stock appears in Table 17.1.

This sample of a market for XYZ is pretty typical of a market quote for a stock. In this quote, 1000 shares of XYZ may be sold for 50.01 and 2000 shares of XYZ could be bought for 50.04. That is as long as no market participant sells shares at 50.01 or purchases shares at 50.04 before a trader gets their order to the market. Also, it is always possible a trader bidding at 50.01 or offering at 50.04 could cancel their order in a millisecond. In this electronic age, markets move extremely fast and many orders are being executed by computers with no human intervention.

Individual option quotes are displayed in a similar manner to stock quotes, but do have some different aspects to them. Table 17.2 is a typical option quote. Note the bid size and ask sizes are both much smaller for the option quote. This is due to the aspect of an option contract representing 100 shares. Ten contracts being bid for represents 1000 shares of the underlying, and 15 contracts being offered, or on the ask, represents 1500 shares of XYZ.

Using this quote line, 10 XYZ Apr 50 Calls may be sold for 1.75, and 15 XYZ Apr 50 Call options may be purchased for 1.80. As with the stock

TABLE 17.1 Typical Market Quote for a Stock

	Bid Size	Bid	Ask	Ask Size	Last	Change	Volume
XYZ	1000	50.01	50.04	2000	50.02	−0.47	205000

TABLE 17.2 Typical Market Quote for an Option Contract

	Bid Size	Bid	Ask	Ask Size	Last	Change	Volume	Open Interest
XYZ Apr 50 Call	10	1.75	1.80	15	1.70	−0.15	155	2107

quote, this is dependent on no market orders jumping in front of a trader entering an order, or a market participant moving their order from the price that represents the current bid or ask.

The major difference between an option quote and a stock quote is an option quote line will usually include a piece of data known as open interest. The open interest would be stagnant throughout the day, as the data needed to calculate it is not accurately available on a real-time basis.

Open interest is the number of contracts that have been opened between buyers and sellers. Until a contract is traded between a buyer and a seller who are initiating new positions, the contract does not exist. Shares of stock are issued by companies and the number of shares outstanding does not change in the way that option contracts do. Options are contacts that are created when a buyer and seller of the agreement come together in a transaction. More information on how the open interest of options is determined and analyzed may be found at www.cboe.com.

In order to execute a stock trade, the action, number of shares, and type of trade would be entered. The action may be to buy, buy to cover, sell, and sell short. Buy and sell are very straightforward. A buy to cover order is done when exiting a short position. As far as selling short, there are a couple of extra steps that may be involved in putting on a short stock position.

When shorting a stock, the shares must be borrowed from a holder of the stock. The shares are borrowed and sold short. If the holder wants their shares back it is possible the short seller may have to buy shares to return to the lender. There are also times when shares may not be available to be borrowed and sold short. In that case, a short position may not be executed.

A rule that seems to come and go over time is the uptick rule. There have been periods where there has been a rule in place regarding the execution of a short sell in a stock. The rule is that the last price change should be a move higher in the stock or an uptick in the price of the stock. The idea behind the uptick rule is to keep a short seller from pushing a stock price down by continuously putting in sell orders. As of this writing, the uptick rule is not in place, but due to market volatility, there is pressure to have the uptick rule reinstated for initiating a short position in a stock.

As far as an option order goes, orders may be buy to open, buy to close, sell to open, and sell to close. Buying to open is exactly what it sounds like, an order to buy an option to create a new position or open a new position. Selling to close would be the action that is taken when a long position is exited.

On the opposite side of this, selling to open would be initiating a new position as a sell or a short option position. When exiting a short option position, the trade would be a buy to close, which is similar to the buy to cover version with a stock.

A SINGLE OPTION SPREAD

The most common strategy that comes to mind for a spread position that involves a stock and an option is the covered call, which was discussed in Chapter 2. Generally, this is discussed in the context of an investor owning shares in a stock and selling a call option against those shares to generate income and possibly be paid for an exit strategy. It is possible to execute a covered call position where the stock is purchased and the call option is executed at the same time. When this position is entered into in this manner it is called a buy-write.

As a reminder, a buy-write obtains this name from the two executions involved in entering the trade. Shares are purchased for the buy part of the term. A call option is sold short, or a trader writes a contract. Very often at the posts on the floor of the Chicago Board Options Exchange, there are quote requests for buy-writes where a trader is trying to enter one of these spread trades on a single transaction.

There are brokers that may have the ability to obtain a single bid and ask quote for executing a buy-write. The bid side would be a price where the stock would be sold and the option bought back. This would be a long sale of stock and a buy to cover the call option. The ask side would involve buying shares and selling to open a call option. The quotes from Table 17.3 will be used to illustrate this further.

TABLE 17.3 Quotes to Illustrate a Buy-Write Execution

	Bid Size	Bid	Ask	Ask Size	Last	Change	Volume	Open Interest
XYZ	1000	48.75	49.00	1200	48.80	−0.30	350700	N/A
XYZ Dec 50 Call	20	1.55	1.70	30	1.70	−0.15	155	2107

The example involves XYZ, which is being currently bid at 48.75 and offered at 49.00 in the marketplace. The option being considered in this buy-write transaction is the XYZ Dec 50 Call. A trader would like a quote on selling an XYZ Dec 50 Call and buying 100 shares of XYZ in a single transaction. Based on the underlying market prices, the quote may appear to be something like a bid ask spread of 47.05 × 47.45.

The bid side—47.05—of this market quote involves a price that a buy-write would be exited. Exiting the buy write at the prevailing market prices would involve selling shares of XYZ at 48.75 and repurchasing the XYZ Dec 50 Call at 1.70. The net proceeds from this transaction would be 47.05, or income of 48.75 for selling shares, then paying out 1.70 to buy back the call option.

The offer or ask side of 47.45 would be the outflow of funds or cost to initiate the buy-write. This would involve buying shares of XYZ for 49.00 and selling the call option for 1.55 of income. The net result is 49.00 minus 1.55, or the offer of 47.45. The quote would be phrased as something like, "XYZ Dec 50 Buy-Write 47.05 bid, 47.45 offered".

A benefit of getting a quote as a single transaction like this is that the quote involves both sides being executed immediately. There is no chance that in the second between when a trader enters the stock order side of the buy-write that the option suddenly moves away from the price at which the trader believed they would be able to execute their trade. Another potential benefit is the ability to get a quote from a market maker that is possibly better than executing them as separate orders. Option market makers base their quotes on what their models indicate the fair value is for an option contract. This fair value is based on a number of factors, and includes the ability to hedge their positions very quickly in the underlying security. When a spread trade is executed, if the spread has lower directional exposure to the underlying security then there will be less of a hedge that would need to be executed by the market maker. In a case where there is less hedging that needs to be done, a better quote than what is prevailing in the market may be obtained. The result of an improved quote would be a less costly execution.

For example, in the case of the XYZ December 50 Buy-Write, the bid was 47.05 and the offer price was 47.45. This equates to a .40 spread between the bid and ask price. It is possible a market maker on the exchange floor or at another professional execution firm might quote a bid–ask for this spread as 47.10 bid by 47.40 offered, or another quote that is a bit better than the market prices.

Another execution approach to take is if there is a relatively wide range between the bid and ask on each part of a spread order, using a limit order that falls somewhere in the range might work out as an improved execution. However, using a limit order in this manner does not guarantee execution, and could result in missing a trade altogether. These decisions are something many professionals refer to as the art of trading.

As quantitative as things have become in the financial industry, there is still the human element to trading and investing that exists. Knowing that element and taking advantage of the emotional side of the market does put some traders on a higher level than others. The ability to improve executions based on knowing when to use a limit order or when to just use what the market is showing is one of those skills that falls under the heading the art of trading.

A SPREAD WITH TWO OPTIONS

A spread trade on the same underlying but with two different option contracts can involve a variety of potential strategies. The one thing these strategies will have in common is each of the contracts will have a spread between the bid and ask which may contribute to the cost of the trade. As with the covered call example in the previous example, a single quote may be ascertained from the quoted prices of each leg of the spread.

Using a straddle based on the two options in Table 17.4 as an example, a price to buy the straddle and a price to sell the straddle can be determined.

To take a long position in the straddle, both the XYZ Aug 40 Call and XYZ Aug 40 Put would be bought. The XYZ Aug 40 Call is offered at 1.90 and the XYZ Aug 40 Put is offered at 1.85. Paying the ask side for both these options would result in a cost of 3.75. To short or sell the straddle, both options would be sold for a total of 3.50. As an individual trade, the bid for the spread is 3.50 and the offer is 3.75. This results in a spread of 25 cents between the bid and the offer.

Once again, option quotes are based on a fair value that results from a pricing model. A market maker's goal is to buy options at a price lower than this fair value and sell options at a price higher than this fair value. When transactions occur, a market maker will execute an offsetting order to hedge their position. Part of their trading strategy involves making small

TABLE 17.4　Quotes to Illustrate a Straddle

	Bid Size	Bid	Ask	Ask Size	Last	Change	Volume	Open Interest
XYZ Aug 40 Call	20	1.80	1.90	10	1.80	+0.15	210	2145
XYZ Aug 40 Put	10	1.70	1.85	15	1.90	−0.10	155	3474

profits and negating price risk related to the underlying security. This is also known as trying to be delta neutral.

When taking a position in a straddle, whether long or short the straddle, if the current price of the underlying is close to the strike price of the options then the position would be close to delta neutral. With XYZ trading at 40.00, the call option from the previous example would have a delta of close to .50 and the put option would have a delta of around −.50. A position that was made up of an equal number of long each option would have a delta of 0.00, as would a position made up of both options being short. Since the market maker would not be exposed to small price changes in the underlying, there would not need to be very much of a hedge implemented to take the other side of a straddle order, short or long.

With very little delta exposure involved in an at-the-money straddle position, market makers have the ability to profit from a straddle at a price better than using both option bid prices when purchasing from a straddle seller, or using both offer prices when selling to a straddle purchaser. Because of this, if a quote is requested on a straddle, the response may be an improvement on the quote based on the individual option's quotes.

Also, there is a good possibility that if an order is entered to sell a little higher than the bid or to buy a little lower than the offer price of the spread, it may be executed. This is possible, but never guaranteed.

A SPREAD WITH MULTIPLE LEGS

There have been a vast number of option spread strategies covered in this book. All the different strategies have a variety of motivations and payouts. They all also have different methods that may be used to try to enter as long or short and exit these spreads. As with the spread that had two legs, spreads with multiple legs may have their bid/ask prices determined through using the bids and offers of the individual options. As a multiple leg spread, the iron condor discussed in Chapter 10 is one of the most popular among individual traders.

The options in Table 17.5 will be used to develop an individual quote for both sides of an iron condor. The iron condor was covered in Chapter 10, but as a reminder when initiating the traditional iron condor the two inside strike options are sold and the two outside strike options are purchased. When the other side of this trade is taken, it is referred to as a reverse iron condor. If a quote were requested for this spread, the result will be a response for both the iron condor and the reverse iron condor.

To get a quote for an iron condor using these options, the bid side of the options that would be sold, or the XYZ Nov 35 Put and XYZ Nov 40 Call

TABLE 17.5 Quotes to Illustrate an Iron Condor

	Bid Size	Bid	Ask	Ask Size	Last	Change	Volume	Open Interest
XYZ Nov 30 Put	10	0.05	0.10	10	0.10	0.00	55	905
XYZ Nov 35 Put	20	0.65	0.70	20	0.65	−0.05	1700	7304
XYZ Nov 40 Call	25	0.75	0.80	25	0.80	+0.05	1250	3523
XYZ Nov 45 Call	10	0.05	0.10	10	0.05	0.00	45	2226

would be used. These two option prices would be combined with the ask side of the XYZ Nov 30 Put and XYZ Nov 45 Call. So assuming the bid side is used for the short options and the ask side of the quote is used for the long options, the result would be income of 1.20 for putting on this spread.

Breaking it down, the XYZ Nov 35 Put could be sold at 0.65 and the XYZ Nov 40 Call would bring in 0.75 for a total of 1.40. Twenty cents would be paid out in the form of paying 0.10 for both the XYZ Nov 30 Put and the XYZ Nov 45 Call.

The other side of this quote, whether it be an order to exit an iron condor or an order to put on a reverse iron condor, would result from paying 0.70 for the XYZ Nov 35 Put and 0.80 for the XYZ Nov 40 Call. This cost of 1.50 would be offset slightly through selling the XYZ Nov 30 Put and XYZ Nov 45 Call for .05 each. The total income from selling these two options is 0.10, for a net result of 1.40 paid for a reverse iron condor. The resulting quote would be 1.20 bid x 1.40 ask.

In Chapter 10 where the iron condor appeared after a discussion of long call and long put condors, it was mentioned that although income is received for the iron condor and a premium is paid to trade the other condors, that it may be possible to have a better payout with one over the other two. Using the quotes in Table 17.6, a price to initiate a long call condor and a long put condor with a similar payout structure will be developed.

To put on a long call condor, the XYZ Nov 30 Call and XYZ Nov 45 Call options would be purchased, and the XYZ Nov 35 Call and XYZ Nov 40 Call options would be sold. Unlike the XYZ Nov 30/35/40/45 Iron Condor which is created by taking in some income, there is a cost associated with the XYZ Nov 30/35/40/45 Long Call Condor.

The cost of the long call condor—if the ask is paid for the long options and the short options are sold at the bid price—comes to 3.70. This is the result of paying 7.15 for the XYZ Nov 30 Call and 0.10 for the XYZ Nov 45 Call at a total cost of 7.25. Income taken in from selling the XYZ Nov 35 Call is 2.80 and the XYZ Nov 40 Call is 0.75 for a sum of 3.55. The key question here is how does this compare to the 1.20 that would have been taken in for putting on the Iron Condor.

TABLE 17.6 Quotes to Illustrate a Comparable Condor Spread

	Bid Size	Bid	Ask	Ask Size	Last	Change	Volume	Open Interest
XYZ Nov 30 Call	10	7.05	7.15	10	7.00	0.00	110	760
XYZ Nov 30 Put	10	0.05	0.10	10	0.10	0.00	55	905
XYZ Nov 35 Call	25	2.80	2.90	20	2.85	−0.05	790	2835
XYZ Nov 35 Put	20	0.65	0.70	20	0.65	−0.05	1700	7304
XYZ Nov 40 Call	25	0.75	0.80	25	0.80	0.05	1250	3523
XYZ Nov 40 Put	20	2.75	2.80	35	2.70	0.00	1230	4725
XYZ Nov 45 Call	10	0.05	0.10	10	0.05	0.00	45	2226
XYZ Nov 45 Put	15	7.10	7.15	15	7.10	0.00	20	978

As with all trades, key levels may be developed for both spreads. Table 17.7 compares the key levels for the iron condor and long call condor using the same option strike prices.

Although the long call condor costs 3.70 and the iron condor has income of 1.20, there is an easy comparison between the two. The maximum profit for the long call condor comes to 1.30, or 5.00 of value at expiration minus the cost of the spread—3.70. The iron condor's maximum profit is the income received of 1.20 with the spread value of 0.00. Using these two scenarios, the market prices for the XYZ 30/35/40/45 Long Call Condor actually result in a slightly superior profit level than the comparable iron condor. All other levels for the long call condor are a little bit better than the iron condor, the maximum loss and break even points are a 0.10 improvement versus the iron condor.

An iron condor is another one of those spreads that is fairly neutral relative to the underlying security and one that may result in a better quote than the bid side of the options to be sold or the offer side of the options

TABLE 17.7 Long Call Condor—Iron Condor Payoff Comparison

	XYZ Nov 30/35/40/45 Long Call Condor	XYZ Nov 30/35/40/45 Iron Condor
Up Break-even Price	41.30	41.30
Down Break-even Price	33.70	33.80
Maximum Dollar Gain	1.30	1.20
Maximum Gain Prices	Between 35.00 and 40.00	Between 35.00 and 40.00
Maximum Dollar Loss	3.70	3.80
Maximum Loss Prices	Under 30.00 Over 45.00	Under 30.00 Over 45.00

TABLE 17.8 Quotes to Illustrate a Long Put Butterfly

	Bid Size	Bid	Ask	Ask Size	Last	Change	Volume	Open Interest
XYZ Mar 50 Put	30	1.05	1.10	20	1.10	−0.15	95	400
XYZ Mar 55 Put	30	3.00	3.10	30	2.95	−0.25	227	1270
XYZ Mar 60 Put	20	5.60	5.65	10	5.50	−0.35	65	345

to be purchased. Again, when a market maker facilitates a trade, he should reduce exposure to the underlying security through another trade. With a spread like a condor that is neutral, not much initial hedging may be needed.

There are two winged spreads, the condor and the butterfly, which comprise the most common type of spread with multiple legs that individual investors like to trade. Butterfly spreads were covered in Chapter 9, but as a reminder a butterfly using all the same type of options involves taking positions in three different strike prices. The center strike price will have twice as many options as the two outside strikes. For instance if call options with 30, 35, and 40 strikes are used to create a butterfly, two 35 strike options would be bought or sold for each of the 30 or 40 strike options that were sold or purchased. The net result is long as many options as the spread is short.

As a second example of a quote for an exotic spread, the quotes in Table 17.8 will be used to create a butterfly spread from put options. The offer price of a long put butterfly using these options would involve the bid side of the middle strike XYZ Mar 55 Put and the offer side of both the XYZ Mar 50 Put and XYZ Mar 60 Put. To create a long butterfly, twice as many Mar 55 Put options would be sold as are purchased of the strikes of the wings. The offer price of this spread represents initiating it as a long put butterfly.

The bid price of the XYZ Mar 55 Put is 3.00, but this should be multiplied by 2, as two of these options would be traded in a butterfly, so the net result is a credit of 6.00. The remainder of the spread offer is determined by the ask side of the other two options. The XYZ Mar 50 Put is offered at 1.10 and the XYZ Mar 60 Put is offered at 5.65, for a net offer of 6.75. Subtracting 6.00 from 6.75 results in an offer price for the butterfly spread of 0.75.

The bid side of this spread would involve taking the opposite side of each of the previous positions. The middle strike would be purchased for 3.10 each, or a total cost of 6.20. The XYZ Nov 50 Put could be sold for the bid side of 1.05 and the Nov 60 Put could be sold for 5.60, which together brings in 6.65. The net result for this would be a 0.45 credit if all these trades were executed simultaneously, this amount is also the bid according to market prices for the XYZ Nov 50/55/60 Put Butterfly.

A bid and offer can be obtained on any option spread position that has two sides to it. For each option in the spread trade, the difference between the individual option's bid and offer will add to the trading cost of entering the spread. With this in mind, any attempt to obtain a better quote or execution than what the market is offering through the individual option pricing is always a worthwhile exercise.

LEGGING INTO A SPREAD TRADE

Although suggested in many cases, there is no rule in place stating that when a spread trade is entered that all legs must be executed at the same time. If a trader feels that they may improve upon the entry price of a trade by timing the execution of various options that will be in the spread they may attempt to trade the options at different times. The result, if successful, will be an improved execution price. However, if unsuccessful the risk may be much higher than the risk associated with the original spread. Either way, there are professional traders that will use their trading ability to attempt to 'leg into' a spread trade and only the most adept traders should try this method on the more exotic spreads.

An initial example of legging into a spread trade may not even be thought of as a legging transaction by many traders or investors. The first spread covered in this book was the covered call. When executed as one transaction this is known as a buy-write. The buy-write can be executed as a single transaction or both parts may be executed with different trades, but at the same time. Also, both parts of the buy-write could be executed on different days—of course then it is referred to as a covered call.

A longer-term investor purchases shares of XYZ at 45.00 with the intention of selling shares at 55.00 or better in the future. To exit the stock, a call option may be sold against those shares as a method to get paid to sell stock at this target price. Table 17.9 shows a variety of call options with a variety of strike prices based on the number of days to expiration. To

TABLE 17.9 Call Option Values

	45 Call	50 Call	55 Call
30 Day	1.30	0.10	0.00
60 Day	1.85	0.40	0.05
90 Day	2.30	0.70	0.15

TABLE 17.10 Call Option Values

	45 Call	50 Call	55 Call
15 Day	7.55	2.90	0.40
45 Day	7.70	3.70	1.25
75 Day	8.00	4.25	1.85

determine these prices, 25 percent implied volatility is assumed with the stock at 45.00.

Only the 55 Call options would result in the stock being called away at an effective target price of 55.00. However, those options are trading for such a small premium that the income taken in probably does not warrant selling a call at this time. If XYZ starts to trade higher or the implied volatility of these options increases, the result will be higher option premiums and possibly enough income to justify selling a call. Planning to sell a call to initiate a covered call in the future may be considered a form of legging into a buy write.

If 15 days later the stock has rallied up to 52.50 and the implied volatility of the options has risen from 25 percent to 30 percent then the options would be priced at the levels indicated in Table 17.10.

It now appears that selling the 45 Day 55 strike call option would be a good way to bring in some extra income and also take on the obligation to sell shares over 55.00, the original target price. Over the course of several days, initiating the long stock position with the intention of selling a call to create a covered call in the future at a certain price can be considered legging into this trade.

On a shorter-term basis, such as in the same day, spreads may also be entered in a more strategic manner. For instance, if a trader was considering a bull call spread on XYZ they may choose to execute one leg with the anticipation of improving the overall profit and loss profile of the trade based on the underlying stock movements during the day. As a reminder, a bull call spread involves selling a higher strike option and purchasing a lower strike option with the anticipation of the stock being above the higher strike at expiration.

For example, XYZ is trading at 33.00 in the morning, up 2.00 over the previous day's closing price. A trader decides he would like to initiate a bull call spread that would involve being long the XYZ 30 Call and short an XYZ 35 Call that both expire in 45 days. However, he also feels like the stock is short-term over bought and should see some selling pressure before the day is over. In this case, he would want to execute the shorting of the XYZ 35 Call first and then purchase the long side of the spread a little later in the day.

TABLE 17.11 Morning Call Option Values

	Bid Size	Bid	Ask	Ask Size	Last	Change	Volume	Open Interest
XYZ 30 Call	50	3.35	3.40	100	3.35	+1.55	980	9525
XYZ 35 Call	25	0.65	0.70	20	0.70	+0.40	450	3206

Using the option pricing in Table 17.11, the trader decides to execute the sell side of the trade first. This involves selling the XYZ 35 Call for 0.65. If he chose to put on the long side of the trade and purchase the XYZ 30 Call he would have paid 3.40 for that option at this time. This would have resulted in a total cost for the bull call spread of 2.75. However, he holds off, believing the stock will trade down by 1.00 to 32.00 by the end of the day. When the stock reaches a price of 32.00, the plan is to buy the long call side of the spread to complete the execution.

With an hour left in the trading day, the trader's price projection has worked out, with XYZ coming in and now trading at 32.00. Table 17.12 is a new option quote line based on XYZ now trading at 32.00.

Now that the stock has traded lower, the trader decides to execute the long side of the trade and purchase the XYZ 30 Call for 2.60. The net result is entering the XYZ 30/35 Bull Call spread at 1.95, paying 2.60, and receiving 0.65 as opposed to 2.75 from paying 3.40 and receiving 0.65. Table 17.13 compares the key levels of a trade with both sides initiated in the morning and the legging trade.

There is a noticeable difference between the potential profit and loss levels with the cost of 1.95 resulting in a potential profit of 3.05 as opposed to the potential loss of 2.75 versus maximum gain of 2.25 from the spread executed at the market in the morning of the day.

Note that if the trader wanted to enter the trade in one spread and did not want to have the naked short option exposure while waiting for the stock to trade lower he could have just waited until the afternoon to execute both sides of the spread. The cost would have been more favorable at 2.25 versus 2.75 through his patience. Also, the risk of being wrong and left with a short call position is eliminated in this case.

TABLE 17.12 Afternoon Call Option Values

	Bid Size	Bid	Ask	Ask Size	Last	Change	Volume	Open Interest
XYZ 30 Call	45	2.55	2.60	75	2.55	+0.75	4900	9525
XYZ 35 Call	10	0.35	0.40	25	0.35	+0.05	2250	3206

TABLE 17.13 Comparison of Legged and Non-legged Payouts

	Legged Bull Call Spread	Non-legged Bull Call Spread
Up Break-even Price	31.95	32.75
Maximum Dollar Gain	3.05	2.25
Maximum Gain Price	Over 35.00	Over 35.00
Maximum Dollar Loss	1.95	2.75
Maximum Loss Prices	Under 30.00	Under 30.00

Finally, be aware that legging into a spread trade can be a risky proposition. In the case of the previous trade, if the stock had climbed by 1.00 to 34.00 by the afternoon the cost of the XYZ 30 Call would have increased to 4.30. This would result in the spread costing 3.65 with a potential profit of only 1.35.

Again, legging into a spread can be rewarding relative to the profitability of a trade, but it also may result in only entering one leg of a spread, and in that case, the leg will almost certainly be a loser if the other leg is not entered.

About the Author

R ussell Rhoads, CFA, is an instructor with The Options Institute at the Chicago Board Options Exchange. He joined the Institute in 2009 after a career as an investment analyst and trader with a variety of firms. He also is a financial author and editor, having contributed to *Technical Analysis of Stocks and Commodities* magazine and edited several books for Wiley publishing. In 2008 he wrote *Candlestick Charting For Dummies*. He is a double graduate of the University of Memphis with a BBA (92) and an MS (94) in Finance and also received a Master's Certificate in Financial Engineering from the Illinois Institute of Technology in 2003. Also, he instructs a graduate level options course at the University of Illinois–Chicago.

Personally, Russell lives in Hinsdale, Illinois, with his wife Merribeth and their two daughters, Emmy and Maggie. Between his job and writing books, he also serves on the Board of Education for Community Consolidated School District 181, which covers five suburban Chicago communities.

Index

American-style options, 3, 16
Arbitrage trading, 50–52
Ask, 256
At the money, 5–6

Backspreads
    calls, 199–207
    puts, 207–211
Bear spreads
    calls, 121–127, 167
    puts, 121–122, 124, 127–133, 141–142
Bid, 256
Break-even point, 17
Bull spreads
    calls, 114–119, 266–268
    puts, 107–114, 109, 141–142, 167
Butterfly spreads
    iron butterfly, 85–88, 142–148
    long call, 136–139
    long put, 139–142, 193–195, 264–265
    reverse iron butterfly, 154–158
    short call, 149–152
    short put, 152–154, 207–209
Buy-write. *See also* Covered calls
        16–17, 25–26, 258–259, 265

Calendar spreads. *See also* Diagonal
        spreads
    combined, 227–230
    long call, 221–223
    long puts, 224–227
    time value effect, 220–221
Call options. *See also* Covered calls;
        LEAPS
    backspreads, 199–207
    bear spreads, 121–127, 167

bull spreads, 114–119, 266–268
butterfly spreads, 136–139, 149–152
calendar spreads, 221–223
condors, 160–163, 172–174, 262–263
definition and overview, 1–5
delta and, 56, 58–59, 246
diagonal, 231–234
doubling down and, 214–215
gamma and, 59–60
Greeks, 9–10
in-at-out of the money, 5–6
intrinsic *vs.* time value, 6–7
legging in, 265–266
ratio spreads, 184–189
spreads, 8–9
stock repair trade and, 216–218
synthetic, 40–50
theta and, 61–65
vega and, 66–67
Cash-secured puts, 26–31
Cash settled index, 3–4
Catalysts
    straddles and, 74, 78–81
    strangles and, 91, 95, 97
Closing transactions, 258
Collar, 33–35
Condor spreads
    iron condor, 166–172, 261–264
    long call, 160–163
    long put, 163–166
    overview, 159–160
    quotes, 262–263
    reverse iron condor, 176–181, 262
    short call, 172–174
    short put, 174–176

Covered calls
  buy-write, 16–17, 25–26, 258–259, 265
  definition and overview, 8, 15–16
  diagonal spread *vs.*, 233–234, 236
  key levels, 17–19
  LEAPS, 22–25, 67–68
  risk, 21–22
  systematic, 25–26
  theta and, 19–21

Delta, 9, 55–59, 245–246
Delta-neutral positions, 246–254, 261
Diagonal spreads. *See also* Calendar
    spreads
  calls, 231–234
  double, 241–244
  LEAPS, 234–241
  puts, 237–239
Double diagonal spread, 241–244
Doubling down, 214–215

Earnings reports
  straddles and, 73–74, 76–78
  strangles and, 95–98, 100
Equity index options. *See* Index
    options
European-style options, 3
Event trading, 76–78
Exchange traded funds (ETF), 2, 16
Executions
  legging into spread trades, 265–268
  multiple legs, 261–265
  single option spread, 258–260
  stock/option trade, 256–258
  two option spread, 260–261
Expiration dates, 3–4, 22–25, 68

Front spreads, 183

Gamma, 9, 59–60, 250–251
Good til canceled orders, 26–27
Greeks, 9–10, 69. *See also specific
    Greeks, such as* Delta

Implied volatility. *See also* Volatility
    65–67, 87–88, 96–98, 100, 105
Index options, 3

Interest rates, 67–68
In the money, 5–6
Intrinsic value, 6–7, 61–65
Iron butterfly, 85–88, 142–148, 154–158
Iron condor spreads, 101–105,
    166–172, 261–264

Key levels, 17–18

LEAPS (Long-term Equity AnticiPation
    Securities), 22–25, 67–68, 234–241
Legging into spread trades, 265–267
Leverage, 93–98
Limit orders, 16, 26–27, 259–260
Long positions
  butterfly spreads, 136–142, 183, 188,
    193–195, 264–265
  calendar spreads, 221–223, 224–227
  condor spreads, 160–166, 262–263
  straddles, 72–81, 207–208, 210–211,
    248–249
  strangles, 89–98, 179–181
  synthetic, 40–44
Long-term Equity AnticiPation
    Securities. *See* LEAPS

Market maker trading, 251–254, 259,
    261, 264
Maximum profit/loss, 17

Naked short positions, 26, 83–84, 87,
    101–102, 105, 185, 197

Open interest, 257
Opening transaction, 258
Option orders, 258
Option quotes, 256–265, 267
Out of the money, 5–6

Payoff tables/diagrams, 10–11, 17–19
Point of indifference, 19
Pricing calculators, 12–13, 23, 65–66
Protective puts, 32–33
Put-call parity, 34, 37–40, 50–53
Put options
  backspreads, 207–211
  bear spreads, 127–133, 141–142

bull spreads, 107–114, 141–142, 167

butterfly spreads, 139–142, 152–154, 193–195, 207–209, 264–265

calendar spreads, 224–227

cash-secured, 26–31

condors, 163–166, 174–176

definition and overview, 1–5

delta and, 56–59, 246

diagonal spreads, 237–239

gamma and, 59–60

Greeks, 9–10

in-at-out of the money, 5–6

intrinsic *vs.* time value, 6–7

LEAPS, 239–241

protective, 32–33

ratio spreads, 189–197

spreads, 8–9

synthetic long, 40–42

synthetic short, 45–46

systematic cash-secured, 31–32

theta and, 61, 64–65

vega and, 66–67

Quarterly earnings reports. *See* Earnings reports

Quotes, 256–265, 267

Ratio spreads
  calls, 184–189
  puts, 189–197

Rho, 10, 67–68

Selling to close/open, 258

Short call butterfly spreads, 149–152

Short call condor spreads, 172–174

Size, 256

Spreads, overview, 8–9. *See also* Executions

Standard option contracts, 2–3

Stock options
  executing, 257
  expiration, 3
  standard number of shares, 2–3
  synthetic long, 42–44
  synthetic short, 48–50

Stock repair strategy, 213–218

Straddles
  executions, 260–261
  leverage and, 93–98
  long, 72–81, 207–208, 210–211, 248–249
  iron butterfly *vs.*, 156–158
  short, 81–88, 146–148, 183, 195–196
  strangles and, 89–98

Strangles
  iron condor *vs.* 101–105
  leverage and, 93–98
  long, 89–98, 179–181
  short, 98–105, 170–172
  straddles *vs.*, 89–98

Strike price, 3–4, 37–38, 107

Synthetic positions
  long, 40–44
  put-call parity, 34, 37–40, 50–53
  short, 44–50

Systematic cash-secured puts, 31–32

Systematic covered calls, 25–26

Theta, 9, 61–65, 220–221

Time value, 6–7, 22–25, 61–65, 220–221. *See also* Theta

Trading spreads. *See* Executions

Underlying securities
  defined, 2
  delta and, 246
  LEAPS and, 22–25
  systematic cash-secured puts, 31–32
  systematic covered calls, 25–26

Uptick rule, 257

Vega, 9, 66–67, 74. *See also* Volatility

Vertical spreads
  bearish, 121–122, 124, 127–133, 141–142
  bullish, 107–114, 109, 141–142, 167

Volatility. *See also* Implied Volatility
  greeks and, 65–67
  historical, 65
  long straddles and, 74–81
  long strangles and, 89–90, 92, 95–98
  short straddles and, 83–85, 87–88
  short strangles and, 98–105

Printed and bound by CPI Group (UK) Ltd, Croydon, CR0 4YY

16/04/2025

14658508-0003